How to Do **Everything**™

Samsung GALAXY Tab™

Guy Hart-Davis

Mc
Graw
Hill

New York Chicago San Francisco Lisbon
London Madrid Mexico City Milan New Delhi
San Juan Seoul Singapore Sydney Toronto

Cataloging-in-Publication Data is on file with the Library of Congress

McGraw-Hill books are available at special quantity discounts to use as premiums and sales promotions, or for use in corporate training programs. To contact a representative, please e-mail us at bulksales@mcgraw-hill.com.

How to Do Everything™: Samsung GALAXY Tab™

1 2 3 4 5 6 7 8 9 0   QFR QFR   1 0 9 8 7 6 5 4 3 2

ISBN   978-0-07-177109-2
MHID   0-07-177109-3

Sponsoring Editor
Megg Morin

Editorial Supervisor
Janet Walden

Project Editor
Howie Severson,
Fortuitous Publishing Services

Acquisitions Coordinator
Stephanie Evans

Technical Editor
Matt Miller

Copy Editor
Bill McManus

Proofreader
Paul Tyler

Indexer
Jack Lewis

Production Supervisor
George Anderson

Composition
Cenveo Publisher Services

Illustration
Cenveo Publisher Services

Art Director, Cover
Jeff Weeks

Cover Designer
Jeff Weeks

This book is dedicated to Teddy

About the Author

Guy Hart-Davis is the author of more than 70 computer books, including *iPhone 4S Geekery, How to Do Everything: iPhone 4S, iPad and iPhone Administrator's Guide, Integrating Macs into Windows Networks, Mac OS X System Administration,* and *How to Do Everything: iPod touch.*

About the Technical Editor

Matthew Miller is the writer of the ZDNet Mobile Gadgeteer and Smartphones & Cell Phones blogs and author of four books: *Windows Phone 7 Companion, Facebook Companion, BlackBerry PlayBook Companion, and Master Visually Windows Mobile 2003.*

Contents at a Glance

Contents

Introduction

Packing a full-featured computer into an easy-to-carry touch-screen tablet, the Galaxy Tab is the best way to stay connected and productive today. You can do everything essential—from keeping your e-mail under control to creating business documents, from watching a movie to posting updates on Facebook—right from the palm of your hand.

But you already know that. That's why you've got a Galaxy Tab—and why you're looking at this book for ways to get the most out of the tablet.

I can see a question is forming on your lips...

What Does This Book Cover?

Glad you asked. Here's a quick taste of what you'll learn from this book:

- Chapter 1 shows you how to unpack the Galaxy Tab and get it charged, add a SIM card or USIM card if necessary, and go through the Galaxy Tab's initial setup routine. You'll meet the home screen and learn how to use it. You'll install the Samsung Kies program on your PC or Mac and connect your Galaxy Tab to the computer.
- Chapter 2 tells you how to customize the Galaxy Tab to suit the way you want to use it. You'll learn how to customize the home screen panels and choose the most important settings for day-to-day use. You'll also learn how to connect a Bluetooth device to the Galaxy Tab, manage your wireless network connections, and outfit the Galaxy Tab with accessories.
- Chapter 3 goes through using Kies to manage the Galaxy Tab and load it with music, videos, and data. You'll learn tricks for making Kies recognize the Galaxy Tab on a USB connection and find out how to keep Kies up to date. If you're using a PC rather than a Mac, you'll learn how to connect the Galaxy Tab via Wi-Fi or Bluetooth as well as via USB.
- Chapter 4 shows you how to play music on the Galaxy Tab. First, we talk about how to get suitable music files for the Galaxy Tab. Then we look at how to play music with the Music Player app, which is friendly and straightforward, and how to set a song as an alarm tone.

- Chapter 5 explains how to watch movies and videos on the Galaxy Tab. You can load video files on the Galaxy Tab using Kies and watch them on it. But you can also use the Galaxy Tab's YouTube app to enjoy raw footage on YouTube, or use the Google Videos app to watch videos available on Google.

- Chapter 6 walks you through using the camera and making the most of photos and videos. You can point and shoot with the default settings, but you'll usually get better results by configuring the camera and camcorder to take the kinds of photos and videos you want—anything from self-portraits and panoramas to videos suitable for sending via multimedia messaging. And no matter how you take the photos and videos, you'll want to review how they came out and share the best ones.

- Chapter 7 shows you how to browse the Web on the Galaxy Tab. You'll learn how to perform basic maneuvers such as scrolling, zooming, and navigating from page to page; open multiple web pages at once using tabs; and use bookmarks, your browsing history, and the search feature. You'll also learn how to choose custom settings for the Browser app and use other web browsers when you need them.

- Chapter 8 explains how to use e-mail on the Galaxy Tab. You'll learn how to set up the built-in Email app to access your various e-mail accounts; how to read incoming messages (and delete or file them); and how to send new messages, reply to messages you've received, or forward messages to other people. You'll also learn how to send and receive attachments, because e-mail can be an easy way of getting files from one computer to another. If you use Gmail, you'll learn how to use the Gmail app to make the most of Google's greatest gift to humankind.

- Chapter 9 takes you through using the Galaxy Tab to keep up with your social networks. If you're lucky, your Galaxy Tab includes the Social Hub app, which lets you track your e-mail accounts and social networking accounts from within a single app. If not, you can access Facebook, LinkedIn, or Twitter by using either their custom Android apps or their websites.

- Chapter 10 tells you how to use the Galaxy Tab to stay in touch via instant messaging. You'll learn how to configure the Messaging app, use it to send and receive instant messages, and read and manage the messages you receive.

- Chapter 11 covers reading e-books, newspapers, and magazines on the Galaxy Tab. Most Galaxy Tab models include the eBook app, which you can use to read not only e-books but also PDF files, and the Pulse newsreader, which gives you quick and easy access to articles from a wide range of newspapers and magazines. This chapter shows you how to use these apps and how to create e-books and PDF files from your own content.

- Chapter 12 shows you how to make the most of apps on the Galaxy Tab. As you know, the Galaxy Tab is a sleek and impressive piece of hardware, but the apps are essential for getting your work (and play) done. You'll learn how to use the apps the Galaxy Tab comes with, add third-party apps from Android Market (and reinstall them if you lose them) and other sources, create app shortcuts on the home screen, manage the apps, and squelch both apps and services when they misbehave.

- Chapter 13 teaches you three handy tricks to take your use of the Galaxy Tab to the next level. First, you learn how to connect other computers to the Internet through the Galaxy Tab's Internet connection, either tethering the Galaxy Tab to your PC via USB or turning it into a mobile access point via Wi-Fi. Second, you learn how to connect the Galaxy Tab to your work network using virtual private networking, so that you can connect to network resources no matter where you are. And third, you find out how to take control of your PC or Mac from the Galaxy Tab across either a network or the Internet.
- Chapter 14 teaches you how to troubleshoot the Galaxy Tab and keep it updated with the latest fixes. You'll learn how to deal with crashed apps, recover from operating system crashes, and restart the Galaxy Tab when it stops responding to the touch screen. You'll also meet heavy-duty troubleshooting maneuvers, such as backing up your data and settings, restoring the Galaxy Tab to its factory settings, and restoring your data from a backup.

Conventions Used in This Book

To make its meaning clear without using far more words than necessary, this book uses a number of conventions, four of which are worth mentioning here:

- Note, Tip, and Caution paragraphs highlight information to draw it to your notice.
- The pipe character or vertical bar denotes choosing an item from a menu on your PC or Mac. For example, "choose File | Open" means that you should click the File menu and select the Open item on it. Use the keyboard, mouse, or a combination of the two as you wish.
- The ⌘ symbol represents the Command key on the Mac—the key that bears the Apple symbol and the quad-infinity mark on most Mac keyboards.
- Both the Galaxy Tab and its computer partners (PCs and Macs) use check boxes— boxes that have two states: *selected* (with a check mark in them) and *cleared* (without a check mark in them). This book tells you to *select* a check box or *clear* a check box rather than "tap to place a check mark in the box" or "tap to remove the check mark from the box." Often, you'll be verifying the state of the check box, so it may already have the required setting—in which case, you don't need to tap at all.

Acknowledgments

I'd like to thank the following people for their help with this book:

- Megg Morin for getting the book approved and choosing me to write it
- Stephanie Evans for handling the acquisitions end of the book
- Matthew Miller for reviewing the manuscript for technical accuracy—twice—and contributing many helpful suggestions
- Bill McManus for editing yet another manuscript of mine with a light touch and good humor—twice

- Howie Severson for coordinating the production of the book—twice
- Janet Walden for keeping the schedule and production of the book within industry-approved norms—twice
- Cenveo Publisher Services for laying out the pages
- Paul Tyler for proofreading the book
- Jack Lewis for creating the index

The Publisher would like to thank Allie Weibring at MWW Group for her help on the cover.

1

Get Up and Running with the Galaxy Tab

HOW TO...

- Unpack and charge the Galaxy Tab
- Install a SIM card or USIM card in a 3G Galaxy Tab
- Identify the hardware controls
- Go through the Galaxy Tab's initial setup routine
- Navigate the home screen
- Connect the Galaxy Tab to your PC

In this chapter, we'll get you started using the Galaxy Tab.

We'll begin by unpacking the Galaxy Tab from its box and setting it to charge the battery so you'll get the best battery life. We'll install a SIM card or USIM card (if the Galaxy Tab needs one) to provide a cellular connection. Then I'll point out the hardware controls and what they do, after which I'll take you through the Galaxy Tab's initial setup routine. You'll then be ready to meet the home screen and learn what its components are, what they do, and how you manipulate them.

Toward the end of the chapter, we'll connect the Galaxy Tab to your PC or Mac so that you can manage it with the Samsung Kies software. I'll show you how to get Kies, install it, and make the Galaxy Tab connect to it. Finally, I'll show you how to disconnect the Galaxy Tab from your PC or Mac.

Unpack the Galaxy Tab and Identify What You Get

Your first step when you get the Galaxy Tab is to open the box and identify the contents. This takes only a moment, although the contents vary depending on the country you buy the Galaxy Tab in and the retailer or service provider you buy it from. Here's what you'll typically find in the box:

- **Galaxy Tab**   The Galaxy Tab comes with protective film on the front and back. Peel this film off by pulling the tabs.
- **Headset**   The headset has ear-bud headphones and a clicker switch with a built-in microphone for making calls.
- **Data cable**   You use this cable for connecting the Galaxy Tab to your PC or Mac or to the USB power adapter. One end of the cable has a standard USB connector, while the other end has a Samsung-proprietary connector for connecting to the Galaxy Tab.
- **USB power adapter**   The USB power adapter is the fastest way of charging the Galaxy Tab. You connect the Galaxy Tab to the USB power adapter using the data cable.
- **Quick Start Guide booklet**   This booklet contains brief information to get you started with the Galaxy Tab. Browse it quickly, and then put it back in the box and return to this book for in-depth information.

Charge the Galaxy Tab

Once you've unpacked the Galaxy Tab, you'll likely be itching to use it—but what you should do immediately is set it to charge fully. You can use the Galaxy Tab while it charges, but it's best not to connect the Galaxy Tab to your PC until it has charged fully.

Unless the Galaxy Tab has spent months in its box waiting for a buyer, the battery will probably have some charge, but you'll get best battery performance by charging the battery fully as soon as possible. See the sidebar "How to Condition the Galaxy Tab's Battery to Extend Its Life" for advice on conditioning the battery.

To charge the battery, plug the USB power adapter into a power socket, plug the USB end of the data cable into the power adapter, and then plug the other end into the socket on the bottom of the Galaxy Tab. The device's screen lights up when the Galaxy Tab detects the power, so you can tell charging is under way. The battery readout in the notifications area at the right end of the status bar (at the bottom of the screen) shows a charging icon (a lightning bolt on a battery symbol), and the Charging readout shows the percentage of charge the battery currently has.

 If you plug the Galaxy Tab in when it's powered off, the Galaxy Tab displays a large battery icon in the middle of the display for a few seconds before dimming the display and then turning it off. If you want to see the progress of the charging, press the power button to display the battery icon for a few more seconds.

The battery takes about six hours to charge from exhaustion to full potency; if you're using the Galaxy Tab, charging takes longer, because you're using power even as it's feeding in to the battery. As usual with lithium-polymer batteries, the battery charges quickly until it is 80 percent full, and then trickle-charges the rest of the way to avoid overcharging (which can cause fire).

When the Galaxy Tab finishes charging, it gives a couple of electronic squeaks of satisfaction and briefly displays the message Battery Fully Charged in the notifications area. The battery icon then sheds its lightning bolt symbol, and the Charging readout changes to Charged.

How to... Condition the Galaxy Tab's Battery to Extend Its Life

To enjoy the Galaxy Tab to the full, you'll want to get the most life possible out of its battery. To do this, you need to condition the battery, which takes some time and patience up front.

To condition the battery, give it three full charges and discharges at the beginning of its life:

- **Charge the battery all the way up to 100 percent**   Use the USB power adapter—it's quicker than a USB cable plugged into your computer, and it doesn't go to sleep.
- **Run the battery all the way down until the Galaxy Tab shuts itself down**   The easiest way to do this is to wind up the screen brightness all the way to high and set a marathon playlist of videos running. You can also simply use the Galaxy Tab normally as long as you don't plug it into your computer or into the USB power adapter.
- **Repeat the process twice**   Plug the Galaxy Tab back into the USB power adapter, leave it until the battery is fully charged, and then run the battery down all the way again. Do that once more, and the battery should be in good shape.

This conditioning technique is simple enough to describe, but it takes real patience to do, because it takes two or three days—the Galaxy Tab can usually manage five to eight hours of playback or other vigorous activity, and takes about six hours to recharge fully, so each cycle takes the better part of a day. This tends to be grueling if you want to start using the Galaxy Tab right the moment you get it. But if you can manage the three full charges and discharges, you'll get the best performance out of the battery.

After conditioning the battery, you can plug the Galaxy Tab into a power source (a computer or the USB power adapter) whenever you need to. Lithium-polymer batteries don't suffer the "memory effect" that plagued older battery technologies, in which charging the battery when it was only partly discharged could take a hefty chunk out of the battery's capacity to store power.

While we're on the subject, two more quick things on charging:

- Don't leave the Galaxy Tab plugged into power for more than a day or two at a time, as doing this can shorten the battery life. Normally, this isn't a problem, as you'll likely be using the Galaxy Tab out and about rather than chaining yourself to a socket.
- Unplug the USB power adapter from the electric socket when you're not using it. This helps both keep the power adapter happy and your electric bill down.

Install a SIM Card or USIM Card

If your Galaxy Tab model is designed to connect to a cellular service, it will need a Subscriber Identity Module card, usually called a SIM card. Some carriers and retailers sell the Galaxy Tab with a suitable SIM card already installed, but for others you'll need to install a SIM card yourself.

 If the Galaxy Tab needs but lacks a SIM card, it displays a message such as "Please insert a SIM card" on the lock screen. During the setup process, the Galaxy Tab also prompts you to install a SIM card if it needs one. If your Galaxy Tab model doesn't need a SIM card, it won't prompt you for one.

Similarly, if your Galaxy Tab model is designed to connect to 3G data networks using the Universal Mobile Telecommunications System (UMTS) or the High-Speed Downlink Packet Access (HSDPA) communications protocol, you'll need to insert a Universal SIM card, or USIM. Usually, you'll need to insert the USIM in the Galaxy Tab yourself.

The SIM card slot is on the top edge of the Galaxy Tab, to the right of the headphone socket. To install the SIM card, dig your fingernail into the open corner of the cover, making it swing out toward the back of the Galaxy Tab. Then slide in the SIM card with the cut-off corner inward and the contacts facing the back of the Galaxy Tab. Push the SIM card in until it clicks into place, and then swing the cover back into place.

 If the Galaxy Tab is running when you install the SIM card, it may reboot when it detects the SIM card. If you install the SIM card before firing up the Galaxy Tab, you don't need to worry about this.

Identify the Hardware Controls

The Galaxy Tab has only two hardware controls:

- **Power button**   The power button is at the left of the top edge of the Galaxy Tab. As you'd expect, you press this button to turn the Galaxy Tab on or to turn it off. You also press this button to wake the Galaxy Tab from sleep and (when it's awake) to put it to sleep. But the power button also has other uses, which you'll learn about later in this book.
- **Volume rocker**   The volume rocker is to the right of the power button on the top edge of the Galaxy Tab. Press the left half of the rocker to lower the volume; press the right half to increase the volume.

For most of the actions you take with the Galaxy Tab, you use the touch screen rather than hardware controls. The touch screen includes four soft buttons that appear most of the time. You'll meet these as soon as we get to the home screen.

Start the Galaxy Tab and Perform Initial Setup

In this section, you'll start the Galaxy Tab and then go through the initial setup routine. This routine involves the following four steps:

- Choose your language on the Welcome screen.
- Decide whether to use Google's Location Service.
- Set the date and time.
- Set up your Google account on the Galaxy Tab.

If your Galaxy Tab is a Wi-Fi-only model rather than a Wi-Fi-and-3G model, you'll also need to connect it to a wireless network.

Choose Your Language on the Welcome Screen

To begin, press the power button for a second or two to start the Galaxy Tab. After a few seconds, the Welcome screen appears. This screen shows the word "Welcome" or its equivalent in whichever language the Galaxy Tab is set to use, a Language pop-up menu button bearing the name of the current language, and a button called Start (or its equivalent in the language).

If the Language pop-up menu button shows a language other than the one you want to use, tap the button to display the pop-up menu, and then tap the correct language. Tap your finger and drag up or down to display other options beyond those that appear at first in the pop-up menu.

Tap the Start button to move along to the Use Google Location Service screen.

Decide Whether to Use Google's Location Service

On the Use Google Location Service screen, select or clear the check boxes as appropriate:

- **Use WiFi And Mobile Networks To Determine My Location**   Select this check box if you want Google's Location Service to collect anonymous location data when you're using the Galaxy Tab. Clear this check box if you want to maintain your privacy.
- **Use My Location For Improved Google Search Results And Other Google Services**   Select this check box if you want the Galaxy Tab to provide your location when you use services such as Google Search. Providing the location may get you more helpful results—assuming you want local items. Clear this check box if you don't want to provide your location.

When you've made your choices, tap the Next button to move along to the Set Date And Time screen.

Set the Date and Time

In the upper-left corner of the Set Date And Time screen, tap the Time Zone pop-up menu button, and then tap the time zone you're in. For example, tap Pacific Time, Central Time, or GMT. Again, you may need to tap and drag up or down to display other options in the pop-up menu.

To have the Galaxy Tab set the date and time automatically from a time server on the Internet, move the Use Network-Provided Time switch to the On position. Otherwise, with the Use Network-Provided Time switch in the Off position, use the Date dials to set the date and the Time dials to set the time.

When you've chosen date and time settings, tap the Next button. The Sign In With Your Google Account screen appears.

Set Up Your Google Account on the Galaxy Tab

To get the most out of your Galaxy Tab, you'll want to have a Google account. If you already have one, you can set it up on the Galaxy Tab in a few moments. If you don't have a Google account, you can sign up for one right on the Galaxy Tab.

On the Sign In With Your Google Account screen, tap the Next button. The Galaxy Tab displays a second Sign In With Your Google Account screen that has an Email field and a Password field (see Figure 1-1). Type your user name and password on the keyboard, and then tap the Sign In button.

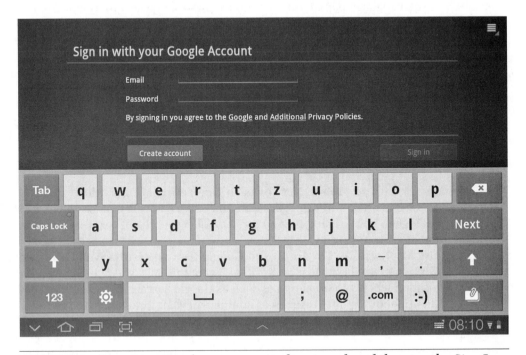

FIGURE 1-1   Type your Google user name and password, and then tap the Sign In button to sign in.

If you don't have a Google account yet, tap the Create Account button, and then follow through the process of creating an account. When you've created it, sign in.

 If you don't want to set up a Google account, tap the Skip button on the first Sign In With Your Google Account screen. Go ahead to the next section, "Meet and Navigate the Home Screen."

On the Backup And Restore screen (see Figure 1-2), choose whether to have the Galaxy Tab automatically synchronize your data with Google's servers so that you can restore the Galaxy Tab if things go wrong. This is usually a good idea, so you'll normally want to select the Keep This Device Backed Up With My Google Account check box.

Tap the Done button to finish setting up your account.

If your Galaxy Tab has a 3G connection, it should now be able to connect to Google's servers and authenticate your account. If your Galaxy Tab has only Wi-Fi, it displays the Google Account Sign-In Failure screen, which tells you that you don't have a network connection. Tap the Connect To Wi-Fi button to display the Wi-Fi Settings screen.

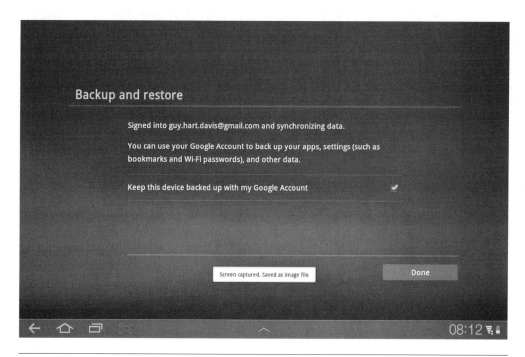

FIGURE 1-2   On the Backup And Restore screen, select the Keep This Device Backed Up With My Google Account check box if you want the Galaxy Tab to automatically synchronize your data with Google's servers.

Tap the network you want to connect to. In the dialog box the Galaxy Tab displays (shown here), type the network's password and any other information needed, and then tap the OK button.

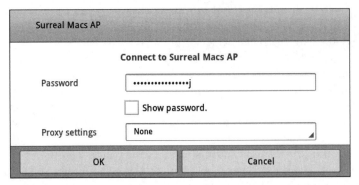

When the Galaxy Tab has connected to the wireless network, tap the Next button. The Sign In With Your Google Account screen appears again. Type your password, and then tap the Sign In button. This time, the Galaxy Tab connects to the Google servers via the wireless network (assuming it has an Internet connection), and then displays the Backup And Restore screen, as discussed above.

Meet and Navigate the Home Screen

At this point, you should be seeing the home screen. If not, follow these steps:

1. If the Galaxy Tab is off, press the power button to turn it on.
2. On the lock screen, tap the lock circle, and then drag it for a short distance in any direction until it unlocks.
3. Tap the Home button, the second button from the left in the lower-left corner of the Galaxy Tab's screen.

Figure 1-3 shows the first panel of the home screen with its key features labeled.

 What you see on the home screen depends on your Galaxy Tab model, its capabilities, and your carrier (if any). The screens shown here are typical—but yours may well be different.

The following sections explain the main features of the home screen.

Home Screen Panels

The home screen is divided into panels represented by the dots near the top of the home screen. For the home screen panel that's displayed, a number replaces the dot

FIGURE 1-3 From the home screen, you can quickly access the features and apps you need.

(for example, the 3 circle in Figure 1-3). You can change the number of home screen panels; see Chapter 2 for details.

You can move from panel to panel by tapping the dot of the panel you want to see, by dragging your finger across the screen, or by tapping at the left edge of the screen (to move to the previous panel) or the right edge of the screen (to move to the next panel). For example, tap the fourth dot to display the fourth panel, or drag from right to left to move from the first panel to the second panel. From the last panel, you need to go back or jump to another panel by tapping its dot—the panels don't wrap around from last to first.

The Buttons at the Top of the Home Screen

At the top of the home screen, there are four buttons—two on the left, and two on the right. These are the buttons on the left:

- **Google Search button**   Tap this button to open a screen for searching Google for whatever tickles your fancy.
- **Voice Actions button**   Tap this button to display the Speak Now panel, into which you can speak to give the Galaxy Tab a command. For example, if you say "Go to www.amazon.com," the Galaxy Tab switches to its browser and loads the Amazon.com home page.

These are the buttons on the right:

- **Apps button**   Tap this button to display the Apps screen, which gives you quick access to your apps.
- **Customize Home Screen button**   Tap this button to display the screen for customizing the home screen.

The Status Bar and Its Contents

Across the bottom of the screen is the Status bar, which contains the four navigation soft buttons, the Open Shortcuts Panel button, and the notifications area, which contains indicator icons.

The Four Soft Buttons

The four soft buttons appear at the left side of the Status bar most of the time you are using the Galaxy Tab. These are the buttons:

- **Back button**   Tap this button to move back to the previous screen or app.
- **Home button**   Tap this button to display the home screen, or tap and hold it to display the Task Manager.
- **Recent Apps button**   Tap this button to display the list of recent apps. Tap and hold this button to display the Apps screen.
- **Screen Capture button**   Tap this button to capture whatever is currently displayed onscreen. The Galaxy Tab saves each screen capture to the ScreenCapture folder in the file system, giving it a name based on the current date and time, and also copies the screen capture to the Clipboard so that you can paste it into a document or e-mail message.

The Open Shortcuts Panel Button

In the middle of the Status bar is the Open Shortcuts Panel button, which shows a caret icon (^). Tap this button to display the Shortcuts panel, a pop-up panel at the bottom of the screen that contains icons for essential items such as the Task Manager,

Calendar, Calculator, and Music Player. Tap the item you want to open. The Galaxy Tab then closes the Shortcuts panel automatically.

 You can't customize the shortcuts in the Shortcuts panel.

At the left end of the Shortcuts panel is the Close Shortcuts Panel button, which shows an inverted caret icon (∨). Tap this button if you need to close the Shortcuts panel without launching an app from it.

The Notifications Area

The indicator icons in the notifications area at the right end of the Status bar show the Galaxy Tab's status. Figure 1-4 shows the four items that normally appear in the notifications area:

- **Updates**   This icon indicates whether updates are available for the Galaxy Tab and its apps.
- **Clock**   This readout indicates the current time. You can change the time in the Date and Time settings.
- **Network**   This icon indicates the strength of the wireless network connection or the cellular network connection (in a 3G Galaxy Tab). A wireless network connection appears as a symbol shaped like an inverted pyramid, as shown below in the left illustration. A cellular connection appears as an inverted pyramid leaning to the left, and has characters next to it indicating its type: H for an HSDPA connection, 3G (as shown below in the right illustration) for a 3G connection, and so on.

- **Battery**   This icon indicates the battery level and whether the battery is charging.

 Different icons may appear in the notifications area on your Galaxy Tab—for example, notifications of new e-mail messages, calendar appointments, and the wireless network you've connected to.

FIGURE 1-4   The notifications area at the right end of the Status bar shows notification icons such as the Updates, Clock, Network, and Battery icons.

You can tap the notifications area to open the notifications panel, which gives you quick access to the following:

- **Date and time**   For example, 2:32 PM, Friday, January 30, 2012.
- **Battery percentage**   For example, 64%.
- **Wireless network or cellular network signal strength and name**   For example, the Surreal PCs wireless network at a three-out-of-four-bars strength, or the AT&T 3G cellular network at a four-out-of-four-bars strength.
- **Wi-Fi**   Tap this icon to turn Wi-Fi on or off.
- **Notifications**   Tap this icon to turn notifications on or off.
- **GPS**   Tap this icon to turn the GPS on or off.
- **Sound/Vibration**   Tap this icon to toggle between playing sounds and getting vibrations when the Galaxy Tab needs your attention.
- **Auto Rotation**   Tap this icon to turn Auto Rotation on or off. When Auto Rotation is on, the Galaxy Tab rotates the screen's contents to match the tablet's orientation.
- **Brightness**   Tap the slider and drag it left to dim the screen or right to brighten the screen. Tap the Auto check box to turn automatic brightness on or off.

 Automatic brightness helps to save power and make the battery last longer. But if you find automatic brightness makes the screen too dim for comfortable use, clear the Auto check box to turn automatic brightness off.

- **Settings**   Tap this icon to access the Settings app quickly.
- **Updates**   Tap this icon to see which updates are available for the Galaxy Tab's software and apps.

When you've finished using the notifications panel, tap the × button in its upper-right corner to close it. You can also tap elsewhere on the screen—for example, tap open space on the desktop.

Widgets

On the home screen panel shown in Figure 1-3, you see the Time widget, the Weather widget, and the Images widget. Widgets are small apps you use to manage the Galaxy Tab and display content on the home screens, as you'll see later in this book.

Apps

You can run an app in two ways:

- By tapping the app shortcut you've placed on the home screen. This is the best way to run apps you need frequently.

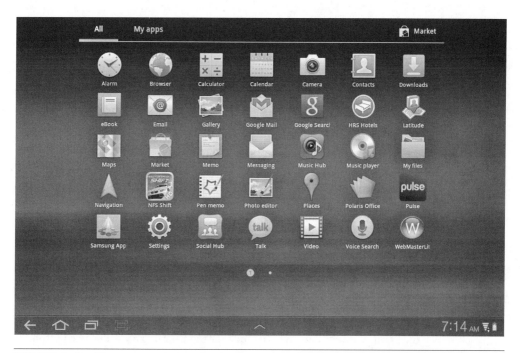

FIGURE 1-5   You can navigate the Apps screens by dragging to the left or right or by tapping the appropriate dot at the top. When you've found the app you want, tap its icon to launch it.

- By tapping the Apps button in the upper-right corner of the home screen, and then tapping the app's icon on the Apps screen that appears. Figure 1-5 shows the first screen of apps that come with a typical Galaxy Tab (as before, your Galaxy Tab model may well be different). You can navigate from one screen of apps to another by dragging your finger across the screen horizontally or by tapping the appropriate dot at the top of the screen. You can switch between viewing all the apps and viewing just your apps by tapping the All tab or the My Apps tab in the upper-left corner.

Tip   You can also display the Apps screen by tapping and holding the Recent Apps button for a couple of seconds.

You now know the essentials of the Galaxy Tab's home screen. We'll dig into all of these topics further in later chapters in the book. But for now, let's look at how you connect the Galaxy Tab to your computer, whether it's a PC (described next) or a Mac (skip ahead several pages).

Connect the Galaxy Tab to Your PC

In this section, we'll look at how to connect the Galaxy Tab to your PC so that you can start syncing data, as discussed in later chapters. As mentioned earlier, it's best to complete the first charge (and ideal to complete the full process of conditioning the battery) using the USB power adapter before you connect the Galaxy Tab to your PC—but circumstances often dictate that you connect it earlier.

Get the Samsung Kies Software

Download the Samsung Kies software from the Samsung web site (www.samsung.com). This web site shunts you to different locations depending on the country you're accessing the site from, but in general, you'll want to follow these steps:

1. Move the mouse pointer over the Support link at the top of the page, and then click the Downloads link on the bar that appears.

 Depending on which Samsung web site you access, you may need to click the Support link, type **galaxy tab** in the Find Your Product box, and then choose your Galaxy Tab model number to reach the relevant web page. After this, click the Get Downloads link, click the Software link, and look for the Samsung Kies, PC Sync button.

2. On the page that appears, click in the Search Product Support box, type **galaxy tab**, and then press ENTER. Your browser will display the Support For Galaxy Tab page.
3. Make sure the Downloads tab in the middle of the page is displayed, and then click the Software link under it.
4. In the table of software, find the row called "Samsung Kies, PC Sync," and then click the icon in the File column.
5. In the File Download – Security Warning dialog box (see Figure 1-6), click the Save button rather than the Run button—the Kies Installer is a big download, so it's better to save it to your PC's hard disk in case you need to install it again. In the Save As dialog box that opens, choose where to save the file (your Downloads folder is a good choice), and then click the Save button.

When you see the Download Complete dialog box (see Figure 1-7), click the Run button. Then install the software as described in the next section.

Install the Samsung Kies Software

If you clicked the Run button in the Download Complete dialog box (or in the File Download – Security Warning dialog box), the Kies Installer will be running at this point. If not, open a Windows Explorer window to the folder you saved the Samsung Kies Installer file in, and then double-click the file.

Whichever way you launch the installer, Windows first displays the User Account Control dialog box (see Figure 1-8) to make sure that it's you rather than a malware attack that's trying to run the installer. Click the Yes button to proceed.

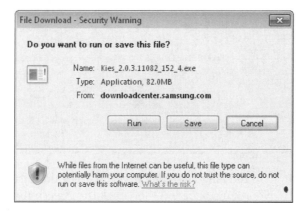

FIGURE 1-6   When downloading the Kies Installer, you'll normally want to save the file to disk.

FIGURE 1-7   When the download has finished, click the Run button in the Download Complete dialog box to launch the Kies Installer.

FIGURE 1-8   Click the Yes button in the User Account Control dialog box to go ahead and install Samsung Kies.

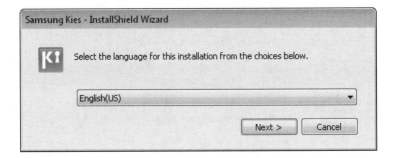

FIGURE 1-9   On the language selection screen of the InstallShield Wizard, choose your language, and then click the Next button.

After the installer cranks up the InstallShield Wizard, you'll see the language selection screen shown in Figure 1-9.

Click the drop-down button and choose your language in the drop-down list. Then click the Next button to move to the License Agreement And Choose Destination Location screen of the wizard (see Figure 1-10).

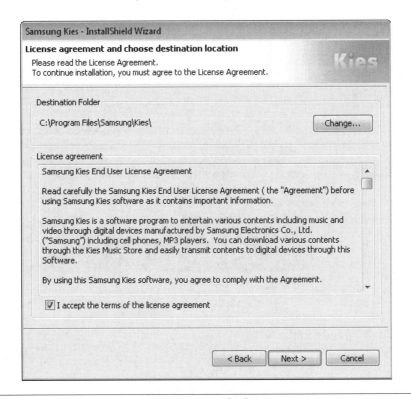

FIGURE 1-10   On the License Agreement And Choose Destination Location screen of the wizard, choose the folder in which to install Kies and select the I Accept The Terms Of The License Agreement check box.

The Destination Folder box shows the default folder for installing the Samsung Kies program: a Kies folder in a Samsung folder in the Program Files folder (for example, C:\Program Files\Samsung\Kies\). Unless you have a pressing need to install the Kies program in a different folder, accept this default choice. If you do need to choose a different folder, click the Change button, choose the folder in the dialog box that opens, and then click the OK button. (You can create a new folder in the current folder by clicking the Make New Folder button and then typing the name.)

Read through as much of the license agreement as you can bear, and select the I Accept The Terms Of The License Agreement check box if you agree to it (as you must do if you want to install it).

Click the Next button to proceed with the installation. The InstallShield Wizard then evaluates your PC and runs the installation, displaying the Setup Status screen as it does so. When installation finishes, the wizard displays the Installation Complete screen (see Figure 1-11).

Clear the Create Shortcut On Desktop check box (which is selected by default) unless you want a Kies shortcut on your Windows Desktop. Usually it's easier to run Kies from the Start menu or from the Taskbar.

Leave the Run Samsung Kies check box selected (as it is by default) if you want to run Kies immediately when the InstallShield Wizard quits. Chances are you'll want to do this.

Click the Finish button to close the InstallShield Wizard. If you left the Run Samsung Kies check box selected, Kies starts automatically. If not, you can launch

FIGURE 1-11   On the Installation Complete screen of the wizard, choose whether to create a Desktop shortcut and whether to run Kies immediately.

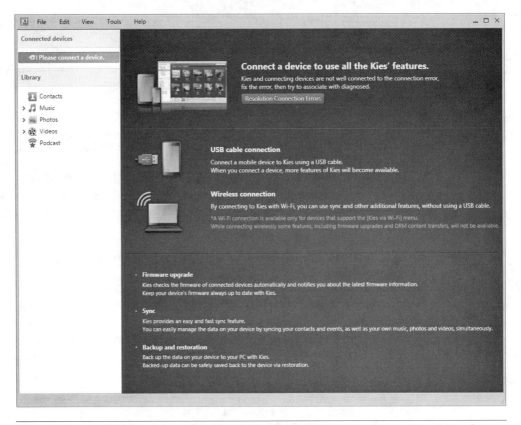

FIGURE 1-12 When you see the Please Connect A Device screen, Kies is ready for you to connect your Galaxy Tab.

it by double-clicking the Desktop shortcut (if you created one) or by choosing Start | All Programs | Samsung | Kies | Samsung Kies.

At first, Kies automatically displays the Please Connect A Device screen (see Figure 1-12).

Connect the Galaxy Tab to Your PC

When you've installed Kies and launched it, you're ready to connect the Galaxy Tab to your PC and start synchronizing it.

 You can also connect the Galaxy Tab to your PC via Wi-Fi. We'll look at how to do this in Chapter 3.

Connect the Galaxy Tab to your PC using the USB cable that came with the Galaxy Tab. Kies then displays the Connecting screen (shown here) as it establishes the connection between your PC and the Galaxy Tab.

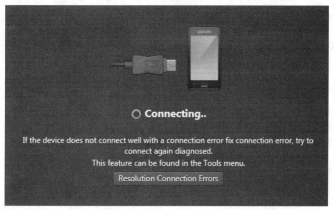

○ **Connecting..**

If the device does not connect well with a connection error fix connection error, try to connect again diagnosed.
This feature can be found in the Tools menu.

Resolution Connection Errors

Note   If Kies displays a Samsung Kies dialog box telling you that a new firmware version is available, it's a good idea to apply it. See the section "Update the Galaxy Tab's Firmware" in Chapter 14 for instructions on updating the firmware.

When you connect the Galaxy Tab to Kies, Kies displays the Galaxy Tab in the Connected Devices list in the left pane. The main pane displays the control screens for the Galaxy Tab as a whole (see Figure 1-13).

How to...   # Make Samsung Kies Recognize the Galaxy Tab

When you connect the Galaxy Tab to your PC, you may find that Samsung Kies simply doesn't recognize the device. If this happens, try these two troubleshooting moves.

First, make sure the Galaxy Tab is connected to a USB port on the PC itself rather than through a USB hub. A direct connection ensures that the Galaxy Tab gets a full-power connection, which helps avoid problems caused by underpowered connections. In particular, avoid connecting the Galaxy Tab through a USB port on a keyboard—these ports are tempting because they're convenient, but usually they have enough power only for undemanding devices such as mouses.

If even a direct connection doesn't make Kies recognize the Galaxy Tab, you may need to reregister the msxml dynamic link library (DLL) files. This sounds technical, but it's easy enough to do, and it often makes all the difference. Follow these steps:

1. Choose Start | All Programs | Accessories | Command Prompt to open a Command Prompt window.

(Continued)

2. Type **cd %windir%\system32** and press ENTER to change the directory to the System32 folder in your PC's Windows folder. (Here, cd is the "change directory" command, and %windir% is an environmental variable that stores the path to the Windows folder, no matter where the folder is or what it's called.)

3. Type **regsvr32 msxml3.dll** and press ENTER to register the msxml3.dll file. You'll see a RegSvr32 dialog box (as shown here) saying that the registration succeeded. Click the OK button.

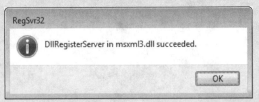

4. Type **regsvr32 msxml6.dll** and press ENTER to register the msxml6.dll file. Again, you should see the RegSvr32 dialog box saying that the registration succeeded. Click the OK button. If you get an error instead (as shown here), follow the instructions later in this sidebar.

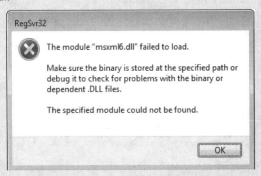

5. Click the Close button (the X button) to close the Command Prompt window.

If you get the RegSvr32 error shown in the previous illustration, the vital file named msxml6.dll is missing. Follow these steps to get it and install it:

1. Open your web browser and steer it to the Microsoft Downloads web site (www .microsoft.com/downloads/).

2. Click in the search box at the top and type **microsoft core xml services msxml** (lowercase is fine unless you're feeling formal) and then press ENTER or click the Search button.

3. On the page of search results, click the Microsoft Core XML Services (MSXML) 6.0 result to display the download page.

4. Click the Download button on the line for the msxml6.msi file. (If you're running 64-bit Windows—lucky you—click the Download button on the msxml6_x64.msi line.)

5. Open a Windows Explorer window to the folder to which you downloaded the file, and then double-click it. Follow through the Installer prompts to install the file.

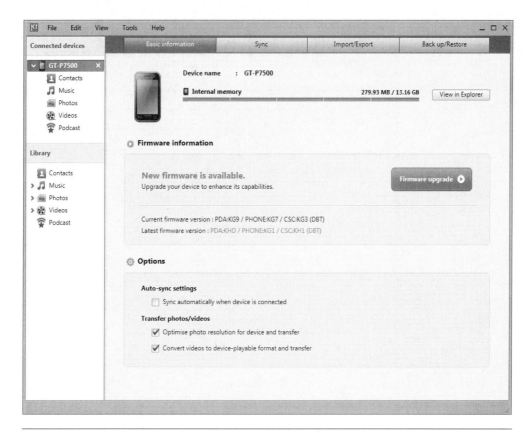

FIGURE 1-13   The Galaxy Tab appears in the Connected Devices list in Kies's left pane. When the Galaxy Tab's entry is selected, the Galaxy Tab's control screens appear in the main pane.

Set Kies to Launch Automatically When You Connect the Galaxy Tab

You'll probably find it useful to set Kies to launch automatically when you connect the Galaxy Tab to your PC. To make Kies launch automatically, follow these steps:

1. Launch Kies from the Start menu, from the Taskbar, or from a Desktop shortcut as usual.
2. Choose Tools | Preferences to display the Preferences dialog box. The General pane appears at the front (see Figure 1-14).
3. Select the Have The Components Reside In Memory When The Operating System Starts, So That Kies Can Run Faster check box to make Kies's components load at startup, so that they're ready when your PC needs them. This is a good idea if you regularly use Kies to manage your Galaxy Tab.

FIGURE 1-14 Select the two check boxes in the Auto-Run area of the General tab of the Preferences dialog box to make Kies start automatically when you connect the Galaxy Tab to your PC.

4. Select the Run Samsung Kies Automatically When A Device Is Connected check box to make Windows launch Kies when the Kies helper program detects that you've connected the Galaxy Tab to the PC.
5. Click the OK button to close the Preferences dialog box.

 If you choose Start | Computer to open a Windows Explorer window in Computer view, you'll see that the Galaxy Tab appears as a Portable Device named GT-P7500 (or a similar model number) and is identified as a Portable Media Player. You can double-click the GT-P7500 entry to display the Tablet folder, which contains the parts of the Galaxy Tab's file system that are readable to Windows.

You're now ready to use Kies on your PC to manage the Galaxy Tab—for example, to put music onto it and to copy pictures from the Galaxy Tab to your PC. I'll show you how to use Kies in Chapter 3.

Disconnect the Galaxy Tab from Your PC

When you've finished working with the Galaxy Tab from your PC, disconnect the Galaxy Tab from the PC. In Kies, take one of these actions:

- Click the Disconnect button, the × button to the right of the Galaxy Tab's listing in the Connected Devices list in the left pane in Kies.
- Right-click the Galaxy Tab's listing in the Connected Devices list, and then click the Disconnect item on the context menu.

When the Galaxy Tab's entry disappears from the Connected Devices list, you can unplug its connector cable.

 Always tell your PC to disconnect the Galaxy Tab before you unplug the cable. Otherwise, data on the Galaxy Tab may get corrupted.

Connect the Galaxy Tab to Your Mac

In this section, I'll show you how to connect the Galaxy Tab to your Mac so that you can load your media files, contacts, and other data onto it. We'll leave the process of loading and syncing information to Chapter 3.

 You can also connect the Galaxy Tab to your Mac via Wi-Fi. We'll look at how to do this in Chapter 3.

Download and Install Kies for Mac

To get Kies for Mac, steer your web browser to the Samsung web site (www.samsung .com) and download the Kies for Mac disk image. How to find Kies for Mac depends on which Samsung web site you access and how Samsung has changed it, but you should be able to locate it in either of these ways:

- Click the Support link, type **galaxy tab** in the Find Your Product box, and then choose your Galaxy Tab model number to reach the relevant web page. After this, click the Get Downloads link, click the Software link, and look for the Samsung Kies (Mac) button.
- Search for **Kies for Mac**.

When you find Kies for Mac, click its Download button. If Mac OS X doesn't automatically mount the disk image when the download finishes, click the Downloads icon on the Dock, and then click the Kies DMG file to mount it.

Once the Kies DMG file is open, double-click the Kies package (PKG) file inside it to launch the Kies Mac Installer. Click the Continue button on the first screen, and then proceed through the installation. The only choice you get is whether to install Kies on your Mac's hard drive (or SSD) or on another drive; using the hard drive (the default location) is the best choice.

When the installation completes, click the Close button. You can then launch Kies from Launchpad (in Mac OS X Lion), from Spotlight, or from the Applications folder.

 If you will use Kies frequently, keep it on the Dock. After launching Kies, CTRL-click or right-click its icon on the Dock, and then choose Options | Keep In Dock. If you want Kies to launch automatically when you log in, CTRL-click or right-click the Kies icon on the Dock, and then choose Options | Open At Login.

Run Kies for the First Time

The first time you run Kies, the application displays the Samsung Kies dialog box shown in Figure 1-15, asking if you want to add multimedia files automatically to the Kies Library.

If you want to let Kies scan, select the Automatically Scan For Multimedia Files And Add Them To The Library option button. You can then either leave the All option button selected (as it is by default) or select the Select Location option button, click the Browse button, and then use the resulting Open dialog box to pick the folder you want Kies to scan.

If you don't want to let Kies scan, make sure the Skip Auto-Scan option button is selected. You can add music files to Kies manually at any point. We'll look at how to add music files and other files to Kies in Chapter 3.

FIGURE 1-15   In this Samsung Kies dialog box, choose whether to let Kies scan your Mac's disks and folders for multimedia files to add to your Kies Library.

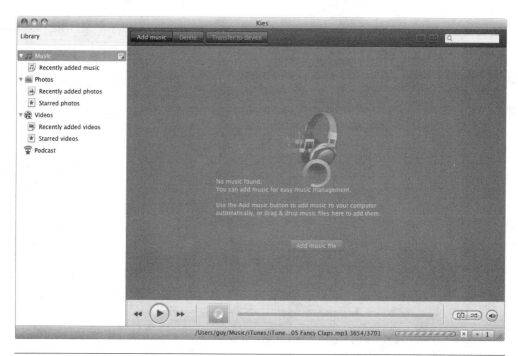

FIGURE 1-16   You can have Kies scan your Mac's drives or folders for music files such as MP3 files.

Kies's preferred audio format is MP3. If you use iTunes and have created files in the Advanced Audio Coding (AAC) format, you will need to convert them to MP3 before you can use them with Kies and the Galaxy Tab.

When you've made your choice, click the OK button. If you chose to allow Kies to scan, it begins scanning, displaying a progress readout as it does so (for example, Figure 1-16 shows Kies scanning the Music folder).

Assuming you scanned for music (and assuming Kies found some files it liked), the list of files appears in the Music category in Kies (see Figure 1-17).

Connect the Galaxy Tab to Your Mac

When you've got Kies running, loaded with your multimedia files (if you so chose), and fully updated (likewise, but advisable), you're ready to connect the Galaxy Tab to your Mac and start synchronizing it.

Connect the Galaxy Tab to your Mac using the USB cable that came with the Galaxy Tab. Kies establishes the connection, and then displays an entry for the Galaxy Tab in the Connected Devices list in the left pane. The main pane displays the control screens for the Galaxy Tab as a whole (see Figure 1-18).

FIGURE 1-17 After you search for music (or add it manually), Kies displays the list of files in the Music category.

FIGURE 1-18 The Galaxy Tab appears in the Connected Devices list in Kies's left pane. When the Galaxy Tab's entry is selected, the Galaxy Tab's control screens appear in the main pane.

How to... Deal with the "A New Network Interface Has Been Detected" Dialog Box

When you connect the Galaxy Tab to Kies, Mac OS X may display the A New Network Interface Has Been Detected dialog box saying that the "Samsung Modem" network interface has not been set up (as shown here).

A new network interface has been detected.

The "SAMSUNG Modem" network interface has not been set up. To set up this interface, use Network Preferences.

Cancel   Network Preferences...

What's happening is your Mac is seeing the Galaxy Tab as a modem that it can use to establish an Internet connection. You don't want to use the Galaxy Tab this way, although you can share the Galaxy Tab's Internet connection with your computer. (You can share the Internet connection either by "tethering" the computer using the USB cable or by turning the Galaxy Tab into a portable Wi-Fi hotspot. We'll look at both these moves in Chapter 13.) But until you tell your Mac how to deal with the Galaxy Tab's modem aspect, your Mac will keep prompting you when you connect the Galaxy Tab.

So click the Network Preferences button in the dialog box to display the Network pane in System Preferences (shown here). You'll see a SAMSUNG Modem entry in the list of network interfaces, marked Not Configured because you haven't configured it.

Instead of configuring the SAMSUNG Modem entry, click the Apply button. This adds the SAMSUNG Modem item to your Mac's network configuration, which stops Mac OS X from prompting you about it when you connect the Galaxy Tab to your Mac in the future.

If Kies displays a Samsung Kies dialog box telling you that a new firmware version is available, it's a good idea to apply it. See the section "Update the Galaxy Tab's Firmware" in Chapter 14 for instructions on updating the firmware.

Disconnect the Galaxy Tab from Your Mac

When you want to disconnect the Galaxy Tab from your Mac, tell Kies to disconnect it. Take either of these actions in Kies:

- Click the Disconnect button, the × button to the right of the Galaxy Tab's listing in the Connected Devices list in the left pane in Kies.
- CTRL-click or right-click the Galaxy Tab's listing in the Connected Devices list, and then click the Disconnect item on the context menu.

When the Galaxy Tab's entry disappears from the Connected Devices list, you can unplug its connector cable.

 Always tell your Mac to disconnect the Galaxy Tab before you unplug the cable. Otherwise, data on the Galaxy Tab may get corrupted.

2

Customize the Galaxy Tab to Suit You

HOW TO...

- Customize the home screen panels
- Switch quickly among the home screen panels
- Rearrange the widgets on the home screen panels
- Add a folder to a home screen panel
- Choose the most important settings
- Choose firewall settings on the Galaxy Tab
- Connect a Bluetooth device
- Manage your wireless network connections
- Tell a 3G Galaxy Tab when to switch from Wi-Fi to mobile data
- Outfit the Galaxy Tab with accessories

In this chapter, I'll show you how to customize your Galaxy Tab to suit the way you work and play.

We'll start by customizing the home screen panels so that you can quickly access the apps you use most. From there, we'll move on to choosing the most important settings on the Galaxy Tab. The Galaxy Tab has a huge number of settings, so you can make it work the way you prefer—as long as you're prepared to spend a little time exploring the settings and trying different combinations.

Toward the end of the chapter, I'll show you how to connect Bluetooth devices to the Galaxy Tab. For example, you may want to pair a Bluetooth keyboard with the Galaxy Tab so that you can enter text more quickly. We'll then dig into how to manage your wireless network connections, which you'll almost certainly need to do if your Galaxy Tab connects to more than one wireless network.

Finally, I'll discuss how you can add accessories to the Galaxy Tab to protect it, make it easier to use, and extend its functionality.

Customize the Home Screen Panels

Chances are you'll spend a lot of time looking at the Galaxy Tab's home screen, so it's a good idea to take a few minutes to customize it with wallpaper you like, the apps and widgets you want, and however many panels you actually need rather than the default number.

How to... ## Switch Quickly Among the Home Screen Panels

You can switch quickly among the home screen panels in several ways:

- Tap the home screen dots at the top of the screen. For example, tap the fifth dot to display the fifth home screen panel.
- When the Galaxy Tab is in landscape view, you can also tap on the left side of the screen to display the previous panel or the right side of the screen to display the next panel.
- Pan the Galaxy Tab sideways, as described later in this chapter.

Tap the Customize (+) button in the upper-right corner of the screen, or tap and hold on blank space on any of the screens. The Galaxy Tab displays the Add To Home Screen Options screen, whose upper part displays thumbnails of all your home screen panels, as shown here. Tap the panel you want to display.

Change the Wallpaper

The quick way to make the home screen look different is to change the wallpaper, the picture that appears behind everything else on the home screen.

 You can use only a single picture for the wallpaper—you can't use a different picture for each panel, as many of us would like to do. Each home screen panel shows a different part of the picture (if there's enough of the picture to go around).

To change the wallpaper, follow these steps:

1. If you're not already at the home screen, tap the Home button to display it.
2. Tap the Customize (+) button in the upper-right corner, or tap and hold on blank space anywhere in the main part of the screen—in other words, not at the left and right side, where you tap to display the previous home screen or next home screen. The Galaxy Tab displays the Add To Home Screen Options screen. This is the screen you use for customizing most aspects of the home screen.
3. Tap the Wallpapers tab to display the wallpaper categories in the lower half of the screen (as shown here). You then have three choices:
    *   **Gallery**   The Gallery app includes screenshots you've taken with the Galaxy Tab.
    *   **Live Wallpapers**   Live wallpapers feature motion, such as a galaxy of swirling stars.
    *   **Wallpapers**   The Wallpapers Gallery contains static wallpapers, including the default wallpaper.

You can then choose a wallpaper as discussed in the following subsections.

Choose Wallpaper from Your Gallery

To choose a wallpaper from your gallery, follow these steps:

1. On the Wallpapers tab of the Add To Home Screen Options screen, tap the Gallery button. The Galaxy Tab displays the Set As dialog box, shown here.

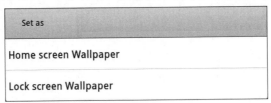

2. Tap the appropriate button to tell the Galaxy Tab which wallpaper you want to change:
   - **Home Screen Wallpaper** Tap this button to set the wallpaper behind the home screens.
   - **Lock Screen Wallpaper** Tap this button to set the wallpaper that appears on the lock screen, the screen you see when the Galaxy Tab is locked.
3. The Galaxy Tab then displays the Select Photo dialog box, shown here.

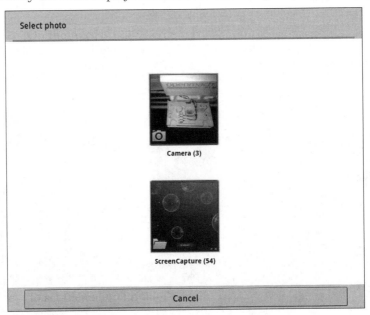

4. Tap the appropriate button:
   - **Camera** Tap this button to see photos you've taken with the camera.
   - **ScreenCapture** Tap this button to see screens you've captured with the ScreenCapture utility.

5. The Galaxy Tab then displays the photos or screen captures in the Select Photo dialog box, as shown here.

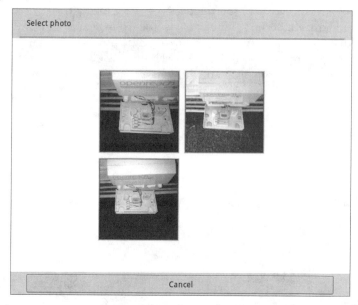

6. Tap the photo or screen capture you want to use. The Galaxy Tab displays it full screen with rectangles showing suggested cropping to fit the screen, as shown in Figure 2-1.

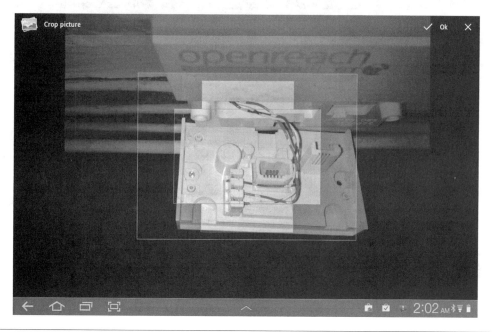

FIGURE 2-1   The Galaxy Tab displays rectangles suggesting how to crop the photo or screen capture to suit the screen.

7. Adjust the cropping as necessary by tapping the crop area and dragging the selection handles that appear.
8. When you have chosen the part you want to keep, tap the OK button in the upper-right corner of the screen. The Galaxy Tab applies the wallpaper and displays the screen for customizing the home screen.
9. Tap the thumbnail of the home screen you want to display. The Galaxy Tab then displays the home screen, and you can get back to work.

Choose a Live Wallpaper

If you want the Galaxy Tab's lock screen or home screen to display movement rather than a static picture, apply one of the live wallpapers. To do so, follow these steps:

1. On the Add To Home Screen Options screen, tap the Live Wallpapers button on the Wallpapers tab. The Galaxy Tab displays the Select Live Wallpaper dialog box (shown here).

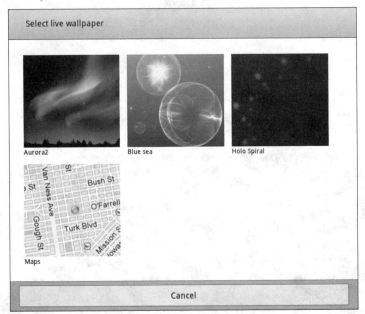

2. Tap the button for the live wallpaper you want. The Galaxy Tab displays a full-screen preview of the wallpaper (see Figure 2-2).

 If the live wallpaper you choose displays a Settings button to the left of the Set Wallpaper button, tap this Settings button to access a screen of settings you can change for the live wallpaper.

3. Tap the Set Wallpaper button. The Galaxy Tab applies the wallpaper to the home screen.

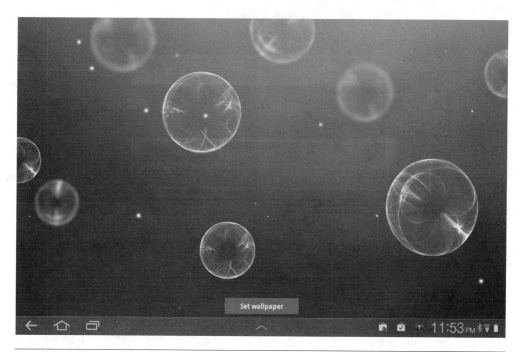

FIGURE 2-2   On the wallpaper preview screen, make sure you like the live wallpaper, and then tap the Set Wallpaper button at the bottom of the screen.

 The live wallpapers look great, but they make the processor work harder and shorten the Galaxy Tab's battery life. To get the best battery life, choose a static wallpaper.

Choose Wallpaper from the Wallpaper Gallery

To choose one of the Galaxy Tab's built-in wallpapers, follow these steps:

1. On the Add To Home Screen Options screen, tap the Wallpapers button on the Wallpapers tab. The Galaxy Tab displays the Set As dialog box (shown here).

2. Tap the appropriate button to tell the Galaxy Tab which wallpaper you want to change:
   - **Home Screen Wallpaper**   Tap this button to set the wallpaper behind the home screens.

- **Lock Screen Wallpaper** Tap this button to set the wallpaper that appears on the lock screen, the screen you see when the Galaxy Tab is locked.

3. The Galaxy Tab then displays the Select Wallpaper dialog box (shown here).

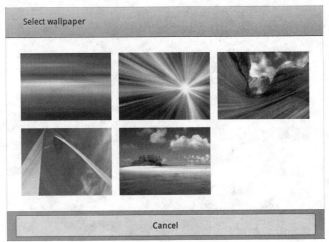

4. Tap the wallpaper picture you want to apply. The Galaxy Tab applies the wallpaper and displays the screen for customizing the home screen.
5. Tap the thumbnail of the home screen you want to display. The Galaxy Tab then displays the home screen, and you can get back to work.

Add an App Shortcut to a Home Screen Panel

Chances are you'll need to run some apps much more often than others. To save time launching an app, you can place an app shortcut on a home screen panel like this:

1. Tap the Home button to display the home screen if you're not already there.
2. Tap or scroll to display the home screen panel you want to add the app shortcut to.
3. Tap the Customize (+) button in the upper-right corner to display the Add To Home Screen Options screen. You can also tap and hold on blank space anywhere in the main part of the screen (not at the left side or right side in landscape view).
4. Tap the App Shortcuts tab in the middle of the screen. The list of apps appears in the lower part of the screen (see Figure 2-3).
5. If necessary, scroll left or right to locate the app you want to add.
6. Tap the app to add it to the selected home screen panel.

 You can also tap an app and drag it to one of the other home screen panels.

7. When you finish customizing the home screen, tap the Back button to leave the Add To Home Screen Options screen and return to the home screen.

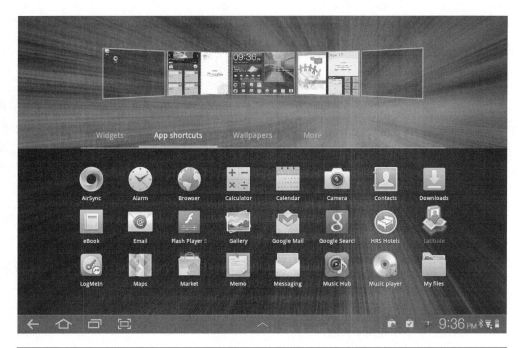

FIGURE 2-3   To add an app shortcut icon to the selected home screen panel, tap the App Shortcuts tab on the Add To Home Screen Options screen, and then tap the icon for the app you want to add. The selected home screen panel has a blue border around it.

Add a Widget to a Home Screen Panel

The Galaxy Tab includes various *widgets*, small apps that you can run on a home screen panel to provide an ever-present feed of information.

To add a widget to a home screen panel, follow these steps:

1. Tap the Home button to display the home screen if you're not already there.
2. Tap or scroll to display the home screen panel you want to add the widget to.
3. Tap the Customize (+) button in the upper-right corner to display the Add To Home Screen Options screen. You can also tap and hold on blank space anywhere in the main part of the screen (not at the left side or right side in landscape view).
4. Tap the Widgets tab in the middle of the screen. The list of widgets appears in the lower part of the screen.
5. If necessary, scroll left or right to locate the widget you want to add.
6. Tap the widget to add it to the home screen panel. You can also tap an app and drag it to one of the other home screen panels, as shown with the Google Maps widget in Figure 2-4.

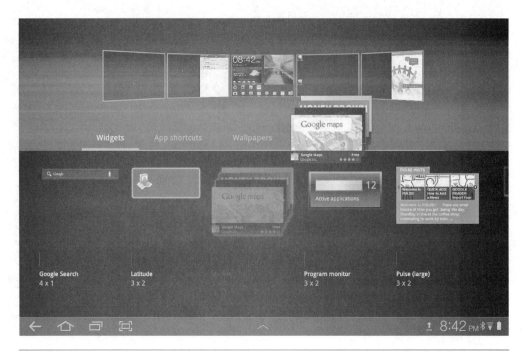

FIGURE 2-4 To add a widget to the selected home screen panel, tap the Widgets tab on the Add To Home Screen Options screen, and then tap the widget you want to add. The selected home screen panel has a blue border around it.

Note If the home screen panel you've chosen doesn't have room for the widget you're trying to put on it, the Galaxy Tab displays a message saying "No more room on this home screen."

7. When you finish customizing the home screen, tap either the Back button or the Home button to return to the home screen so that you can see the items you've added.

How to... **Rearrange the Widgets on the Home Screen Panels**

To move a widget to a different position on the home screen panel, tap and hold the widget until the widget grows slightly and the Remove button appears in the upper-right corner of the screen. Drag the widget to where you want it, and then let go of it. The Galaxy Tab displays blue guidelines to help you position the widget.

Add Other Items to Your Home Screen Panels

You can also add items such as bookmarks, contacts, and Kies Via Wi-Fi to your home screen panels. To do so, follow these steps:

1. Tap the Home button to display the home screen if you're not already there.
2. Tap or scroll to display the home screen panel you want to add the item to.
3. Tap the Customize (+) button in the upper-right corner to display the Add To Home Screen Options screen. You can also tap and hold on blank space anywhere in the main part of the screen (not at the left side or right side in landscape view).
4. Tap the More tab in the middle of the screen. The list of items appears in the lower part of the screen (see Figure 2-5).
5. Tap the item you want to add to the home screen panel.

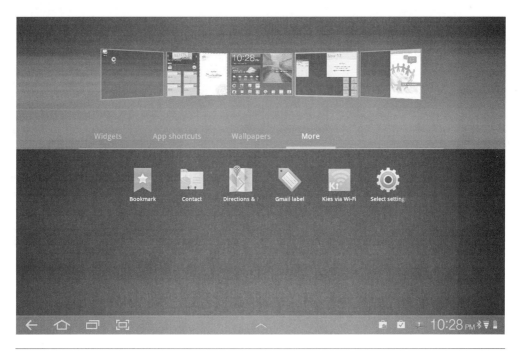

FIGURE 2-5   Tap the More tab on the Add To Home Screen Options screen to add items such as bookmarks, contacts, Gmail labels, and Kies Via Wi-Fi to a home screen panel.

6. If the Galaxy Tab prompts you for extra information, provide it. For example:
   - When you tap the Select Setting item, the Galaxy Tab displays the Select Settings Shortcut dialog box (shown here) so that you can pick the Settings shortcut you want.

Select settings shortcut

Language and input

Location and security

Manage applications

Memory usage

Running services

Screen

Sound

VPN settings

Wi-Fi settings

Cancel

   - When you tap the Contact item, the Galaxy Tab displays the Select Contact Shortcut dialog box so that you can choose which contact to put on the home screen panel.
7. When you finish customizing the home screen panels, tap either the Back button or the Home button to return to the home screen so that you can see the items you've added.

Remove an Item from a Home Screen Panel

To remove an item from a home screen panel, tap and hold the item's icon until it grows slightly and the Remove button appears in the upper-right corner of the screen. Then drag the item over the Remove button. When the item turns red, release it, and the Galaxy Tab removes it from the home screen panel.

Add a Folder to a Home Screen Panel

To keep your files in order, you may find it useful to create shortcuts to one or more folders on your Galaxy Tab's home screen panels. The Galaxy Tab's Android Honeycomb operating system lets you put a shortcut to the My Files app on the home screen, but it doesn't provide a way to put a folder shortcut on a home screen panel.

To put a folder shortcut on a home screen panel, you need to use an app such as ES File Explorer. Tap the folder's name in ES File Explorer to display the Operations dialog box (shown here), and then tap the Shortcut button.

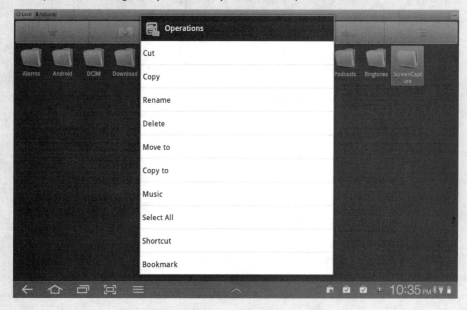

You can get ES File Explorer from Android Market; at this writing, it's free.

Choose the Most Important Settings

The Galaxy Tab's Android Honeycomb operating system has a vast number of settings that enable you to customize the Galaxy Tab's behavior as needed. In this section, I'll show you the settings you'll often want to change to make the Galaxy Tab behave the way you want.

Note   Some of the settings are more esoteric. We'll look at these settings later in the book along with their topics. For example, we'll examine the Applications settings in Chapter 12, which shows you how to get the most out of apps.

Open the Settings App

To start working with settings, open the Settings app. From the home screen, tap the Apps icon in the upper-right corner, and then tap the Settings icon. (You may have to scroll to the second Apps screen to find the Settings icon.)

Figure 2-6 shows the Settings screen in portrait orientation, so that you can see the full list of settings categories on the left.

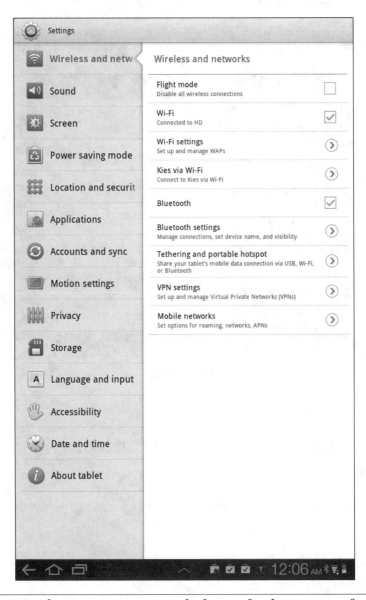

FIGURE 2-6 On the Settings screen, tap the button for the category of settings you want to adjust.

The first category of settings is Wireless And Network. We'll look at these in the section "Manage Your Wireless Network Connections," toward the end of this chapter. So we'll start with Sound settings, the second category.

Choose Sound Settings

Your Galaxy Tab comes equipped with a full range of sound options—and chances are that you'll want to set most of them. Tap the Sound button on the Settings screen to display the Sound screen (shown in Figure 2-7), and then work through the General settings, Notifications setting, and Feedback settings as discussed in the following subsections.

Choose General Sound Settings

In the General area of the Sound screen, you can choose the following settings:

- **Vibrate**   To change when the Galaxy Tab gives you a tickle, tap this button, and then choose the appropriate option button in the Vibrate dialog box

FIGURE 2-7   The Sound screen includes settings for vibration and volume; setting a notification ringtone; and getting feedback.

(shown here): Always, Never, Only In Silent Mode, or Only When Not In Silent Mode. The Galaxy Tab closes the dialog box when you tap one of the option buttons.

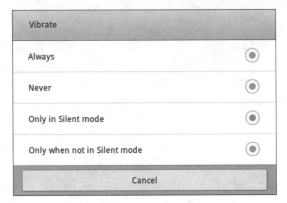

- **Volume** To set the volume at which the Galaxy Tab plays notifications, media (for example, music), and alarms, tap this button, and then drag the sliders in the Volume dialog box (shown here). The System Volume slider controls the overall volume—for example, turn it down if you find the Galaxy Tab's sound too loud overall. Tap the OK button when you've made your choices.

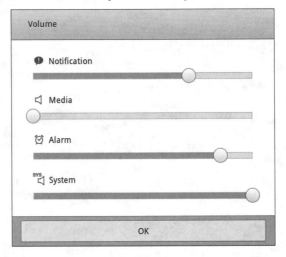

Choose Notifications Settings

To help you distinguish your notifications from those on all the other devices around you, the Galaxy Tab lets you choose from a wide variety of ringtones.

To set a ringtone, follow these steps:

1. Tap the Notification Ringtone button. The Galaxy Tab displays the Ringtones dialog box.

2. Tap a ringtone to play it and to select its option button. Scroll up and down to see the full range of ringtones.

 Tip Tap the Silent option button at the top if you do not want any sound to play for notifications.

3. When you find the ringtone you want, tap the OK button to close the Ringtones dialog box.

Choose Feedback Settings

In the Feedback area of the Sound screen, you can set the following four settings:

- **Audible Selection**   Select this check box to have the Galaxy Tab play a feedback tone when you select an item. For example, when you tap a folder on the home screen, the Galaxy Tab plays a *plink* noise. This feedback can be helpful when you're getting the hang of the tap screen, but it quickly becomes annoying.
- **Screen Lock Sounds**   Select this check box if you want the Galaxy Tab to play tones when you lock and unlock the screen. This feedback tends to be helpful as confirmation that you've applied or removed the locking.
- **Haptic Feedback**   Select this check box if you want the Galaxy Tab to vibrate gently when you press soft keys and take other actions onscreen. Many people find this response helpful. Others hate it.
- **Vibration Intensity**   To control how much of a buzz the Galaxy Tab gives you, tap the Vibration Intensity button to display the Vibration Intensity dialog box (shown here). Drag the slider to set anything from a frisson to a minor earthquake, and then tap the OK button.

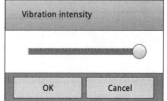

Choose Screen Settings

To control how the Galaxy Tab's screen appears, tap the Screen button on the Settings screen to display the Screen settings screen (shown in Figure 2-8). You can then choose the following settings:

- **Brightness**   To set the screen's brightness, tap the Brightness button, and then drag the slider in the Brightness dialog box (shown here). You can select the Automatic Brightness check box if you want the Galaxy Tab to automatically adjust its brightness to the lighting conditions it detects, but at this writing this feature is too erratic for regular use.

FIGURE 2-8 The Screen settings screen lets you change the font, brightness, colors, and more.

 Two things here. First, decreasing the screen brightness is a great way of saving battery power and extending runtime—but there's little point in turning down the brightness past the point where you can comfortably see the screen. Second, if you find the Automatic Brightness feature suddenly turns the brightness way down for no apparent reason, chances are you've put a finger over the light sensor. Move your fingers, and the Galaxy Tab will stop thinking that night has suddenly fallen.

- **Screen Display** Tap the Screen Display button to display the Screen Display screen (shown here), from which you can change the font style and the wallpaper as discussed next. Tap the Screen link at the top of the screen to return to the Screen settings screen. You can also tap the Back button.

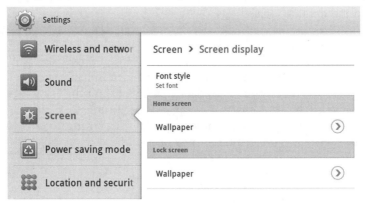

- **Font Style** Tap the Font Style button to display the Choose New Font dialog box (shown here). You can either tap the option button for one of the current fonts or tap the Get Fonts Online button to download further fonts from Android Market. If this is the first time you've used Android Market, you'll need to agree to the Terms of Service—after reading them 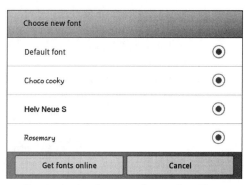 through carefully, of course. Tapping a font's option button closes the Choose New Font dialog box and applies that font.

- **Wallpaper** You can start the process of changing the wallpaper by tapping the Wallpaper button in the Home Screen area or the Wallpaper button in the Lock Screen area. Unless you like working from the Settings app, it's usually easier to change the wallpaper starting from the home screen, as discussed earlier in this chapter.

- **Mode** If the way colors appear onscreen looks wrong to you, tap the Mode button to display the Mode dialog box (shown here). You can then tap the Dynamic option button, the Standard option button, or the Movie option button to see the different color modes available. Tap the OK button when you've picked the best of the three modes for your needs.

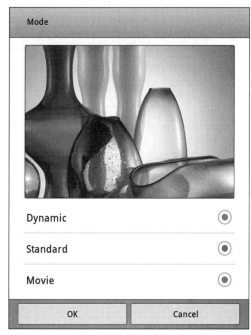

- **Auto-Rotate Screen** Select this check box to allow the Galaxy Tab to rotate the screen automatically to match the orientation it detects. Clear the check box to fix the orientation.
- **Animation** To choose how many animations the Galaxy Tab displays when opening, closing, and moving windows, tap the Animation button. In the Animation dialog box (shown here), select the No Animations option button, the Some Animations option button, or the All Animations option button (the default).

- **Timeout** To change the length of time the screen stays lit, tap the Timeout button. In the Timeout dialog box (shown here), tap the option button for the length of time you want: 15 Seconds, 30 Seconds, 1 Minute, 2 Minutes, 5 Minutes, 10 Minutes, or 30 Minutes. If saving power is more important than convenience, set the timeout to as short an interval as you can tolerate.

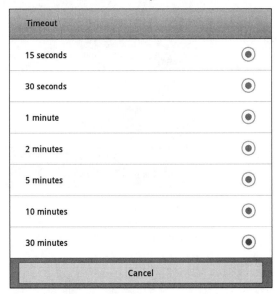

- **Auto Adjust Screen Power** Select this check box if you want the Galaxy Tab to save power by decreasing the screen brightness when you're looking at a bright or contrasty image. This setting is well worth trying, but if you don't like the effects it produces, turn it off again.

- **Horizontal Calibration**   If the Galaxy Tab doesn't react consistently when you tilt it, you may need to reset the horizontal calibration. To do so, follow these steps:

   1. Tap the Horizontal Calibration button on the Screen settings screen to display the Horizontal Calibration dialog box (shown here).

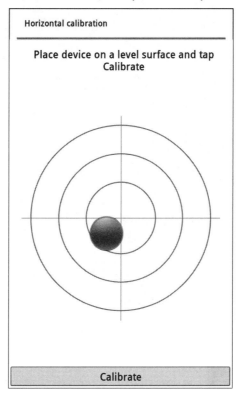

   2. Place the Galaxy Tab on a flat surface—for example, a table or desk.
   3. Tap the Calibrate button.

Choose Power Saving Mode Settings

To make the Galaxy Tab as miserly as possible with its precious power, tap the Power Saving Mode button in the left column of the Settings screen, and then work on the Power Saving Mode screen (see Figure 2-9).

At the top of the Power Saving Mode screen, select the Use Power Saving Mode check box to enable Power Saving mode. Selecting this check box makes the Galaxy Tab automatically turn on Power Saving mode when the battery reaches the level you specify.

FIGURE 2-9 Use the settings on the Power Saving Mode screen to squeeze the most usage out of each charge of the Galaxy Tab's battery.

To control the battery level, tap the Power Saving Mode On button, and then tap the appropriate option button in the Power Saving Mode On dialog box: 10% Battery Power, 30% Battery Power, 50% Battery Power, or 70% Battery Power. Tapping the option button closes the Power Saving Mode On dialog box.

Note   Which option button you should select in the Power Saving Mode On dialog box depends on how aggressively you need to save power. For example, selecting the 50% Battery Power option button lets you burn through the first half of the battery's capacity before switching to frugal mode.

In the Power Saving Mode Settings area of the Power Saving Mode screen, you can choose the following settings:

- **Turn Off Wi-Fi**   Select this check box to turn Wi-Fi off unless the Galaxy Tab is actually connected to a wireless access point. Wi-Fi can burn through a surprising amount of power, so selecting this check box can be a big help in eking out more battery life.
- **Turn Off Bluetooth**   Select this check box to turn off Bluetooth when you're not using it. Unless you use Bluetooth extensively, this is a great way to save power.
- **Turn Off GPS**   Select this check box to turn off the GPS unit when you're not using it.
- **Turn Off Sync**   Select this check box to turn off automatic syncing.
- **Brightness**   To control how bright the screen is when Power Saving mode is on, tap this button, and then tap the appropriate option button in the Brightness dialog box (shown here): 10%, 30%, 50%, 70%, or 100%. Tapping the option button closes the dialog box and applies your choice.

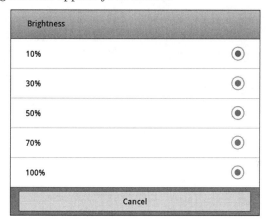

- **Timeout**   To control how long the screen stays on after you finish fondling it, tap this button, and then tap the appropriate option button in the Timeout dialog box: 15 Seconds, 30 Seconds, 1 Minute, 2 Minutes, 5 Minutes, 10 Minutes, or 30 Minutes. For most purposes, 30 Seconds or 1 Minute is a good choice. Tapping the option button closes the dialog box and applies your choice.
- **Power Saving Tips**   Tap this button to display a screen showing tips on saving power.

When the battery level reaches the threshold you set, the Galaxy Tab displays a dialog box prompting you to switch to Power Saving mode. Tap the OK button if you want to do so.

Choose Location and Security Settings

The Location And Security screen (shown in Figure 2-10) contains some settings (such as the My Location settings and the Lock Screen settings) that you'll probably want to set and others (such as the Device Administration settings and the Credential Storage settings) that you will probably not need to set.

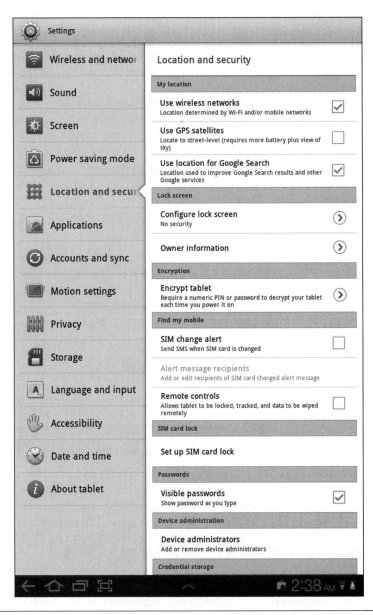

FIGURE 2-10 On the Location And Security screen, you can choose settings for identifying your location and locking the screen.

Choose My Location Settings

In the My Location area, you can control how the Galaxy Tab determines your location:

- **Use Wireless Networks**   Select this check box to use Wi-Fi networks that Google has logged and cellular networks (if your Galaxy Tab has 3G) to determine your location. Using this option gives your approximate location and needs only a modest amount of battery power.
- **Use GPS Satellites**   Select this check box to use Global Positioning System (GPS) satellites to determine your location more exactly. Using GPS takes more battery power, and the Galaxy Tab needs to have a more-or-less unobstructed view of the sky.
- **Use Location For Google Search**   Select this check box to allow the Galaxy Tab to provide your location when searching on Google Search and using other Google services. Providing your location enables you to get more-targeted search results. If you don't want to provide this information, clear this check box.

Set Up a Screen Lock

To prevent anyone else from using the Galaxy Tab if you mislay it, you can apply a screen lock that uses a pattern of movements, a PIN, or a password.

To set up the screen lock, tap the Configure Lock Screen button in the Lock Screen area of the Location And Security screen, and then work with the Configure Lock Screen controls (shown here). Tap the appropriate button (described next), and the Galaxy Tab walks you through the process of setting up the screen lock:

- **Off**   Tap this button to prevent the screen from locking.
- **Unsecure**   Tap this button to allow the screen to lock but not protect it. Anyone can then unlock the screen.
- **Pattern**   Tap this button to set up a pattern that you draw with your finger on a grid of nine dots. The pattern is a neat way of unlocking the screen, because you can draw the pattern more easily than you can type a PIN or a password. The disadvantage is that the pattern is less secure than either a PIN or a password.
- **PIN**   Tap this button to set up a Personal Identification Number (PIN) that you must type to unlock the screen. The PIN must be at least four digits long, but you can make it much longer for greater security.
- **Password**   Tap this button to set up a password that you must type to unlock the screen. The password must be at least four characters long, but you can create a longer password for additional security.

After you apply a Pattern, PIN, or Password screen lock, two more settings appear in the Lock Screen area of the Location And Security screen. To control how quickly the Galaxy Tab locks the screen after the screen turns off, tap the Timeout button, and then tap the appropriate option button in the Timeout dialog box—for example, tap the Immediately option button or the 5 Seconds option button. And if you want the Galaxy Tab to give tactile feedback as you enter the password or PIN, select the Use Tactile Feedback check box.

Add Your Owner Information to the Lock Screen

To increase your chance of getting the Galaxy Tab back if you lose it, you can make the lock screen display owner information—for example, the phone number to call to find out how to return the tablet.

To add the owner information, tap the Owner Information button in the Lock Screen area of the Location And Security screen. On the Owner Information screen (shown here) that appears, select the Show Owner Info On Lock Screen check box, and then type the ransom name and number in the text box.

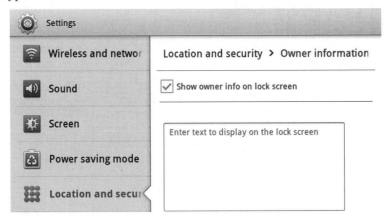

Encrypt the Galaxy Tab and Its Contents

If the Galaxy Tab contains sensitive or confidential data, you can encrypt it so that an attacker can't read it.

 Before turning on encryption, make sure you understand how encryption works.

Here's how encryption works:

- You specify a password or a numeric PIN for the encryption.
- The Galaxy Tab then encrypts its data. This can take an hour or so, depending on how big the Galaxy Tab's storage is and how much data you've stuffed in there.

You mustn't interrupt the encryption process, because doing so may lose data. To avoid power problems, the Galaxy Tab refuses to start encrypting itself until the battery is fully charged *and* the charger is plugged in.

- Once the Galaxy Tab is encrypted, you must enter your password or PIN each time you turn the Galaxy Tab on.

 If you forget your encryption password or PIN, you will not be able to recover the data from the Galaxy Tab. But you can get the Galaxy Tab working again by performing a factory data reset from Kies. This erases all your data from the Galaxy Tab.

After encrypting your Galaxy Tab, you should power it down to protect it fully instead of leaving it running but locked.

To encrypt your Galaxy Tab, follow these steps:

1. Plug the Galaxy Tab into its charger and charge the battery fully.
2. Set a lock screen PIN or password, as described earlier in this chapter.
3. In the Encryption area of the Location And Security screen, tap the Encrypt Tablet button, The Encrypt Tablet screen appears.
4. Tap the Encrypt Tablet button. The Confirm Password screen appears.
5. Type your lock screen PIN or password, and then tap the Continue button. The Confirm Encryption screen appears.
6. Tap the Encrypt Tablet button. The Galaxy Tab launches the encryption process, which includes several restarts.
7. When you see the password prompt, type your password. The Galaxy Tab then starts and displays the lock screen, where you have to type the password again to unlock the Galaxy Tab.

 To decrypt the Galaxy Tab again, tap the Decrypt Device button on the Location And Security screen in the Settings app (the Decrypt Device button appears in place of the Encrypt Tablet button). On the Decrypt Device screen that appears, tap the Decrypt Device button. Type your password on the Confirm Password screen and tap the Continue button, then tap the Decrypt Device button (yes, a third button with this name) on the Confirm Decryption screen. Then wait while the Galaxy Tab decrypts itself; again, this requires several reboots. When the lock screen appears, type your password, and you'll be back in business.

Set Up Find My Mobile Options

The Find My Mobile area of the Location And Security screen for a 3G-capable Galaxy Tab contains three options you can set in case your Galaxy Tab goes missing:

- **SIM Change Alert**   Select this check box to have an SMS message (a text message) sent to you when someone changes the SIM card in the Galaxy Tab. After selecting this check box, you must accept Samsung's terms and conditions for this service and then sign up with a Samsung account.

Signing up for a Samsung account involves providing your e-mail address (real), date of birth (old enough to allay any worries under the Children's Online Privacy Protection Act, COPPA), and a password.

- **Alert Message Recipients**   After selecting the SIM Change Alert check box and accepting the terms and conditions, tap this button, and then set up the list of people who should receive the text message warning of the SIM change. For example, you'll normally want to add your cell phone number to the list.

 On a Wi-Fi–only Galaxy Tab, only the Remote Controls option appears in the Find My Mobile area.

- **Remote Controls**   Select this check box if you want to be able to lock the Galaxy Tab remotely, track where it is, and wipe data from it. After selecting this check box, you must accept Samsung's terms and conditions for this service and then sign up with a Samsung account. (If you've just created a Samsung account for the SIM Change Alert service, you just need to enter your password.)

Lock the SIM Card

If you need to ensure nobody unauthorized makes phone calls with your Galaxy Tab, tap the Set Up SIM Card Lock button in the SIM Card Lock area of the Location And Security screen, and then use the options on the Set Up SIM Card Lock screen to apply a PIN to the SIM card.

Make Passwords Visible

As you've seen already, the Galaxy Tab by default hides the characters of passwords you type, in case someone is snooping over your shoulder. You can reveal the characters of any password when you feel safe. But if you want to see password characters all the time, select the Visible Passwords check box in the Passwords area of the Location And Security screen.

Choose Device Administration Settings

If you are setting up the Galaxy Tab for a managed environment (for example, in a company or organization), you may need to add administrators. To do so, tap the Device Administrators button in the Device Administration area of the Location And Security screen, and then work on the Device Administrators screen.

   If you are using the Galaxy Tab outside a managed environment, the Device Administrators screen shows the message "No device administrators available"—so you can't do anything from this screen.

Choose Credential Storage Settings

If you need to use digital certificates to authenticate the Galaxy Tab to servers, work in the Credential Storage area of the Location And Security screen. For example, you

may need to add a digital certificate to enable the
Galaxy Tab to connect to a virtual private network
(VPN) at your workplace.

To turn on the usage of secure credentials, select
the Use Secure Credentials check box. Type your
password in the Enter Password dialog box (shown
here) that appears, and then tap the OK button.

If the Galaxy Tab has a credential password set, and you have forgotten it, you
need to wipe out the password and existing credentials so that you can set a new
password. Tap the Clear Storage button at the bottom of the Credential Storage
area on the Location And Security screen, and then tap the OK button in the
Attention dialog box that appears.

To add credentials, connect to your Galaxy Tab a USB storage device containing
the credentials. Then tap the Install From USB Storage button.

To change the password for credential storage, tap the Set Password button. Type
the existing password and the new password (twice) in the Set Password dialog box
(shown here), and then tap the OK button.

To clear all your credentials and reset the password, tap the Clear Storage button
at the bottom of the Credential Storage area on the Location And Security screen, and
then tap the OK button in the Attention dialog box (shown here) that appears.

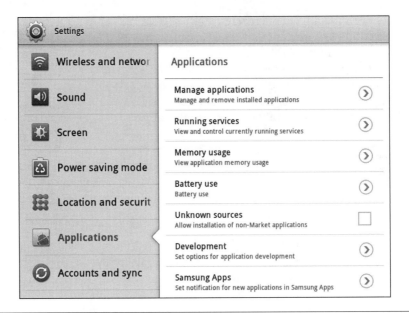

FIGURE 2-11 From the Applications screen in the Settings app, you can manage apps and services, view memory or battery usage, and set extra features for running apps.

Choose Applications Settings

To control how apps run on the Galaxy Tab, tap the Applications button in the left column of the Settings screen to display the Applications screen (see Figure 2-11).

We'll look at how to use the Manage Applications feature, the Running Services feature, and the Memory Usage feature in Chapter 12, which covers apps. So here we'll look just at the Battery Use, Unknown Sources, Development, and Samsung Apps features.

Check Which Features Have Been Consuming the Battery Power

To see what's been consuming the Galaxy Tab's battery power, tap the Battery Use button and look at the Battery Use screen (see Figure 2-12). This screen shows readouts for Android OS, Screen, Wi-Fi, Cell Standby, and Tablet Idle. From it, you can get an idea of how much power you could save by turning down the screen brightness or by turning off Wi-Fi. Tap the Applications link at the top when you're ready to go back to the Applications screen.

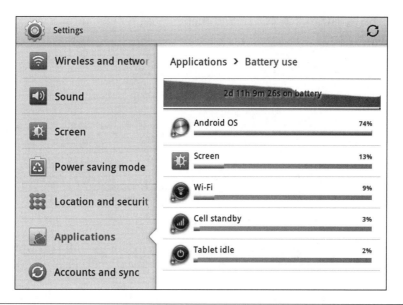

FIGURE 2-12   Use the Battery Use screen to learn which of the Galaxy Tab's features have been consuming the most battery power.

Allow Yourself to Install Apps from Other Sources Than Android Market

The main source of apps for the Galaxy Tab and other devices that run the Android operating system is Android Market, which Google controls. Here, you can find an incredibly wide variety of apps that cater to almost every need you can imagine (and then some).

Normally, you'll want to install only apps from Android Market, because this helps you avoid malware and other dangerous apps. But in some cases you may need to install apps from other sources. For example, if your friend is developing an Android app, you may want to load it to see if it will run on the Galaxy Tab.

To allow yourself to install apps from other sources than Android Market, select the Unknown Sources check box on the Applications screen. See the sidebar "Add Apps from Other Sources" in Chapter 12 for instructions on installing apps.

Set Development Options

If you develop Android apps yourself, and you want to test them on the Galaxy Tab, you may need to set development options. To do so, tap the Development button on the Applications screen, and then choose options on the Development screen (shown here):

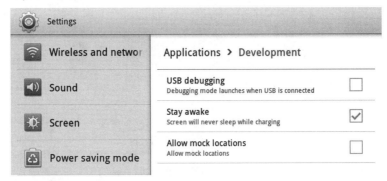

- **USB Debugging**   Select this check box to launch USB Debugging mode when you connect the Galaxy Tab to your computer via USB.
- **Stay Awake**   Select this check box if you want to prevent the Galaxy Tab from going to sleep while it's connected to power. This setting is sometimes useful outside of development—for example, if you're demonstrating the Galaxy Tab at an open day or trade show.
- **Allow Mock Locations**   Select this check box if you want to be able to set the Galaxy Tab to believe it's in a particular location when it isn't—for example, to tell the Galaxy Tab it's in Manhattan when it's actually in Podunk.

Choose Samsung Apps Settings

To choose whether you receive notifications when Samsung apps are using packet data via Wi-Fi or the cellular connection (on a 3G Galaxy Tab), tap the Samsung Apps button. The Samsung Apps screen appears, as shown here.

Now tap the New Application Notification button to display the New Application Notification dialog box (shown next), and then tap the appropriate option button: Off,

Wi-Fi Only, or Mobile Data And Wi-Fi. Tapping an option button closes the dialog box for you.

Choose Accounts and Sync Settings

To choose how apps and accounts synchronize data, tap the Accounts And Sync button on the Settings screen to display the Accounts And Sync screen (shown in Figure 2-13).

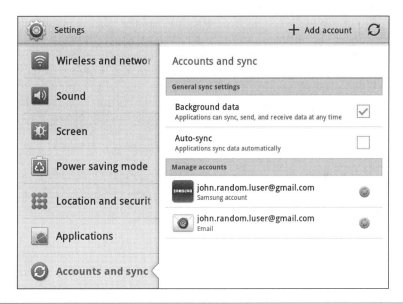

FIGURE 2-13   On the Accounts And Sync screen, choose whether to use background synchronization and auto-sync.

Choose General Sync Settings

In the General Sync Settings area of the Accounts And Sync screen, you can set these two settings:

- **Background Data**   Select this check box if you want apps to be able to send and receive data when they're in the background (in other words, you're working with another app—that's the one in the foreground). Normally, sending and receiving data in the background is helpful.

 Clearing the Background Data check box on the Accounts And Sync screen helps reduce the demand on the Galaxy Tab's battery and should make a battery charge last longer. But even if you clear this check box, some apps may still send data in the background—it doesn't shut off every data connection.

- **Auto-Sync**   If you select the Background Data check box, you can also select this check box to allow apps to sync data automatically on schedules they determine. If you clear the Background Data check box, this check box is unavailable.

Choose Sync Settings for an Account

The Manage Accounts area of the Accounts And Sync screen shows a button for each account you have set up on the Galaxy Tab.

To change the settings for an account, tap the account's name in the Manage Accounts area. On the Sync Settings screen for the account (an example is shown here), tap the button for the item you want to synchronize now. For example, tap the Sync Contacts button to synchronize your contacts. Tap the Accounts And Sync link when you're ready to return to the Accounts And Sync screen.

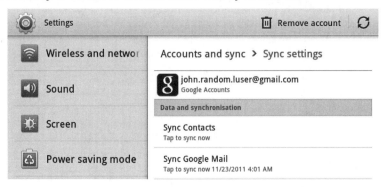

Choose Motion Settings

The Galaxy Tab supports two physical motions that you may find useful:

- **Tilt**   With a picture displayed in the Gallery app, place your thumbs on the screen and tilt the Galaxy Tab away from you to zoom out or toward you to zoom in. (You can use any two fingers, but if you're holding the Galaxy Tab in two hands, using your thumbs is usually easiest.)

- **Pan**   On a home screen panel, tap and hold an icon, then pan the Galaxy Tab left or right to move the icon to another home screen panel.

To control whether the Galaxy Tab uses these motions, tap the Motion Settings button in the left column of the Settings screen, and then work on the Motion Settings screen (shown here).

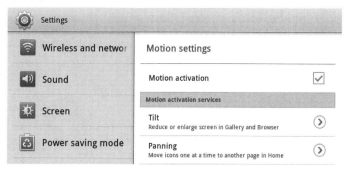

Select the Motion Activation check box if you want to use motion, and then work through the rest of this section. If you don't want to use motion, clear this check box and skip the rest of the section.

In the Motion Activation Services area, tap the Tilt button to display the Tilt screen (see Figure 2-14). Select the Use Tilt check box to turn on tilt if you want to use it. Then tap the Sensitivity button to display the Try Tilt screen, drag the Slow–Fast slider until tilt works the way you want, and then tap the OK button.

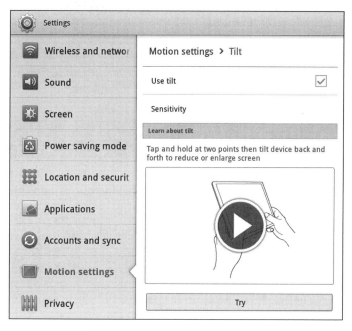

FIGURE 2-14   On the Tilt screen, you can turn the tilt motion on and adjust its sensitivity.

FIGURE 2-15 On the Panning screen, you can turn the panning motion on and adjust its sensitivity.

Tap the Motion Settings link at the top of the screen to go back to the Motion Settings screen, and then tap the Panning button to display the Panning screen (see Figure 2-15).

Select the Use Panning check box if you want to use panning. Then tap the Sensitivity button to display the Try Panning screen, drag the Slow–Fast slider until panning happens at the speed you want, and then tap the OK button.

How to... **Choose Firewall Settings on the Galaxy Tab**

If your Galaxy Tab's Settings screen has a Firewall button in the left column, tap this button to display the Firewall category. You can then choose these settings:

- **Use IP Firewall** Select this check box to turn on the firewall and make the other settings available. (IP here stands for "Internet Protocol," not "Intellectual Property.")
- **IP Firewall Settings** Tap this button to display the IP Firewall Settings screen. You can then tap the app you want to affect, and then tap the Allow option button or the Block option button.
- **Default Policy Settings** To choose whether the default policy is to allow an app or block it, tap this button, and then tap the Allow option button or the Block option button in the Default Policy dialog box that opens.

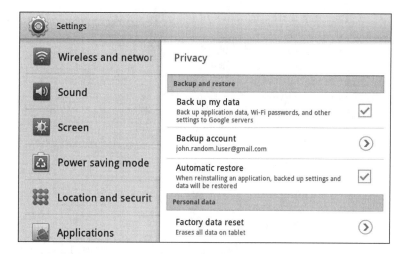

FIGURE 2-16   On the Privacy screen, select the Back Up My Data check box if you
want to back up your settings automatically to the Google server.

Choose Privacy Settings

To control whether the Galaxy Tab backs up your settings to the Google server, tap the
Privacy button on the Settings screen to display the Privacy screen (shown in Figure 2-16).

In the Backup And Restore area of the Privacy screen, you can choose these three
settings:

- **Back Up My Data**   Select this check box to back up your Galaxy Tab's data
  automatically to the Google server. Backing up your data enables you to recover
  it automatically if the Galaxy Tab gets messed up, so it's a good idea—as long as
  you're comfortable with the idea of Google storing your data.
- **Backup Account**   If this button already shows the backup account you want
  to use, you're set. Otherwise, tap this button to display the Set Backup Account
  dialog box (shown here), and either choose the existing account or tap the Add
  Account button to add another account.

- **Automatic Restore**   If you select the Back Up My Data check box, you can
  select this check box to allow the Galaxy Tab to automatically restore an app's
  settings and data from your backup when you reinstall the app. This too is usually
  helpful, but again it means that Google is storing your data online. If the Back Up
  My Data check box is cleared, the Automatic Restore check box is unavailable.

If the Back Up My Data check box was selected, and you clear it, the Galaxy Tab displays the Backup dialog box (shown here) to make sure you know you're about to delete your backups from the Google server. Tap the OK button if you're fine with this; otherwise, tap the Cancel button.

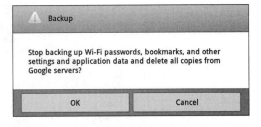

From the Privacy screen, you can also reset the Galaxy Tab to factory settings. We'll go over how to do this—and when you'd need to—in Chapter 14, which shows you how to troubleshoot hardware and software issues.

Work with Storage Settings

To see how much free space you have left in your Galaxy Tab's internal memory, tap the Storage button on the Settings screen and look at the Storage screen (shown in Figure 2-17). You can also see how much space applications, downloads, pictures and videos, audio, and miscellaneous files are taking up.

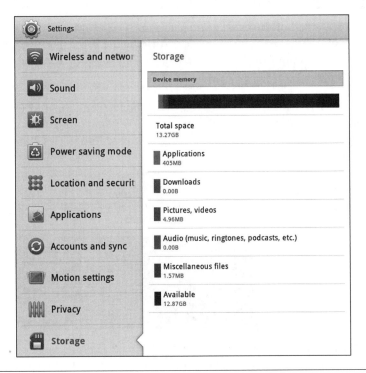

FIGURE 2-17 Use the Storage screen to check how much free space remains on the Galaxy Tab.

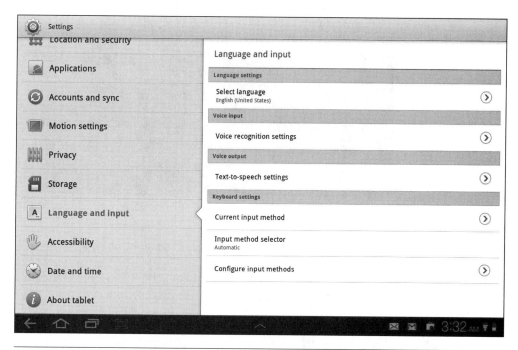

FIGURE 2-18   On the Language And Input screen, you can choose the GUI language, set up voice input and output, and choose keyboard settings.

Choose Language and Input Settings

To choose which language the Galaxy Tab's user interface uses, to set up voice recognition and voice output settings, and to select keyboard settings, tap the Language And Input button in the left column of the Settings screen. Then work on the Language And Input screen (see Figure 2-18).

Choose the Language for the Galaxy Tab's User Interface

If the Galaxy Tab is using the wrong language in its user interface, tap the Select Language button in the Language Settings area. (At least, this is what the controls are called in English. If the Galaxy Tab is set to a different language, just tap the button under the first heading on the screen.) On the Select Language screen, tap the language you want to use.

Choose Voice Input Settings

To set up voice recognition, tap the Voice Recognition Settings button in the Voice Input area of the Language And Input screen. On the Google Voice Recognition

Settings screen (shown here), select the settings you want, and then tap the Back button to return to the Language And Input screen.

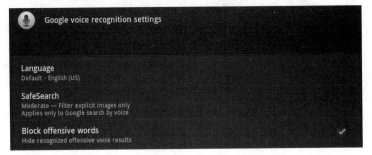

Choose Voice Output Settings

To choose settings for voice output, tap the Text-To-Speech Settings button in the Voice Output area of the Language And Input screen to display the Text-To-Speech Settings screen (see Figure 2-19). Here, you can set various playback options, including the speech synthesis engine, the speech rate, and the language-specific voice to use.

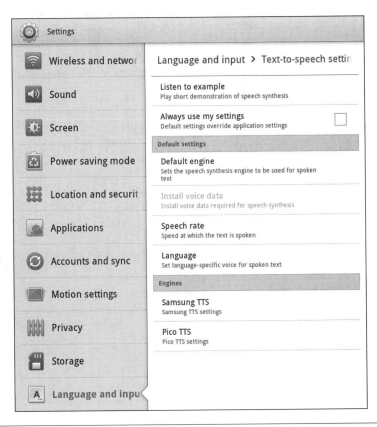

FIGURE 2-19 On the Text-To-Speech Settings screen, choose how the Galaxy Tab should read text to you.

Choose Suitable Keyboard Settings

To enable you to enter text quickly on the Galaxy Tab, Samsung provides five input methods:

- **Keyboard**   This is a regular soft keyboard at the bottom of the screen. You tap each key needed in turn.
- **Voice**   You can dictate the text you want, and the voice recognition software transcribes it for you. Results vary depending on your elocution.
- **Samsung Keypad**   This is a keypad that offers different features from the regular keyboard. The most notable of these is the XT9 predictive text feature, which tries to predict the rest of the word you're typing and offers suggestions. Some people swear by XT9, especially on cell phones with tiny keyboards; rather more people swear *at* XT9 on the Galaxy Tab. But try it yourself and see if you find it helpful. See the nearby Tip about using Auto-Substitution.
- **Swype**   Swype is an app in which you enter a word by dragging your fingertip across each of its letters in turn rather than tapping them in sequence (see Figure 2-20). Swype sounds awkward, but many people find it not only easy but much faster than the regular keypad—so it's well worth spending a few minutes seeing if Swype suits you.
- **TalkBack Keyboard**   This is a keyboard that gives audio feedback to confirm what you've tapped and tell you which screen you're at. Normally, you'd want to use this only if you have trouble seeing the screen.

To choose which input method you use, tap the Current Input Method button in the Keyboard Settings area, and then tap the appropriate option button in the Select

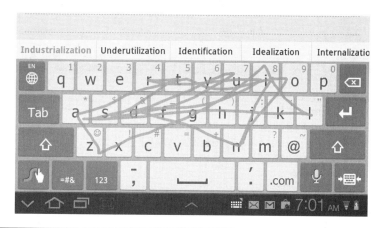

FIGURE 2-20   Swype is an app that enables you to type faster by dragging your finger across each letter of a word in turn. The line here looks messy, but Swype identified "industrialization" just fine.

Input Method dialog box (shown here). Tapping the option button closes the dialog box and returns you to the Language And Input screen.

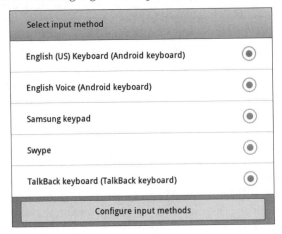

To choose whether the Galaxy Tab automatically selects what it hopes is a suitable input method for you or lets you select automatically, tap the Input Method Selector button. In the Input Method Selector dialog box (shown here), tap the Automatic option button, the Always Show option button, or the Always Hide option button, as needed. Tapping an option button closes the dialog box.

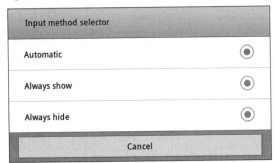

Whichever input method you choose, take a minute to investigate the options it offers. Tap the Configure Input Methods button on the Language And Input screen to display the Configure Input Methods screen (see Figure 2-21), and then tap the Settings button under the appropriate heading to display the Settings screen for that input method. For example, tap the Settings button under the Swype heading to display the Swype Settings screen.

The XT9 predictive text feature for the Samsung Keypad can save you many keystrokes, especially if you add words you need to use frequently. On the Samsung Keypad Settings screen, select the XT9 check box, then tap the XT9 Advanced Settings button to display the XT9 Advanced Settings screen. From here, apart from turning options on and off, you can tap the XT9 My Words button to add your custom words, or tap the XT9 Auto-Substitution button to add spellings that you want XT9 to substitute for what you type in.

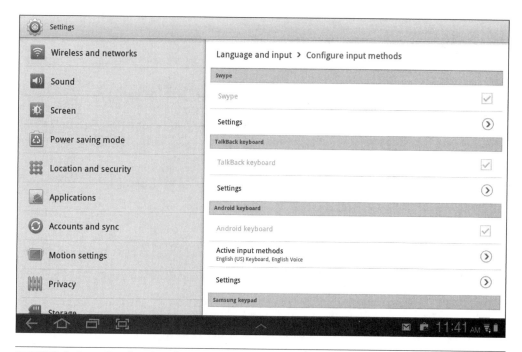

FIGURE 2-21   On the Configure Input Methods screen, tap the Settings button for the input method you want to configure.

Choose Accessibility Settings

To make the Galaxy Tab easier to use, you can use accessibility features such as the TalkBack screen reader and the tap and hold delay.

To choose accessibility settings, tap the Accessibility button in the left column of the Settings screen, and then work on the Accessibility screen (see Figure 2-22).

Select the Accessibility check box if you want to use any of the Accessibility features. If not, clear this check box.

In the Accessibility Applications area, select the TalkBack check box if you want to use the TalkBack screen reader. As mentioned earlier, when TalkBack is on, the Galaxy Tab speaks the names of the screens and the keys you tap.

In the Accessibility Scripts area, select the Download Accessibility Scripts check box if you want apps to be able to download accessibility scripts from Google. If you need accessibility features, this is normally a good idea.

In the Touch Screen Controls area, tap the Tap And Hold Delay button to display the Tap And Hold Delay dialog box (shown here). Tap the Short option button, the Medium option button, or the Long option button, as needed, to make your selection and to close the dialog box.

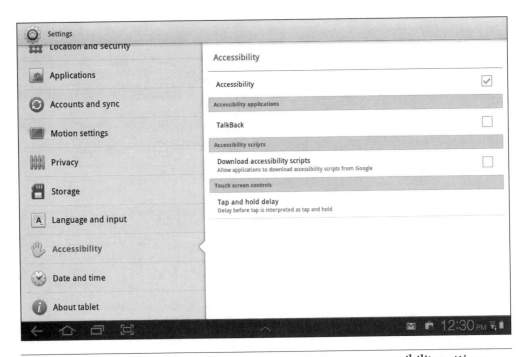

FIGURE 2-22 On the Accessibility screen, you can turn on accessibility settings as a whole, turn TalkBack on, choose whether to let apps download accessibility scripts, and configure the tap and hold delay.

Choose Date and Time Settings

Normally, once you've established an Internet connection, the Galaxy Tab sets its date and time automatically from Internet time servers. If you need to change the date, time, time zone, or format, tap the Date And Time button on the Settings screen, and then work on the Date And Time screen (shown in Figure 2-23).

Choose settings on the Date And Time screen like this:

- **Automatic Date And Time**   Select this check box to make the Galaxy Tab set the date, time, and time zone automatically using an Internet time server. When you select this check box, the Set Date button, the Set Time button, and the Select Time Zone button become unavailable.
- **Set Date**   To set the date manually, tap this button, set the date in the dialog box that opens, and then tap the Set button.
- **Set Time**   To set the time manually, tap this button, set the time in the dialog box that opens, and then tap the Set button.
- **Select Time Zone**   To set the time zone manually, tap this button, and then tap the appropriate time zone on the Select Time Zone screen. The time zones are arranged from earliest (Midway Island, GMT –11:00) to latest (Tonga, GMT +13:00), so scroll up or down as needed.

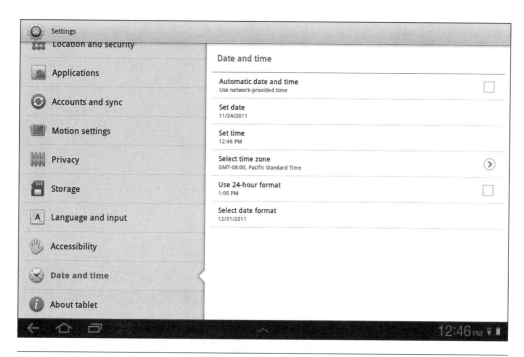

FIGURE 2-23   On the Date And Time screen, you can select the Automatic Date
And Time check box to pick up the date, time zone, and time
automatically, or clear the check box and set all three manually.

- **Use 24-Hour Format**   Select this check box if you want to use 24-hour times
  rather than A.M./P.M. times.
- **Select Date Format**   To control how the Galaxy Tab represents the date, tap
  this button, and then choose the date format in the Select Date Format dialog box
  (shown here).

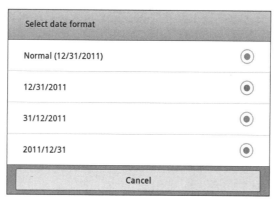

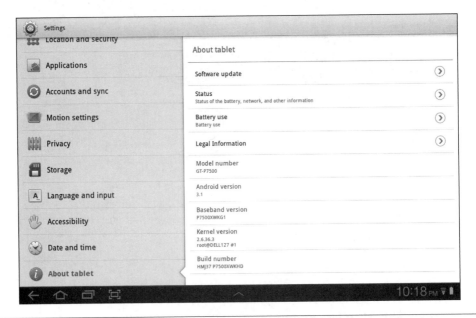

FIGURE 2-24   The About Tablet screen includes the model number, firmware version, and other technical details for the Galaxy Tab.

Examine the About Tablet Settings

When you need to run a software update, find out the battery status or what's using the battery most, or check the details of the Galaxy Tab's firmware or software version, tap the About Tablet button on the Settings screen to display the About Tablet screen (shown in Figure 2-24).

Choose Software Update Settings

To run a software update right now, or to choose settings for the Software Update feature, tap the Software Update button on the About Tablet screen, and then work on the Software Update screen (shown here).

To run a software update, tap the Update button, and then tap the OK button in the Software Update dialog box (shown here) that appears.

 If you have a 3G Galaxy Tab, make sure you use a Wi-Fi network rather than a 3G connection for updating the Galaxy Tab. An update may involve downloading a lot of data, so it can take a big bite out of your data plan.

On the Software Update screen, you can also choose these three settings:

- **Auto Update**   Select this check box to allow the Galaxy Tab to update itself automatically.
- **Wi-Fi Only**   On a 3G Galaxy Tab, select this check box to prevent the Galaxy Tab from updating itself over the 3G network (which may incur extra cost).
- **Push Messages**   Select this check box if you want the Galaxy Tab to receive push messages about software updates. Push messages are messages sent from Samsung's servers to the Galaxy Tab when updates are available. If you turn off push messages, the Galaxy Tab needs to check in with the servers to find out about updates.

Check the Galaxy Tab's Status

To check the Galaxy Tab's status, tap the Status button on the About Tablet screen, and then look at the readouts on the Status screen (see Figure 2-25). Here you can see various pieces of information, from whether the battery is charging or discharging all the way through to the IP address, Wi-Fi MAC address, Bluetooth address, and serial number.

Tap the Back button when you want to leave the Status screen.

 The MAC address is the hardware address for the Galaxy Tab's Wi-Fi adapter. This address is hardwired into the device, so it remains constant, unlike the IP address. If you use a wireless network that allows connections only from approved MAC addresses, this is the number you will need to add to the approved list. But because software can spoof (fake) a MAC address, using MAC addresses to control access to wireless networks is effective only against casual intruders.

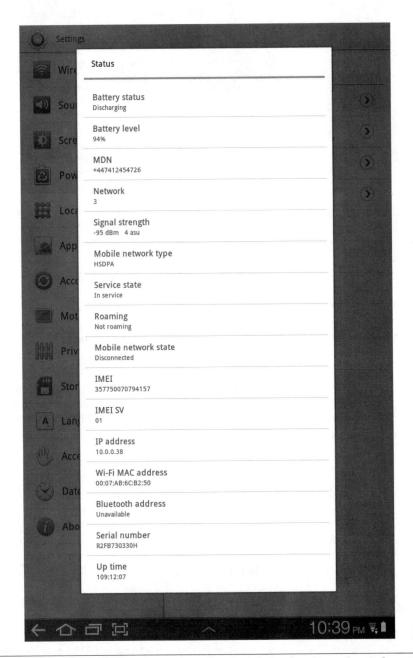

FIGURE 2-25 The Status screen shows a wealth of details about the Galaxy Tab, including its current IP address, the hardware (MAC) address of its wireless adapter, and its Bluetooth address.

Check the Battery Usage

To check the battery usage, tap the Battery Use button on the About Tablet screen. The Galaxy Tab displays the Battery Use screen, which appears in Figure 2-12, earlier in this chapter. See the section "Check Which Features Have Been Consuming the Battery Power" for details.

View Legal Information About the Galaxy Tab's Software

To view legal information about the Galaxy Tab's software, tap the Legal Information button on the About Tablet screen, and then tap the Open Source Licenses button or the Google Legal button on the Legal Information screen.

View the Model Number, Version Numbers, and Build Number

Further down the About Tablet screen, you can view the following information:

- **Model Number**   This is the Galaxy Tab's model number. You may need to know it when calling support or troubleshooting hardware-specific issues.
- **Android Version**   This is the version of the Galaxy Tab's firmware, the permanent software programmed into the device's read-only memory. You may need to check this to see if a new version of the firmware is available.
- **Baseband Version**   This is the version of the communications hardware the Galaxy Tab is using. Again, you may need to know this number for reference.
- **Kernel Version**   This is the version of the Linux kernel that the Android operating system is running on. You may need to know this number for installing updates, but it's mostly of interest to techies.
- **Build Number**   This is the build name and number of the Android operating system. You may need to check this to see if a new build of Android is available.

When you've finished choosing settings, tap the Home button to display the home screen again.

Connect a Bluetooth Device

The Galaxy Tab includes a Bluetooth chip, so you can connect Bluetooth devices such as keyboards and headphones. Follow these steps:

1. From the home screen, tap the Notifications area to display the Notifications panel.
2. Tap the Settings button to display the Settings screen.
3. Tap the Wireless And Networks button at the top to display the Wireless And Networks screen (see Figure 2-26).
4. Tap the Bluetooth Settings button to display the Bluetooth Settings screen (shown in Figure 2-27).

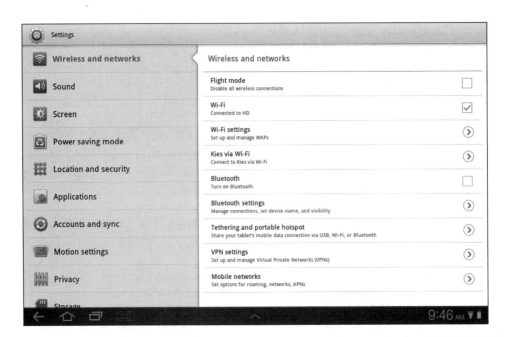

FIGURE 2-26   On the Wireless And Networks screen, tap the Bluetooth Settings button.

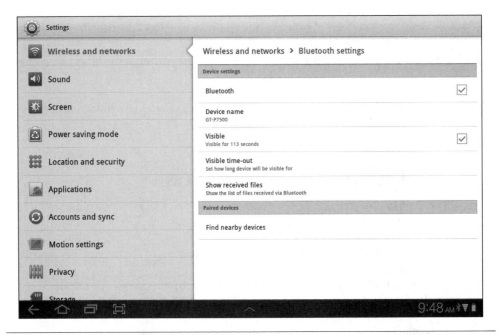

FIGURE 2-27   From the Bluetooth Settings screen, you can turn on Bluetooth, change the Galaxy Tab's Bluetooth name, make the Galaxy Tab visible to other Bluetooth devices, and pair the Galaxy Tab with other devices.

5. Select the Bluetooth check box if it's not already selected.

6. If you want to change the Galaxy Tab's Bluetooth name, tap the Device Name button, type the name in the Device Name dialog box, and then tap the OK button.

7. If you want to make the Galaxy Tab visible to other Bluetooth devices, select the Visible check box. When you're performing the pairing from the Galaxy Tab to a device that's visible itself (for example, a keyboard), you don't need to make the Galaxy Tab visible.

8. Turn on the device you want to pair the Galaxy Tab with.

9. Tap the Find Nearby Devices button to force the Galaxy Tab to sweep the area for Bluetooth devices. The Galaxy Tab displays the Find Nearby Devices screen, which lists the devices found.

10. Tap the device's name. If you're pairing a keyboard, the Galaxy Tab displays a dialog box showing the PIN to use for pairing, as in the example here.

> **ⓘ Bluetooth pairing request**
>
> Enter 3149 on FrogPad to pair, then tap Return or Enter.
>
> Cancel

11. Enter the PIN on the device, and then press RETURN or ENTER. The Galaxy Tab pairs with the device and connects to it. When the Bluetooth Devices list shows the device's status as Connected, you can start using the device.

Note If you connect a Bluetooth keyboard, and the Galaxy Tab is set to use Swype or another alternative text-input method, the Galaxy Tab displays a dialog box prompting you to change the input method to Samsung QWERTY. Tap the OK button (there's no alternative).

When you need to check whether Bluetooth is turned on, look at the notifications area in the lower-right corner of the screen to see if the Bluetooth icon appears there. If so, Bluetooth is turned on; if not, it's turned off.

To turn Bluetooth on or off, follow these steps:

1. Tap the notifications area to reveal the notifications panel.

2. Tap the Settings button to display the Settings screen.

3. Tap the Wireless And Networks button at the top to display the Wireless And Networks screen.

4. Clear the Bluetooth check box.

5. Tap the Home button to return to the home screen.

Manage Your Wireless Network Connections

Cellular connections can be great if your Galaxy Tab has 3G, but you'll probably want to use your Galaxy Tab on wireless network connections as much as possible to conserve your cellular allowances. Most likely, you'll need to connect to two or more wireless networks—perhaps many more. In many cases, you'll need to manage your wireless network connections actively rather than being able to set them and then forget them. This section shows you the moves you'll need.

Set Up a New Wireless Network

Normally, you'll connect to your first wireless network when you first set up the Galaxy Tab, as discussed in Chapter 1. When you need to set up another wireless network, open the Wi-Fi Settings screen like this:

1. From the home screen, tap the notifications area to display the notifications panel.
2. Tap the Settings button to display the Settings screen.
3. Tap the Wireless And Networks button at the top to display the Wireless And Networks screen (shown in Figure 2-26, earlier in this chapter).
4. Tap the Wi-Fi Settings button to display the Wi-Fi Settings screen (see Figure 2-28).

If the wireless network appears in the Wi-Fi Networks list, add it as described in the first subsection, "Add an Open Wireless Network." If the wireless network doesn't appear, add it as described in the second subsection, "Add a Closed Wireless Network."

 An *open* wireless network is one that broadcasts its name or (technical term) service set identifier, SSID for short. A *closed* wireless network is one that doesn't broadcast its name.

Add an Open Wireless Network

To add an open wireless network, follow these steps:

1. Tap the network's name in the Wi-Fi Networks list on the Wi-Fi Settings screen. The Galaxy Tab displays a dialog box showing the network's name, as shown here.

Surreal Macs AP	
	Connect to Surreal Macs AP
Password	●●●●●●●●●●●e
	☐ Show password.
Proxy settings	None ◢
IP settings	DHCP ◢
OK	Cancel

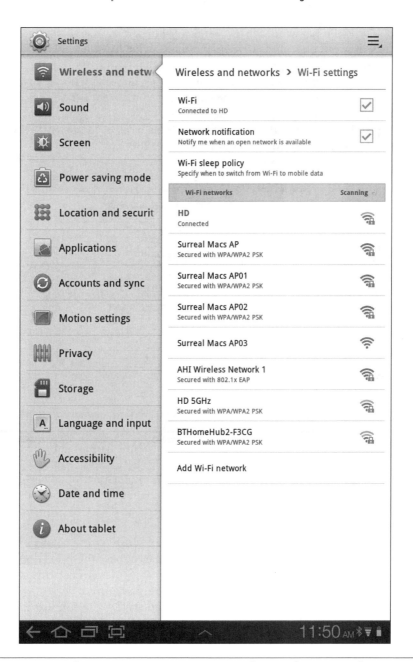

FIGURE 2-28   On the Wi-Fi Settings screen, tap the wireless network you want to connect to. If the wireless network doesn't appear in the Wi-Fi Networks list, tap the Add Wi-Fi Network button.

2. Type the password for the wireless network. As usual, you can select the Show Password check box if you want to see what you've typed.

3. If you need to specify proxy settings for the network, tap the Proxy Settings drop-down button, and then tap the Manual item. The dialog box for the wireless network displays three extra boxes for you to enter the proxy information in, as you see in the illustration here:

   - **Hostname**   Type the name or IP address of the proxy server—for example, **epoxy.surrealmacs.com** or **10.0.1.200**.

Surreal Macs AP		
	Connect to Surreal Macs AP	
Password	••••••••••••	
	☐ Show password.	
Proxy settings	Manual ◢	
	HTTP proxy used by browser but may not be used by other applications	
Hostname	proxy.example.com	
Proxy port	8080	
No Proxy for	example.com,mycomp.test.com,localhost	
IP settings	DHCP ◢	
OK	Cancel	

Normally, you don't need to enter proxy information for a home network—only for a network in a company or organization. If you need to find out the proxy settings, ask the network's administrator.

   - **Proxy Port**   Type the port number to use on the server—for example, **8080**.
   - **No Proxy For**   If you're supposed to bypass the proxy for certain domains, type their names in this text box, putting a comma between them—for example, **surrealmacs.com, surrealpcs.com**.

4. If your network uses DHCP, make sure the DHCP item is selected in the IP Settings drop-down list. If you need to specify a static IP address for the network, tap the IP Settings drop-down button, and then tap the Static item.

The dialog box for the wireless network displays five extra boxes for you to enter the IP address information in, as you see in the illustration here.

- **IP Address**   Enter the IP address—for example, **192.168.0.11**.

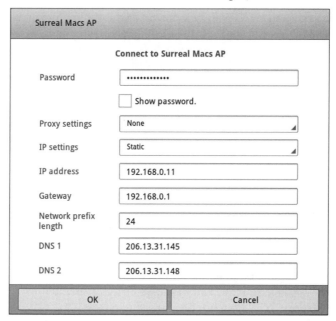

Note	Most home networks use Dynamic Host Configuration Protocol (DHCP) to allocate IP addresses automatically. If your network uses DHCP, you don't need to set a static IP address for the Galaxy Tab. Normally, you'll need to set a static IP address only if your network's administrator tells you to. In this case, the network administrator will give you the details for the network.

- **Gateway**   Enter the IP address of the gateway or router that gives the network access to the Internet—for example, **192.168.0.1**.
- **Network Prefix Length**   Enter the network prefix length here. Depending on the network, this is 8, 16, or 24.
- **DNS 1**   Enter the IP address of the primary DNS server.
- **DNS 2**   Enter the IP address of the secondary DNS server.

5. Tap the OK button to close the dialog box for connecting to the wireless network. The Galaxy Tab connects to the wireless network, and the Wi-Fi Networks list in the Wi-Fi Settings screen shows Connected under the network's name.

Add a Closed Wireless Network

To add a closed wireless network, follow these steps:

1. Tap the Add Wi-Fi Network button at the bottom of the Wi-Fi Settings screen to display the Add Wi-Fi Network dialog box (shown here with settings chosen).

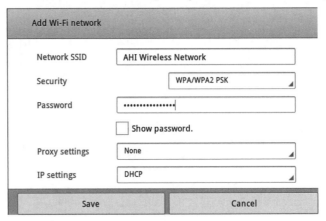

Add Wi-Fi network	
Network SSID	AHI Wireless Network
Security	WPA/WPA2 PSK
Password	••••••••••••••
	☐ Show password.
Proxy settings	None
IP settings	DHCP
Save	Cancel

2. Type the network's name in the Network SSID box.
3. Choose the security type in the Security drop-down list:
   - **Open**   The network has no security.
   - **WEP**   The network uses Wired Equivalent Privacy security. This security is weak because it has known flaws—but some wireless networks still use it.
   - **WPA/WPA2 PSK**   The network uses Wi-Fi Protected Access (WPA) or Wi-Fi Protected Access version 2 (WPA2) security with a pre-shared key (PSK). This is an effective and widely used security type.
   - **802.1x EAP**   The network uses Extensible Authentication Protocol (EAP) security, which involves using multiple means of authentication (such as certificates and passwords). This type of security is mostly used in corporate networks.
4. For WEP or WPA/WPA2 PSK, type the password in the Password text box. For EAP, provide the many details required.
5. If you need to choose proxy settings, do so as explained in step 3 of the previous list.
6. If you need to specify a static IP address, do so as explained in step 4 of the previous list. Otherwise, make sure the DHCP item is selected in the IP Settings drop-down list.
7. Tap the Save button to save the network's details and return to the Wi-Fi Settings screen.
8. Tap the new network's name to connect to it.

Note To have the Galaxy Tab alert you when an open wireless network is available, select the Network Notification check box on the Wi-Fi Settings screen.

How to... Tell a 3G Galaxy Tab When to Switch from Wi-Fi to Mobile Data

If your Galaxy Tab has 3G, it can connect to the Internet via either Wi-Fi or a cellular network. Normally, you'll want to use a Wi-Fi network as long as one's available, to avoid chewing through your cellular data allowance. But you may also want your Galaxy Tab to drop a wireless connection when you stop using the Galaxy Tab, so that it doesn't waste battery life staying connected to the wireless network.

To tell the Galaxy Tab when to switch from Wi-Fi to mobile data, tap the Wi-Fi Sleep Policy button on the Wi-Fi Settings screen, and then tap the appropriate option button in the Wi-Fi Sleep Policy dialog box (shown here).

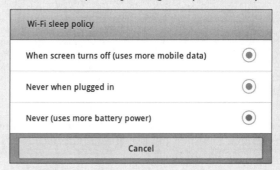

- **When Screen Turns Off (Uses More Mobile Data)**   This setting disconnects the Galaxy Tab from the wireless network when you turn the screen off or it turns off automatically. This saves power but causes the Galaxy Tab to use more mobile data.
- **Never When Plugged In**   This setting uses the power connection to determine when you're somewhere you should be using Wi-Fi rather than cellular.
- **Never (Uses More Battery Power)**   This setting prevents the Galaxy Tab from using the cellular network when a Wi-Fi connection is available. This is normally the best choice unless you have a generous data plan.

Selecting an option button closes the Wi-Fi Sleep Policy dialog box and returns you to the Wi-Fi Settings screen.

You can force the Galaxy Tab to start using a cellular connection at any time by turning off Wi-Fi. Tap the notifications area to display the notifications panel, then tap the Wi-Fi button to turn off Wi-Fi and tap the × button to close the notifications panel.

Turn Wi-Fi On and Off from the Notifications Panel

The quick way to check whether Wi-Fi is turned on or off, and to turn it on or off as needed, is to use the notifications panel.

To check whether Wi-Fi is turned on, look for the Wi-Fi icon (the inverted pyramid of blue bars) in the notifications area. If the icon appears, Wi-Fi is on; if not, Wi-Fi is off.

To turn Wi-Fi on or off quickly using the notifications panel, follow these steps:

1. Tap the notifications area to display the notifications panel.
2. Tap the Wi-Fi icon to turn Wi-Fi on (if it's off) or off (if it's on).
3. Tap the × button in the upper-right corner of the notifications panel to close the panel.

Make the Galaxy Tab Forget a Wireless Network

When you no longer need to use a particular wireless network, tell the Galaxy Tab to forget the network. This helps avoid connecting to the network unintentionally if you stray within range; and even if the network is far away, it shortens the list of Wi-Fi networks you need to manage.

To make the Galaxy Tab forget a network, tap the network's name on the Wi-Fi Settings screen, and then tap the Forget button in the network information dialog box that appears, as shown here.

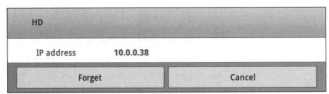

Outfit the Galaxy Tab with Accessories

The Galaxy Tab is great as a self-contained device, but to get the most out of it, you'll probably want to add accessories. This section discusses the most useful accessories: a case and screen protector, a keyboard, a TV-out cable, and a stand.

Protect the Galaxy Tab with a Case and Screen Protector

With its plastic case, the Galaxy Tab is sturdy enough for conventional use. But even so, it's a good idea to protect it with a case. You should also apply a screen protector to the screen to protect it from scratches, oil, and other hazards.

You can find a wide variety of cases in both online stores and bricks-and-mortar stores. In particular, Amazon.com and eBay offer many cases—everything from folding leather cases with a handy stand built in, to silicon sheaths that add a little grip and cushioning to the Galaxy Tab.

 If you intend to use your Galaxy Tab extensively, get a case that gives you full access to the screen and the camera rather than a slip case you have to take the Galaxy Tab out of before you can use it.

Choosing a screen protector tends to be more straightforward than choosing a case, because there's less variation. Even so, it's worth reading reviews of screen protectors before buying to avoid three problems:

- **Too thin or flexible**   If the screen protector is too thin or too flexible, it may be hard to fit without getting air bubbles under it.
- **Too thick**   If the screen protector is too thick, the Galaxy Tab's screen won't respond correctly to your caresses.
- **Not sticky enough**   If the screen protector doesn't stick tightly enough to the Galaxy Tab's screen, it'll start coming off the sides as soon as you put the case on.

 Two things here. First, clean the screen thoroughly with a soft cloth before applying the screen protector. Second, you may find a credit card, a plastic ruler, or a plastic ice scraper (the kind for getting ice off your car's windshield) helpful for applying the screen protector evenly across the screen.

Enter Text Quickly with a Keyboard

The Galaxy Tab's onscreen keyboard works pretty well, and if you learn to use Swype, you can enter text at a good clip. But if you need to enter serious amounts of text, add a hardware keyboard.

The best fit for the Galaxy Tab 10.1 is the Samsung Galaxy Tab 10.1 Keyboard Dock (around $75), which you can buy from retailers both online (for example, Amazon .com) and offline. This keyboard has a built-in stand that holds the Galaxy Tab upright, turning the tablet into a mutant laptop. For the Galaxy Tab 8.9, there's a Samsung Galaxy Tab 8.9 Keyboard Dock, which costs around the same amount.

If the price of the Samsung Galaxy Tab Keyboard Dock seems too steep, look for an equivalent product from a third-party manufacturer. You'll find a good selection available online, especially on eBay.

Because the Galaxy Tab has Bluetooth, you can also connect any standard Bluetooth keyboard to it using the technique described earlier in this chapter. If you already have a Bluetooth keyboard, this can be a great solution—particularly if you put the Galaxy Tab in a stand or a case that incorporates a stand.

The disadvantage of a standard Bluetooth keyboard is that it doesn't have Galaxy Tab–specific buttons and features, but if you're prepared to use your finger on the screen when necessary, a Bluetooth keyboard can be a good solution—especially because you can use it with other computers and devices as necessary. If you use Swype as your text-input method, you'll need to turn it off when using the Bluetooth keyboard.

Output Videos and Photos on a TV

When you want to share your videos or photos with other people, you can connect the Galaxy Tab to a TV and show the images on the big screen.

To make the connection to a regular TV, you need either the Samsung TV-Out Cable (around $20) or a functional equivalent—a cable with the Samsung connector at the Galaxy Tab's end and three composite connectors at the TV's end.

To make the connection to an HD TV, you need an adapter such as the Samsung Galaxy Tab P4 HDTV Adapter (around $50).

Get a Stand for Hands-Free Use

If you've chosen a Galaxy Tab case that includes a built-in stand, or if you've picked up the Samsung Galaxy Tab Keyboard Dock, you already have a stand that will hold the Galaxy Tab at an angle and attitude for you to use it on a desk. If not, you may want to get a stand for the Galaxy Tab so that you can watch movies on it or use it with a Bluetooth keyboard that doesn't have a stand.

As with other accessories, you can find Galaxy Tab stands at various virtual and real-world retailers, but the best selections tend to be on sites such as Amazon.com and eBay.

When choosing a stand, keep these three questions in mind:

- Should you buy a case with a built-in stand instead?
- Should you buy a keyboard with a built-in stand instead?
- Do you want a stand that connects to power and charges the Galaxy Tab? If so, consider getting a stand with an audio connection or built-in speakers.

 Various iPad stands work for the Galaxy Tab in either landscape orientation or portrait orientation. So if you can't find a Galaxy Tab–specific stand you like, it's worth looking at iPad stands too.

3

Load and Manage the Galaxy Tab with Samsung Kies

HOW TO...

- Launch Kies
- Add your multimedia files to the Kies Library
- Import your existing Windows Media Player and iTunes playlists into Kies
- Remove media files from Kies
- Connect the Galaxy Tab to your PC or Mac via USB
- Make Kies recognize the Galaxy Tab on a USB connection
- Make Kies establish the connection to the Galaxy Tab
- Manage the Galaxy Tab using Kies
- Force quit Kies for the Mac if it hogs your Mac's processor
- Load media files onto the Galaxy Tab without using Kies
- Deal with the "USB Storage Blank or Has Unsupported File System" message
- Connect the Galaxy Tab to your PC via Wi-Fi
- Configure how Kies handles the Galaxy Tab
- Keep Kies up to date
- Connect the Galaxy Tab to your PC via Bluetooth

To get the most out of your Galaxy Tab, you'll need to load it with content from your PC or Mac. To do so, you use the Kies application, which you downloaded and installed in Chapter 1.

In this chapter, I'll show you how to use Kies to manage the Galaxy Tab from your PC or your Mac. You'll learn how to add media files to Kies either automatically or manually thereafter, so that your Kies Library contains the files you want to put on the Galaxy Tab.

Next, I'll show you how to connect the Galaxy Tab to your PC or Mac via USB and manage it using Kies. We'll go through how to choose settings for the Galaxy Tab, how to choose which items to sync, and how to copy items between the Galaxy Tab and your PC or Mac. You'll also learn how to configure the way Kies handles the Galaxy Tab. And I'll show you how to connect the Galaxy Tab to your PC via Wi-Fi; this feature isn't available on the Mac at this writing.

Toward the end of the chapter, we'll look at how to make Kies run the way you prefer and how to keep Kies up to date. I'll also show you how to connect the Galaxy Tab to your PC using Bluetooth, for those times when you don't want to use USB. As with Wi-Fi, you can't use Bluetooth to connect the Galaxy Tab to a Mac at this writing.

 You can also use Kies to back up the Galaxy Tab to your PC (not to a Mac) and to restore the Galaxy Tab from a backup. Chapter 14 covers backup and restore.

Launch Kies

Start by launching Kies if it's not already running.

On Windows, launch Kies in one of these ways:

- Click the Kies icon on the Taskbar in Windows 7.
- Double-click the Kies icon on the Desktop.
- Choose Start | Kies.
- Choose Start | All Programs | Samsung | Kies | Samsung Kies.

On the Mac, launch Kies in one of these ways:

- Click the Kies icon on the Dock.

 If the Kies icon doesn't appear on the Dock, and you want it there, launch Kies in one of the following ways. Then CTRL-click or right-click the Kies icon on the Dock, highlight or click the Options item on the context menu to display the submenu, and then click the Keep In Dock item.

- On Mac OS X Lion, click the Launchpad icon on the Dock, and then click the Kies icon on the Launchpad screen.
- Click the desktop, choose Go | Applications to open a Finder window showing the Applications folder, and then double-click the Kies icon.

Add Your Multimedia Files to the Kies Library

What you probably need to do at this point is add your multimedia files to the Kies Library so that you can transfer them easily to the Galaxy Tab when you connect it.

You can import your multimedia files manually at any time, but the best way to start is by using Kies's feature for automatically importing either all the multimedia files in a particular folder you select or all the multimedia files Kies can scare up on the computer.

 The first time you launch Kies on the Mac, it displays a dialog box asking if you want to add multimedia files automatically to the Kies Library, as discussed in the section "Run Kies for the First Time" in Chapter 1. If you accepted this offer, you may have already added all the files you need to Kies—in which case, feel free to skip this section until you need to add further files.

Use Kies's Feature for Importing Multimedia Files Automatically on the PC

Normally, the first time you run Kies on your PC and click the Music item in the Library category of the list on the left, Kies notices that your library contains no music and displays the Automatically Add Multimedia Files dialog box (see Figure 3-1). From here, you can quickly add files to the library. You can also install extra codecs—and you should do this before you add the files to the library, because you can't easily summon up the Automatically Add Multimedia Files dialog box again.

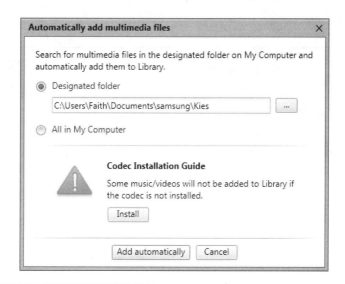

FIGURE 3-1 From the Automatically Add Multimedia Files dialog box, you can make Kies search either a particular folder or your PC's entire file system for multimedia files.

Install Extra Codecs if Necessary

If the lower part of the Automatically Add Multimedia Files dialog box bears a triangular icon containing an exclamation mark, as in Figure 3-1, you will need to install extra codecs, software to make Kies import all your music.

 A *codec* is a *co*der/*deco*der, software that can encode audio or video file formats or decode them to play them back. Kies includes codecs for widely used audio and video file formats, such as the MP3 audio format. But if you have audio or video files in other formats—for example, songs in the Advanced Audio Coding (AAC) format that Apple favors—you may need to install codecs to enable Kies to deal with them. Kies won't import any files it can't play.

To sort out any codec issues, click the Install button in the Code Installation Guide area of the Automatically Add Multimedia Files dialog box.

Next, Windows normally displays the User Account Control dialog box shown next. Check that there's a verified publisher, and that it's a credible Samsung company (which company varies depending on where you are), and then click the Yes button to let the installation proceed.

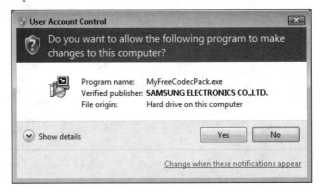

In the Installer Language dialog box, open the drop-down list and click your language, and then click the OK button. You then need to agree to the license agreement to reach the Installation Options screen (shown here).

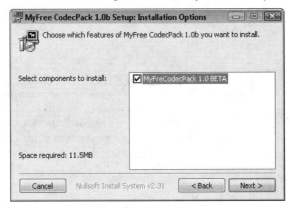

In the Select Components To Install list box, make sure the check box to the MyFreeCodecPack item is selected (the name varies, but usually it's pretty clear—or the only item).

Click the Next button to display the Installation Folder screen (shown here).

Normally, you'll want to accept the default folder here, but if you need to use a different folder, click the Browse button, and then use the Browse For Folder dialog box to select it. When you've made your choice, click the Install button.

The installation finally runs. When you see the Completed dialog box, click the Close button. Kies is then able to add the music or videos files it wouldn't have been able to play without the codecs.

Choose Which Files to Import

After sorting out your codecs, select the appropriate option button in the Automatically Add Multimedia Files dialog box (shown earlier, in Figure 3-1):

- **Designated Folder**   Select this option button if you want Kies to search only a particular folder. Click the ... button to display the Select Folder dialog box, navigate to the folder and select it, and then click the Select Folder button. Kies closes the Select Folder dialog box and enters the folder's path and name in the Designated Folder text box.
- **All In My Computer**   Select this option button to have Kies search your PC's entire file system for multimedia files.

When you've made your choice, click the Add Automatically button. You'll then see the songs start to appear in the Music category. The readout in the status bar shows Kies's progress, as in the next illustration.

How to... Import Your Existing Windows Media Player and iTunes Playlists into Kies

If you have created playlists on your PC or Mac, you can import them into Kies quickly and easily. This saves you from having to re-create the playlists in Kies.

To import playlists you've created in Windows Media Player on Windows, choose File | Import Windows Media Player Playlist To Library. Kies searches for your Windows Media Player playlists and imports them automatically. You'll see the playlists appear in the Music category.

To import playlists you've created in iTunes on Windows or the Mac, choose File | Import iTunes Playlist To Library. Again, Kies searches for the playlists and imports them automatically, adding them to the Music category.

Add Media Files to Kies Manually

As discussed earlier in this chapter, you'll probably want to have Kies scan your computer for multimedia files at first to start building your library as quickly as possible. After that, you can add music files, video files, photo files, and podcast files to Kies manually at any time.

Add Files by Using Drag and Drop

The easiest way to add files is by opening a Windows Explorer window (on Windows) or a Finder window (on the Mac) so that you can see the folder that contains the files, and then drag the folder to the Library item at the top of the left pane in Kies. When you see a + sign, which indicates that Kies will add the files, release the mouse button. Kies copies the files.

If you want to add just some of the files in a folder, or just one file, select the files, and then drag them to the Library item.

Add Files by Using the Open Dialog Box or the Select Folder Dialog Box

To add individual files, you can also choose File | Add File To Library or press CTRL-O to display the Open dialog box. Navigate to the folder that contains the files, select the file or files, and then click the Open button.

 Tip You can also display the Open dialog box by selecting the Music item, the Photos item, the Video item, or the Podcast item in the Library area of the left pane and then clicking the Add Music button, Add Photo button, Add Video button, or Add Podcast button on the Kies toolbar.

If you want to add a folder of files, choose File | Add Folder To Library or press CTRL-SHIFT-O to display the Select Folder dialog box. Navigate to the folder that contains the files, click the folder, and then click the Select Folder button.

Remove Media Files from Kies

To remove media files from Kies, follow these steps:

1. Click the appropriate item (Music, Photos, Video, or Podcast) in the Library area to display the list of those items.
2. Select the item or items you want to delete.
3. Click the Delete button on the toolbar. Kies displays the Delete dialog box. The next illustration shows the Mac version of this dialog box.

4. If you want to suppress this dialog box in the future, select the Do Not Ask Me Again check box.
5. Click the Delete button (on Windows) or the OK button (on the Mac).

Connect the Galaxy Tab to Your PC or Mac via USB

Now that you've added your media files to Kies, you're ready to connect the Galaxy Tab to your PC or Mac and start synchronizing it.

Connect the Galaxy Tab to your PC or Mac using the USB cable that came with the Galaxy Tab. When you've made the connection, press the Galaxy Tab's power button to turn it on, and then slide the Unlock slider to the right to unlock the device.

If the Galaxy Tab and your computer seem to be having trouble establishing a connection, try tapping the Home button to display the home screen. Sometimes having the home screen displayed helps establish the connection.

When you connect the Galaxy Tab to your computer, and Kies recognizes it, Kies displays the Galaxy Tab in the Connected Devices list at the top of the Source list on the left side of the Kies window. We'll look at the Kies interface in the next section.

Did You Know?

When to Connect the Galaxy Tab to Your PC via USB and When to Use Wi-Fi or Bluetooth

You can connect the Galaxy Tab to your PC via USB, Wi-Fi, or Bluetooth—but normally you'll want to use USB. (For the Mac, you're stuck with USB.)

USB has two advantages over Wi-Fi:

- **USB is faster than Wi-Fi**   Even if you establish the fastest wireless connection possible, a USB connection will usually be substantially faster.
- **You can back up and restore via USB**   You can't back up your Galaxy Tab or restore it via Wi-Fi, only via USB.

USB has two main advantages over Bluetooth:

- **USB is much faster than Bluetooth**   USB is more than 100 times faster than Bluetooth, so use USB when you need to transfer lots of data quickly—for example, when you're initially loading music, videos, and photos on the Galaxy Tab or backing up the Galaxy Tab.
- **You can use Kies to manage the Galaxy Tab**   At this writing, Kies works with a USB connection but not with a Bluetooth connection.

Bluetooth works fine for transferring smaller amounts of data, as you'll see later in this chapter. And sometimes, connecting across the airwaves is more convenient than using a physical cable. See the end of this chapter for instructions on connecting the Galaxy Tab to your PC via Bluetooth.

How to...

Make Kies Recognize the Galaxy Tab on a USB Connection

When you connect the Galaxy Tab to your PC, you may find that Kies simply doesn't recognize the device. If this happens, try these two troubleshooting moves.

First, make sure the Galaxy Tab is connected to a USB port on the PC itself rather than connecting through a USB hub. A direct connection makes sure that the Galaxy Tab gets a full-power connection, which helps avoid problems caused by underpowered connections. In particular, avoid connecting the Galaxy Tab through a USB port on a keyboard—these ports are tempting because they're convenient, but usually they have enough power only for undemanding devices such as mouses.

If even a direct connection doesn't make Kies recognize the Galaxy Tab, you may need to reregister the msxml dynamic link library (DLL) files. This sounds technical, but it's easy enough to do, and it often makes all the difference. Follow these steps:

1. Choose Start | All Programs | Accessories | Command Prompt to open a Command Prompt window.

2. Type **cd %windir%\system32** and press ENTER to change directory to the System32 folder in your PC's Windows folder. (Here, cd is the "change directory" command, and %windir% is an environmental variable that stores the path to the Windows folder, no matter where the folder is or what it's called.)

3. Type **regsvr32 msxml3.dll** and press ENTER to register the msxml3.dll file. You'll see a RegSvr32 dialog box (as shown here) saying that the registration succeeded. Click the OK button.

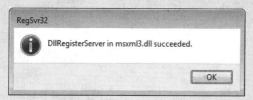

4. Type **regsvr32 msxml6.dll** and press ENTER to register the msxml6.dll file. Again, you should see the RegSvr32 dialog box saying that the registration succeeded. Click the OK button. If you get an error instead (as shown here), follow the instructions later in this sidebar.

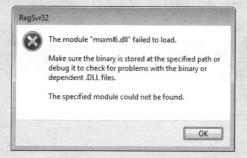

5. Click the Close button (the X button) to close the Command Prompt window.

If you get the RegSvr32 error shown in the previous illustration, the vital file named msxml6.dll is missing. Follow these steps to get it and install it:

1. Open your web browser and steer it to the Microsoft Download Center web site (www.microsoft.com/downloads/).
2. Click in the search box at the top and type **microsoft core xml services msxml** (lowercase is fine unless you're feeling formal) and then press ENTER or click the Search button.
3. On the page of search results, click the Microsoft Core XML Services (MSXML) 6.0 result to display the download page.
4. Click the Download button on the line for the msxml6.msi file. (If you're running 64-bit Windows, click the Download button on the msxml6_x64.msi line.)
5. In the File Download – Security Warning dialog box, click the Save button.
6. Open a Windows Explorer window to the folder to which you downloaded the file, and then double-click it. Follow through the Installer prompts to install the file.

| How to... | # Make Kies Establish the Connection to the Galaxy Tab |

If the Connected Devices area at the top of the left pane in Kies shows the status Connecting (as shown here), but the circular arrows continue to spin fruitlessly, you may need to reinstall the Samsung USB Driver for Mobile Phones. Even though most Galaxy Tab models aren't mobile phones, they use the same driver as many of Samsung's phones.

Disconnect the USB cable from the Galaxy Tab, then click the Troubleshoot Connection Error button or choose Tools | Troubleshoot Connection Error. Then follow through the wizard that opens (shown here).

This wizard removes and then reinstalls the Kies driver, which typically takes several minutes. Along the way you'll need to go through User Account Control (as shown here) to authorize Kies to reinstall the USB driver.

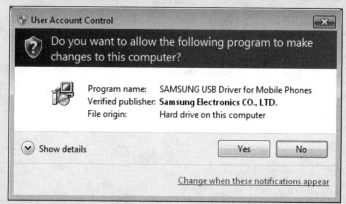

When the wizard finishes, connect the USB cable to your Galaxy Tab again. Kies should now be able to make the connection, and the Galaxy Tab will appear in the Connected Devices list.

Manage the Galaxy Tab Using Kies

After recognizing the Galaxy Tab, Kies displays an entry for the device in the Connected Devices list at the top of the left pane in the window. Click the Galaxy Tab's item to see the device's control screens. At first, you'll see the Basic Information screen, as shown in Figure 3-2.

 Normally, Kies expands the Galaxy Tab's entry, so you can see the Contacts folder, Music folder, Photos folder, Videos folder, and Podcast folder, as in Figure 3-2. If the Galaxy Tab's entry isn't expanded, click the > button (on Windows) or the disclosure triangle (on the Mac) to the left of the Galaxy Tab's name to expand it; if you want to collapse the Galaxy Tab's entry, click the down-arrow button (on Windows) or the disclosure triangle (on the Mac) to the left of the name.

With the Galaxy Tab's control screens displayed, you can click one of the other tabs—the Sync tab, the Import/Export tab, or the Back Up/Restore tab—at the top of the window to display the related screen. We'll look at how to use these screens later in this chapter (except the Back Up/Restore screen, which is covered in Chapter 14).

 At this writing, Kies for Mac doesn't have the Back Up/Restore screen.

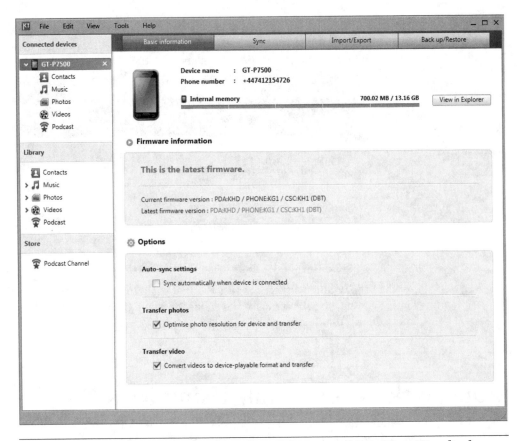

FIGURE 3-2 When you connect the Galaxy Tab to your PC or Mac, Kies displays an entry for the Galaxy Tab in the Connected Devices list in the Source list on the left side of the Kies window.

Choose Settings on the Basic Information Screen

From the Basic Information screen (shown in Figure 3-2), you can do the following:

- **View the internal memory**   The Internal Memory readout shows how much of the Galaxy Tab's internal memory is in use. On Windows, you can click the View In Explorer button next to the readout to open a Windows Explorer window showing the contents of the internal memory. On the Mac, you can click the Internal Memory button to open a window that shows the contents of the Tablet part of the Galaxy Tab's file system in a navigable format. This Internal Memory window looks and acts mostly like a Finder window, but it is still a part of Kies.
- **Update the firmware**   The Firmware Information area shows details of the current firmware version the Galaxy Tab is using. If the Galaxy Tab is up to date, this area shows the message "This is the latest firmware." If a firmware update is available, this area shows a button for updating the firmware to the latest version.

- **Choose whether to sync the Galaxy Tab automatically** Select the Sync Automatically When Device Is Connected check box in the Auto-Sync Settings area if you want Kies to sync data automatically when you connect the Galaxy Tab.

On the Mac, the Basic Information screen may display the Memory Order area, which lets you choose the order in which to use the Galaxy Tab's internal memory and external memory. The controls in this area apply only to Galaxy Tab models that have external memory as well as internal memory—but on the Mac, they currently appear even for Galaxy Tab models that don't have external memory.

- **Choose whether to optimize photos for the Galaxy Tab** (Windows only.) In the Transfer Photos area, select the Optimize Photo Resolution For Device And Transfer check box if you want Kies to create versions of photos that will work best on the Galaxy Tab and then transfer them to the device. This is normally a good idea, as it makes sure the photos on the Galaxy Tab are the right resolution for its screen and that they don't waste a huge amount of space by being a larger resolution than the screen can show.
- **Choose whether to convert video to formats the Galaxy Tab can play** (Windows only.) In the Transfer Video area, select the Convert Videos To Device-Playable Format And Transfer check box if you want Kies to convert videos to formats the Galaxy Tab can play, and then transfer them. This too is usually helpful, as it enables you to view the videos on the Galaxy Tab.

If you want to transfer photos and videos to the Galaxy Tab manually, and to keep them at higher resolutions or in different formats so that you can then transfer them to different devices, clear the Optimize Photo Resolution For Device And Transfer check box in the Transfer Photos area and the Convert Videos To Device-Playable Format And Transfer check box in the Transfer Video area of the Basic Information screen.

Choose Which Items to Sync with the Galaxy Tab

When you've chosen settings on the Basic Information screen, click the Sync tab to display the Sync screen. Figure 3-3 shows the Sync screen on Windows; the Sync screen on the Mac is similar, but it has fewer controls. You can then choose which items to sync, as described in the following subsections—or you can simply select the Select All Items check box at the top to sync all the items shown on the screen.

Sync Your Personal Information

In the Personal Information box on Windows, select the check boxes for the items you want to sync to the Galaxy Tab:

- **Sync Contacts With** To sync contacts, select this check box, and then choose the program in the drop-down list: Google, Yahoo!, Windows Contacts, or Outlook (if you have Outlook installed on your PC). If the Account Preferences button appears when you choose the program, click this button, and then follow through the steps for setting up your account.

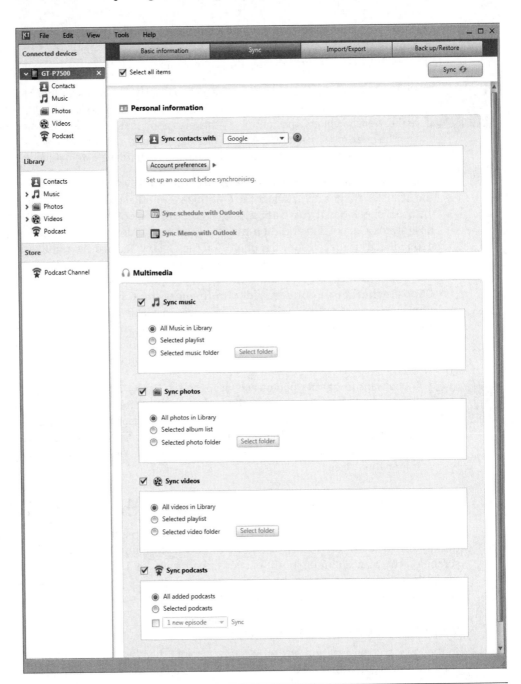

FIGURE 3-3 On the Sync screen in the Galaxy Tab's control screens, choose which items to synchronize automatically between the Galaxy Tab and your PC or Mac.

- **Sync Schedule With Outlook** If you have Outlook, select this check box to sync your Outlook calendar with the Galaxy Tab.
- **Sync Memo With Outlook** If you have Outlook, select this check box to sync memos between Outlook and the Galaxy Tab.

Similarly, on the Mac, select the check boxes in the Personal Information box to control what to sync to the Galaxy Tab:

- **Sync With Address Book** Select this check box to sync the contacts in your Address Book with the Galaxy Tab.
- **Sync Schedules With iCal** Select this check box to sync your iCal calendars with the Galaxy Tab.

Sync Your Multimedia Files

In the Multimedia box, specify which items to sync by selecting the Sync Music check box, the Sync Photos check box, the Sync Videos check box, and the Sync Podcasts check box, as needed.

On the Mac, that's the full extent of your choices at this writing—you can't pick and choose. But on Windows, you can then choose whether to sync all of the files or just some of them. For example, these are your choices if you select the Sync Music check box:

- **All Music In Library** Select this option button to sync all the music you've added to the Kies Library with the Galaxy Tab. If the Galaxy Tab has enough space to take all the music, you may want to do this.
- **Selected Playlist** Select this option button to sync just a playlist that you create in Kies. A playlist can be a convenient way of adding to the Galaxy Tab only those songs you want to play on the device.
- **Selected Music Folder** Select this option button to specify one or more folders containing the music you want to sync with the Galaxy Tab. Click the Select Folder button to display the Select Folder dialog box, navigate to and click the folder, and then click the Select Folder button to close the dialog box. Kies adds the folder to the gray box below the line, and displays a check box for each subfolder that contains music files. You can then clear the check box for any folder you don't want to sync.

The Sync Photos controls, the Sync Videos controls, and the Sync Podcasts controls work in a similar way, except that the Sync Podcasts controls don't have a Selected Podcast Folder option button—instead, there's a check box you can select to sync only the number of new episodes you choose in the drop-down list.

When you've chosen sync options, click the Sync button in the upper-right corner of the Sync screen to perform the sync. The readout in the lower-right corner of the Kies window shows the sync's progress.

Copy Files to and from the Galaxy Tab

Instead of syncing files between your computer and the Galaxy Tab, you may simply want to copy files from one to the other. Copying rather than syncing is especially helpful if you load the Galaxy Tab from two or more computers or if you want to use the Galaxy Tab to transfer files from one computer to another.

Kies makes it easy to copy your personal information files (your contacts, schedule, and memos) and your multimedia files (your music files, photos, and videos) between your computer and the Galaxy Tab. Kies calls copying the files from the computer to the Galaxy Tab *importing from PC* and copying files from the Galaxy Tab to the computer *exporting to PC*. (At this writing, Kies uses the term "PC" for Macs as well as for Windows computers.)

To copy files to and from the Galaxy Tab, click the Import/Export tab at the top of the Kies window to display the Import/Export screen. Figure 3-4 shows the Import/Export screen for Kies on Windows, but the Import/Export screen in Kies for Mac is functionally identical. You can then import or export information by following these steps:

1. In the left pane of the Import/Export screen, click the Import tab or the Export tab, as needed.
   - **Import** Click this tab to copy contacts, calendars, music, or whatever from the computer to the Galaxy Tab. When you're loading the Galaxy Tab, this is the tab you need.
   - **Export** Click this tab to copy data from the Galaxy Tab to the computer.

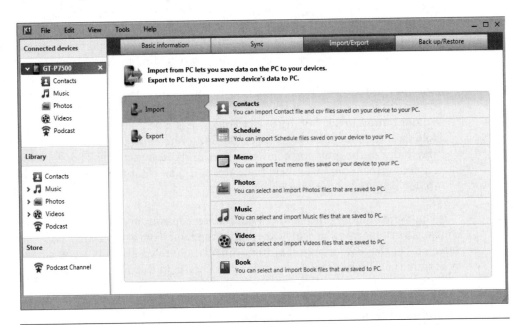

FIGURE 3-4 Use the Import/Export screen in Kies to copy your contacts, schedule, memos, and multimedia files from your computer to the Galaxy Tab or vice versa.

2. In the right pane, click the Contacts button, the Schedule button, the Memo button, the Photos button, the Music button, the Videos button, or the Book button, as appropriate. Kies displays an Import button or an Export button to the right of the item, depending on whether you are importing data or exporting data.
3. Click the Import button or the Export button.
4. In the Open dialog box or Save dialog box that opens, choose the source or destination for the information you're importing or exporting, and then click the Open button or the Save button.

How to... Force Quit Kies for the Mac if It Hogs Your Mac's Processor

At this writing, the current version of Kies for the Mac appears to suffer from various bugs. In particular, you may find that Kies starts hogging your Mac's processor, making other apps run slowly.

If you think this is happening, run Activity Monitor and have a look. Follow these steps:

1. Click in the Spotlight field at the right end of the menu bar.
2. Type **activ** and then click the Activity Monitor result to launch Activity Monitor.
3. On the tab bar at the bottom, click the CPU tab to display the CPU screen, as shown here.

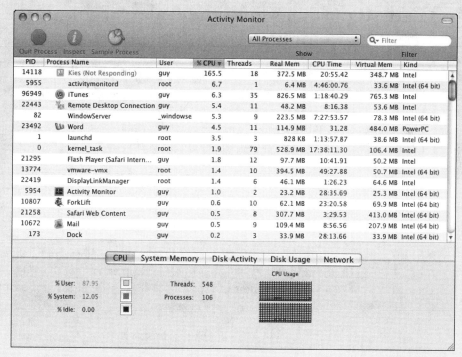

(Continued)

4. Click the % CPU column once or twice, as needed, to produce a descending sort. This shows you the application that's taking most processor cycles at the top.

If the hungriest application is Kies, and it's taking up a lot of cycles (say, more than 100% of the 200% that a dual-core processor has), you may need to quit it. To do so, CTRL-click or right-click the Kies icon on the Dock, and then click the Quit item on the context menu.

If Kies won't quit normally, or if Activity Monitor lists it in red and marked as "(Not Responding)", you will need to force quit Kies. To do so, OPTION-click the Kies icon on the Dock, and then click the Force Quit item on the context menu.

Load Media Files onto Your Galaxy Tab Without Using Kies

Instead of loading media files onto the Galaxy Tab using Kies, you can load them directly from a USB drive or an SD card. You can also load files from a PC by using Windows Explorer instead of Kies. This section shows you how to perform these two moves.

Load Media Files onto the Galaxy Tab from a USB Drive or an SD Card

Loading media files onto your Galaxy Tab from your computer is usually fast and easy, but other times you may need to load media files onto the Galaxy Tab without connecting it to a computer. You can do so by putting the media files on a USB drive or SD card, connecting that drive to the Galaxy Tab, and copying the files from it.

To connect a USB drive or SD card to the Galaxy Tab, you need a device that plugs into the Galaxy Tab's 30-pin port and that provides a USB port or SD card slot at the other end. If you need to be able to connect both USB drives and SD cards to your Galaxy Tab (one at a time), the easiest solution is to get the Samsung USB & SD Connection Kit for Samsung Galaxy Tab, which costs around $30. This kit provides one connector with a USB port and another connector with an SD card slot. You can find third-party equivalents or near-equivalents that provide similar functionality for less outlay.

When you connect a USB drive or SD card to the 30-pin port using the connector, the Galaxy Tab automatically displays the My Files app showing the contents of the USB drive or SD card. You can then work with the files or folders. For example, you can copy music files like this:

1. In the My Files app, select the check box for each file or folder you want to affect.
2. Tap the Copy button on the toolbar to copy the files or folders.

How to... **Deal with the "USB Storage Blank or Has Unsupported File System" Message**

If you see the message "USB storage blank or has unsupported file system" in the notifications area when you connect a USB drive or SD card to the Galaxy Tab, there are two possibilities:

- **The drive is blank**   If so, fine—you can put all the more files on it. Normally, you'll know whether the drive is blank or not.
- **The drive uses a file system the Galaxy Tab can't read**   The Galaxy Tab can read only the FAT32 file system. So if you connect a drive formatted with a different file system, such as the Mac OS Extended file system, the Galaxy Tab won't be able to read it.

If the drive uses a file system other than FAT32, you will need to reformat the drive before you can use it with the Galaxy Tab. You can reformat the drive by using Windows Explorer on the PC or Drive Utility on the Mac. Before you reformat the drive, copy from it any files that you want to keep, because reformatting the drive removes all the files from it.

After reformatting the drive, you can copy the files back to it, and then connect the drive to the Galaxy Tab again.

3. In the left column, tap the Music folder to switch to it.
4. Tap the Paste button on the toolbar to paste in the copied files or folders.

The Galaxy Tab mounts a USB drive or SD card in the /Root/Storages/usb/sda/ folder. You can navigate to this folder manually if you need to—for example, if you want to copy files from the Galaxy Tab to the USB drive or SD card.

To unmount the USB drive or SD card, tap the notifications area, and then tap the USB Device Connected button on the notifications panel. The Galaxy Tab ejects the USB device and displays the message "USB Device Removed Safely" onscreen for a moment. After this message appears, you can safely disconnect the device.

You can also tap the USB symbol that appears at the left end of the notifications area, and then tap the USB Device Connected button to eject the USB device. But usually it's easiest to tap anywhere in the notifications area and then tap the USB Device Connected button on the notifications panel.

Add Files to the Galaxy Tab Using Windows Explorer

As you've seen earlier in this chapter, Kies is the program Samsung provides for managing the Galaxy Tab on Windows. But you don't have to use Kies if you don't want to. Instead, you can open a Windows Explorer window to show the contents of the Galaxy Tab's internal memory, and then simply copy or move files back and forth.

(In case you're wondering, the Galaxy Tab doesn't appear in the Finder on the Mac—but iPhoto may detect the Galaxy Tab as an attached camera and offer to import its photos.)

To display the contents of the Galaxy Tab, follow these steps:

1. Choose Start | Computer to open a Windows Explorer window in Computer view.

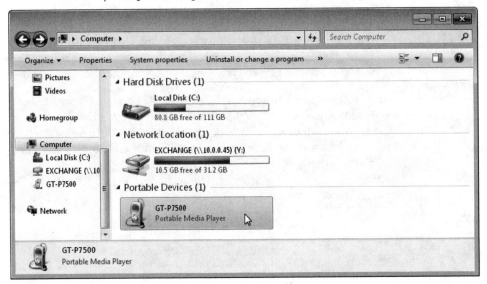

2. In the default view, double-click the item named GT and the Galaxy Tab's model number (for example, GT-P7500) in the Portable Devices area. The Windows Explorer window shows the Galaxy Tab's contents as a drive named Tablet, as shown here.

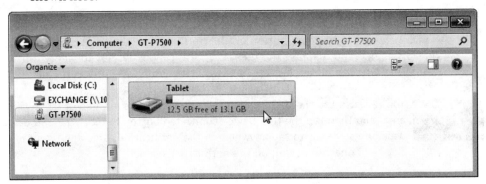

3. Double-click the Tablet item to display its contents.

You can now add files to the Galaxy Tab's file system, or copy or move files from the Galaxy Tab to your PC, as needed.

Connect the Galaxy Tab to Your PC via Wi-Fi

The normal way of connecting the Galaxy Tab to your PC is via USB, which gives the highest possible connection speeds and so makes file transfer, sync, and backup as swift as possible. But you can also connect the Galaxy Tab to your PC via Wi-Fi. Connecting via Wi-Fi is often more convenient, because you don't need to use the USB cable and you can leave the Galaxy Tab charging from its power adapter during the sync.

 At this writing, Kies for the Mac doesn't support connecting the Galaxy Tab via Wi-Fi. And even Kies for Windows doesn't support backing up and restoring the Galaxy Tab via Wi-Fi.

To connect the Galaxy Tab to your PC via Wi-Fi, follow these steps:

1. On the PC, make sure Kies is running, and that the PC is connected to the same wireless network as the Galaxy Tab.
2. On the Galaxy Tab, tap the notifications area to display the notifications panel.
3. Tap the Settings button to display the Settings screen.
4. In the left panel, tap the Wireless And Networks button to display the Wireless And Networks screen.
5. Tap the Kies Via Wi-Fi button to display the Kies Via Wi-Fi dialog box (shown at right).

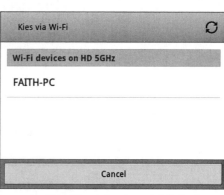

6. In the Wi-Fi Devices list, tap the button for your PC. Kies tries to establish the connection, as shown here.

7. When the Wi-Fi Connection Request dialog box appears on the PC, as shown here, tap the Yes button.

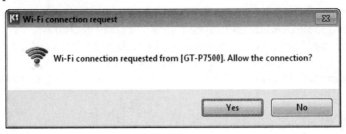

8. When the Kies Via Wi-Fi dialog box shows that the connection is established, as shown here, you can start the sync in Kies on your PC, as described earlier in this chapter.

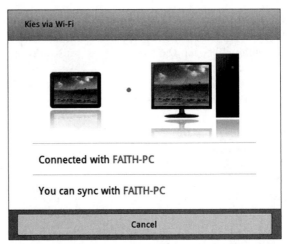

9. In Kies on the PC, the Galaxy Tab's icon shows a Wi-Fi symbol, as shown here. When you finish syncing, eject the Galaxy Tab in Kies by clicking its × button.

10. On the Galaxy Tab, tap the Cancel button to close the Kies Via Wi-Fi dialog box.

Configure How Kies Handles the Galaxy Tab

To configure how Kies handles the Galaxy Tab, choose Tools | Preferences, and then work on the three screens of the Preferences dialog box. Kies for Windows and Kies for the Mac have different preferences, so we'll look at them separately—Windows first, and then Mac.

Configure Kies on Windows

The Preferences dialog box for Kies for Windows has three screens: the General screen, the Device screen, and the Update screen.

Choose Auto-Run, Folder Location, Language Preferences, and Log Preferences

On the General screen in the Preferences dialog box (see Figure 3-5), you can choose five settings:

- **Run Samsung Kies Automatically When A Device Is Connected**   Select this check box if you want Kies to launch automatically when you connect the Galaxy Tab to your PC. This is usually helpful if you use Kies to sync files and data between your PC and the Galaxy Tab.
- **Have The Components Reside In Memory When The Operating System Starts, So That Kies Can Run Faster**   Select this check box if you want Windows to load Kies's components automatically during startup (after you log on) so that Kies will launch more quickly. If you use Kies regularly, this is usually a good idea—but it does mean that your PC will take longer to log you in and get your Windows session underway.
- **Folder Location**   In the Default Folder text box, enter the name of the folder you want Kies to use as the default location. The standard setting is the Documents\ Samsung\Kies folder in your user folder. This folder works fine unless you have a folder you prefer—in which case, click the Change button, click the folder in the Select Folder dialog box, and then click the Select Folder button.
- **Language**   In this drop-down list, you can change the language the Kies user interface uses. If you picked the right language when setting up Kies, you shouldn't need to change this setting.
- **Automatically Send Log Information Of Mobile Device**   In this area, select the check box (which has a three-line name) if you want to allow Kies to send error information and usage information about your Galaxy Tab to Samsung. Samsung doesn't provide the guarantees of anonymity and privacy that are customary with such features, so you may want to clear this check box.

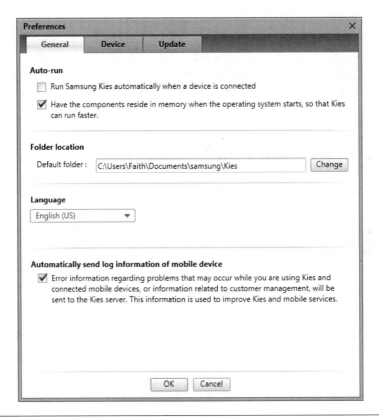

FIGURE 3-5 On the General screen in the Preferences dialog box, you can set Kies to run automatically when you connect the Galaxy Tab, change the default folder, set the language, and decide whether to automatically send log information to Samsung.

Choose Device Preferences

On the Device screen in the Preferences dialog box (see Figure 3-6), you may or may not be able to initialize the syncing logs for contacts, scheduling information, and memos. If the check boxes in the Initialize Syncing Log box are available, you can select one or more of them and then click the Initialize Syncing Log button.

Initializing the syncing log wipes out the existing sync status but doesn't delete the contact information, scheduling information, or memos. You may never need to initialize the syncing log.

What you may well want to do on the Device screen is delete old backup files you no longer need. To delete a backup file, follow these steps:

1. In the Backup File list box, select the backup file's check box.

FIGURE 3-6   On the Device screen in the Preferences dialog box, you can delete unwanted backup files. You may also be able to initialize your syncing log.

2. Click the Delete Backup button. Kies displays the Notification dialog box (shown here.)

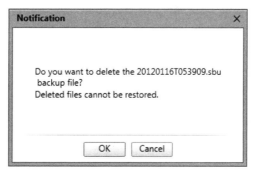

3. Click the OK button.

Choose Update Preferences

On the Update screen in the Preferences dialog box (see Figure 3-7), you can control Kies updates:

- **Update Now** If this button is available, click it to start updating Kies to the version shown in the readout. If the Check For Updates button appears instead, click this button to find out whether an update is available.
- **Notify When Updates Are Available** Select this check box if you want Kies to check for updates and prompt you to install them. This automatic checking is usually helpful.

 We'll look at the process of updating Kies later in this chapter.

FIGURE 3-7 On the Update screen in the Preferences dialog box, you can choose whether to have Kies notify you when updates are available. You can also check manually for updates.

Configure Kies on the Mac

The Preferences dialog box for Kies for Mac has three screens: the General screen, the Device screen, and the Update screen.

Choose the Location of the Default Folder

On the General screen in the Preferences dialog box (see Figure 3-8), you can choose only the location of the default folder. See if the folder shown in the Default Folder box is the one you want. If not, click the Change button, navigate to the correct folder in the Open dialog box, and then click the Open button.

Choose Device Preferences

On the Device screen in the Preferences dialog box (see Figure 3-9), you should in theory be able to initialize the syncing logs for contacts, scheduling information, and memos. At this writing, the Device screen isn't complete, and the controls on it don't work.

Choose Update Preferences

On the Update screen in the Preferences dialog box (see Figure 3-10), you can control Kies updates:

- **Update Now**   If this button is available, click it to start updating Kies to the version shown in the readout.

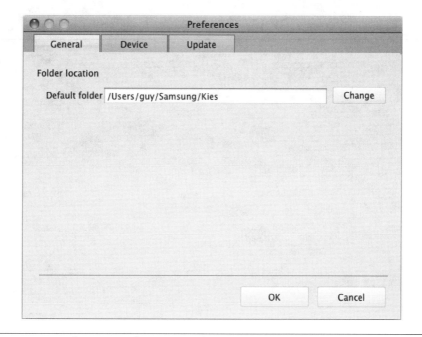

FIGURE 3-8   On the General screen in the Preferences dialog box, you can set the default folder for Kies for Mac.

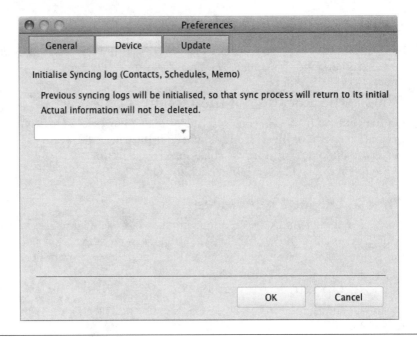

FIGURE 3-9   The Device screen in the Preferences dialog box of Kies for Mac is a work in progress.

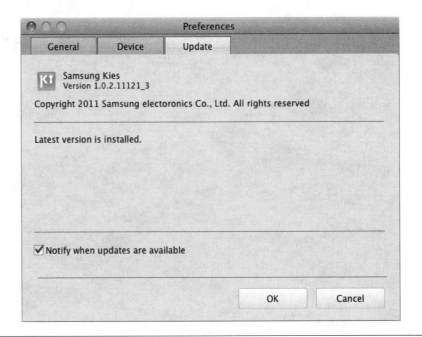

FIGURE 3-10   On the Update screen in the Preferences dialog box, you can choose whether to have Kies notify you when updates are available.

- **Notify When Updates Are Available**   Select this check box if you want Kies to check for updates and prompt you to install them. This automatic checking is usually helpful.

 We'll look at the process of updating Kies next.

Keep Kies Up to Date

To get the best performance and results with Kies, you need to update it to the latest version. In this section, we'll look at how to update Kies first on the PC and then on the Mac.

Keep Kies Up to Date on Windows

If you set Kies to alert you to updates, it displays the Kies Update dialog box (shown here) when it detects one.

In the Auto Check Update drop-down list, choose the frequency: Always, Everyday, Every 3 Days, Every Week, Every 15 Days, or Every Month. The frequency is up to you, but Every Week is a sensible compromise between frantic checking and leaving Kies too long without important updates.

Click the OK button to tell Kies to download the files (as it is shown doing here).

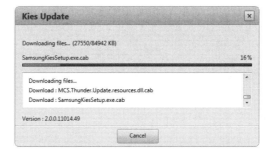

If the Kies download seems to get stuck, look at the Taskbar to see if a User Account Control button is flashing there. If so, click this button to display the User Account Control dialog box, and then click the Continue button. For reasons unknown, the User Account Control dialog box tends to get stuck behind the Kies Update dialog box.

When Kies finishes downloading the files, the Kies Installer runs, and the Samsung Kies – InstallShield Wizard dialog box (shown here) appears, telling you that you need to uninstall the previous version of Kies before you can install the new version.

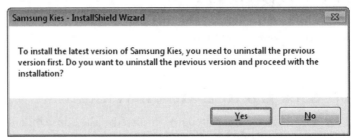

Click the Yes button. The InstallShield Wizard then removes Kies, launches the installation routine, and walks you through it. This uses the same steps described earlier in the chapter.

At the end of the installation, make sure the Run Samsung Kies check box is selected, and then click the Finish button. The installer launches Kies, and you can start using it again.

Keep Kies Up to Date on Your Mac

To help you keep it updated, Kies automatically checks for updates and prompts you to install any it finds.

If you have time, go ahead and update Kies. Click the Update button, and follow through the prompts for downloading and installing the update. This is less straightforward than it should be, because performing the update involves running another application called LUI.app, which asks you to authenticate yourself to prove your authority to run it (as shown here).

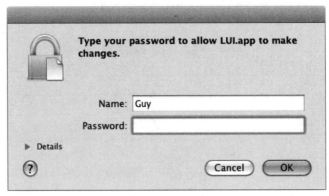

Once you've agreed to run LUI.app, the Kies Update dialog box appears (as shown here), keeping you updated on Kies's progress getting the files and installing them.

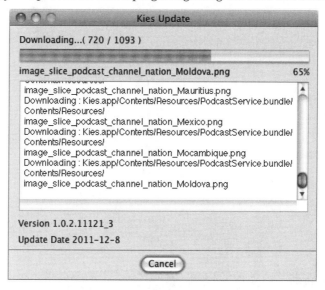

Connect the Galaxy Tab to Your PC via Bluetooth

Before you can connect the Galaxy Tab to your PC via Bluetooth, you need to turn Bluetooth on and make the Galaxy Tab visible via Bluetooth. You can then pair the Galaxy Tab with your PC, establish a connection, and transfer files back and forth.

 Kies has a Tools | Connect Using Bluetooth command, but it doesn't work for devices that use the Android operating system, as the Galaxy Tab does. So you need to establish the Bluetooth connection using Windows instead.

Turn On Bluetooth and Make the Galaxy Tab Visible

To turn on Bluetooth and make the Galaxy Tab visible so that you can pair it with the PC, follow these steps:

1. From the home screen, tap the notifications area to display the notifications panel.
2. Tap the Settings button to display the Settings screen.

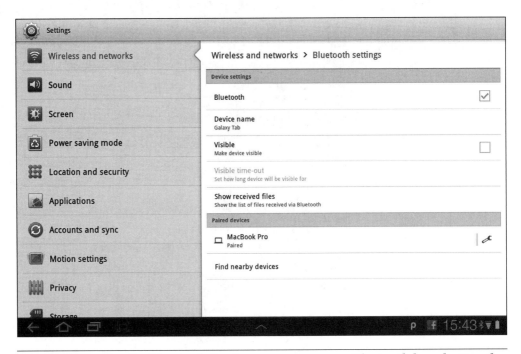

FIGURE 3-11 On the Bluetooth Settings screen, turn on Bluetooth by selecting the Bluetooth check box, and then make the Galaxy Tab visible to other Bluetooth devices by selecting the Visible check box.

3. Tap the Wireless And Networks button to display the Wireless And Networks screen.
4. Tap the Bluetooth Settings button to display the Bluetooth Settings screen (shown in Figure 3-11).
5. Select the Bluetooth check box to turn Bluetooth on.

When Bluetooth is turned on, the Bluetooth symbol appears in the Galaxy Tab's notifications area, so you can instantly tell whether Bluetooth is on.

6. If you want to change the Galaxy Tab's Bluetooth name, tap the Device Name button, type the name in the Device Name dialog box, and then tap the OK button.

In this section, I've used the name "Galaxy Tab" for my Galaxy Tab, because I like to keep things straightforward. When you connect to your Galaxy Tab via Bluetooth, you'll see the Bluetooth name you've set.

7. Select the Visible check box. The Galaxy Tab makes itself visible to other Bluetooth devices for 120 seconds, which it counts down on the Visible line.

Pair the Galaxy Tab with Your PC

Now that Bluetooth is on and the Galaxy Tab is visible via Bluetooth, you can pair the Galaxy Tab with your PC. To do so, follow these steps:

1. Choose Start | Control Panel to open a Control Panel window.

 These steps are for Windows 7. For Windows XP or Windows Vista, you need to take similar but different steps.

2. Click in the Search Control Panel box in the upper-right corner of the Control Panel window, and then type **Bluetooth** to display a list of Bluetooth-related tasks.
3. Click the Add A Bluetooth Device link to launch the Add A Device wizard, which displays the Select A Device To Add To This Computer screen (shown in Figure 3-12 with the Galaxy Tab found).

FIGURE 3-12   On the Select A Device To Add To This Computer screen of the Add A Device wizard, select the Galaxy Tab, and then click the Next button.

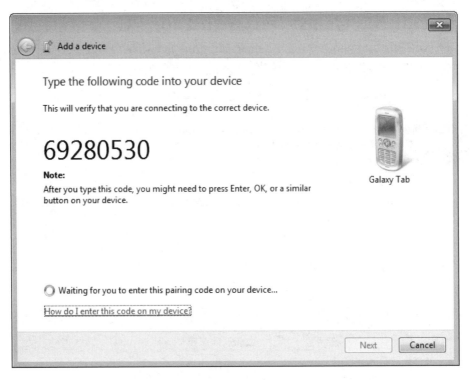

FIGURE 3-13 When you see the Type The Following Code Into Your Device screen on your PC (top), type the code into the Bluetooth Pairing Request dialog box on the Galaxy Tab (bottom).

4. Click the Galaxy Tab's icon in the list box, and then click the Next button to display the Type The Following Code Into Your Device screen (shown in the upper part of Figure 3-13).

5. Type the code into the Bluetooth Pairing Request dialog box on the Galaxy Tab (shown in the lower part of Figure 3-13).

6. The Add A Device wizard then displays the This Device Has Been Successfully Added To This Computer screen (see Figure 3-14).

7. Click the Close button.

FIGURE 3-14   The Add A Device wizard displays the This Device Has Been Successfully Added To This Computer screen when you've paired the Galaxy Tab.

Transfer Files to and from the Galaxy Tab Using Bluetooth

When you've paired the Galaxy Tab with your PC, you can send files to it and receive files from it by using the Bluetooth File Transfer wizard. Choose Start | All Programs | Accessories | Bluetooth File Transfer to launch the Bluetooth File Transfer wizard, which displays its Transfer Files Using Bluetooth screen (see Figure 3-15).

To send one or more files to the Galaxy Tab, follow these steps:

1. On the Transfer Files Using Bluetooth screen, click the Send Files button. The Bluetooth File Transfer wizard displays the Select Where To Send Your Files screen (see Figure 3-16).
2. Click the Galaxy Tab's entry.
3. Click the Next button. The Bluetooth File Transfer wizard displays the Select The Files screen.

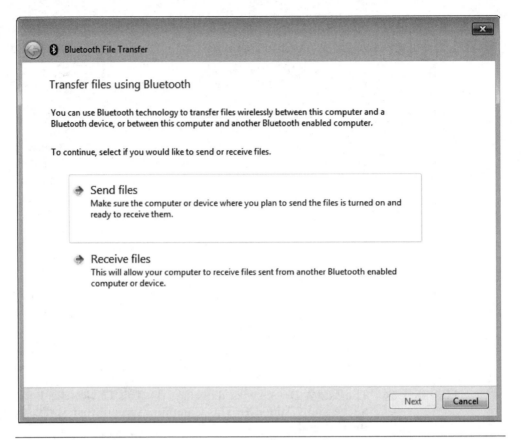

FIGURE 3-15 Use the Bluetooth File Transfer wizard to send files from your PC to the Galaxy Tab or to receive files from the Galaxy Tab.

4. Select the files you want to transfer:
   a. Click the Browse button to display the Browse dialog box.
   b. Navigate to the folder that contains the files.
   c. Select the file or files.
   d. Click the Open button. The Bluetooth File Transfer wizard adds the file name or names to the File Names text box, separating the names with semicolons.
5. Click the Next button. The Bluetooth File Transfer wizard displays its The File Is Being Sent screen.
6. The Galaxy Tab then displays a message telling you that there's a Bluetooth request you need to authorize. To do so, follow these steps:
   a. Tap the notifications area to open the notifications panel.
   b. Tap the Authorization Request button to display the Bluetooth Authorization Request dialog box.

FIGURE 3-16   On the Select Where To Send Your Files screen of the Bluetooth File Transfer wizard, click the Galaxy Tab's entry, and then click the Next button.

    c. Select the Always Allow This Device check box if you want to receive files more easily from your PC in the future.

    d. Tap the Accept button. The Galaxy Tab starts receiving the file or files.

7. The Bluetooth File Transfer wizard shows the progress of sending the file or files, and the notifications panel shows the Galaxy Tab's progress of receiving the data.

8. When the transfer is complete, the Bluetooth File Transfer wizard displays the File Successfully Transferred screen. Click the Finish button to close the wizard.

9. When the Galaxy Tab has finished receiving the files, tap the Bluetooth Share: Received notification in the notifications panel to display the Inbound Transfers screen (shown here). You can then tap the button for a file to open it.

You'll find files you receive via Bluetooth in the Bluetooth folder, which you can access using the My Files app.

To transfer one or more files from the Galaxy Tab to your PC, follow these steps:

1. Choose Start | All Programs | Accessories | Bluetooth File Transfer to launch the Bluetooth File Transfer wizard. The wizard displays the Transfer Files Using Bluetooth screen (shown in Figure 3-15, earlier in this chapter).
2. Click the Receive Files button. The Bluetooth File Transfer wizard displays the Waiting For A Connection screen.
3. On the Galaxy Tab, start sending a file like this:
   a. Open the file you want to send.
   b. Tap the Share button on the toolbar to display the Share menu.
   c. Tap the Bluetooth button to display the Bluetooth Device Picker screen (shown here).

Bluetooth device picker
Scan for devices
Found devices
💻 MacBook Pro Paired
💻 FAITH-PC Paired
💻 Guy's PowerBook G4 17" Pair with this device
💻 macserver Pair with this device

   d. Tap the button for the device to which you want to send the file. The Galaxy Tab starts sending the file, and the Bluetooth File Transfer wizard starts receiving it.
4. When the Bluetooth File Transfer wizard displays the Save The Received File screen (see Figure 3-17), you can either accept the default folder shown in the Location text box or click the Browse button and use the Browse dialog box to choose another folder. Then click the Finish button to save the file to that folder.

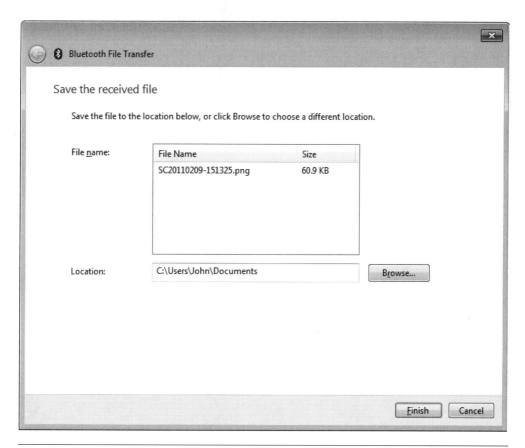

FIGURE 3-17   On the Save The Received File screen of the Bluetooth File Transfer wizard, choose whether to use the default folder or a folder you select.

4

Play Music on the Galaxy Tab

HOW TO...

- Get suitable music files for the Galaxy Tab
- Play music with the Music Player app
- Set a song as an alarm tone

In this chapter, I'll show you how to play and enjoy music on the Galaxy Tab. If you've made the Galaxy Tab part of your everyday life, and music is as important to you as it is to me, the two go together like waffles and maple syrup.

We'll start by briefly covering how to get suitable music files for the Galaxy Tab. The best way to get started is to create audio files from your CDs so that you can load them on the Galaxy Tab using Kies (as described in Chapter 3). You can also buy music online, using either the Galaxy Tab or your computer, or download music files for free—but you'll need to know about the dangers before you do either.

After you load some music on the Galaxy Tab, you'll want to enjoy it. You can play the music by artist, by album, or (with some luck) by genre—or you can create custom playlists that contain the songs you want to hear in the order you want to hear them.

Ready? Right, let's get started.

Get Suitable Music Files for the Galaxy Tab

Before you can enjoy music on the Galaxy Tab, you need to get suitable music files. This section outlines the four main sources you'll probably want to explore:

- Creating music files from your own CDs
- Buying music online using the Galaxy Tab
- Buying music online using your computer
- Finding free music online

Rip Your CDs to Create Music Files You Can Play on the Galaxy Tab

If the music you want to play on the Galaxy Tab is on CDs, you will need to create audio files of the songs on the CDs. Creating audio files is called *ripping*, because it technically involves extracting the audio files from the CD rather than just copying them (as you would do if music were software).

To rip CDs, you can use any of a variety of programs—but these are arguably the best two:

- **Windows Media Player**   Windows 7 (and most known versions of Windows) includes Microsoft's Windows Media Player, which you can launch by choosing Start | All Programs | Windows Media Player.
- **iTunes**   iTunes is the program that Apple provides for creating and converting music files and for managing iPads, iPhones, and iPods. Even if you totally lack i-devices, you can download iTunes for free from Apple's web site (www.apple .com/itunes/download).

After creating music files, you can put them on the Galaxy Tab using Kies or doubleTwist, as discussed in Chapter 3.

Buy Music Online Using the Galaxy Tab

If you want to buy music online, you may be able to do so by using an app that the Galaxy Tab includes. Whether you have such an app depends on your Galaxy Tab model and (if it's a 3G Galaxy Tab) your carrier, so display the Apps screen and see if one of these applications is there:

- **Amazon MP3**   This app gives you an easy way to browse and buy the millions of songs Amazon.com offers in the MP3 format.
- **Music Hub**   This app gives you easy access to an online music service or online media service from which you can preview and buy songs. Figure 4-1 shows the Music Hub app.
- **Media Hub**   This app connects you to an online service for TV, movies, and in some cases music.

Buy Music Online Using Your Computer

Instead of buying music from a proprietary music service such as the service you can access through the Music Hub app or Media Hub app, you can buy music from web sites and online services using your computer.

Because most of the music stores mentioned here work with most any web browser, you can access them using the Galaxy Tab and buy music from them. But unless you're in a tearing hurry, it's usually easier to buy the music using your computer and then copy it to the Galaxy Tab.

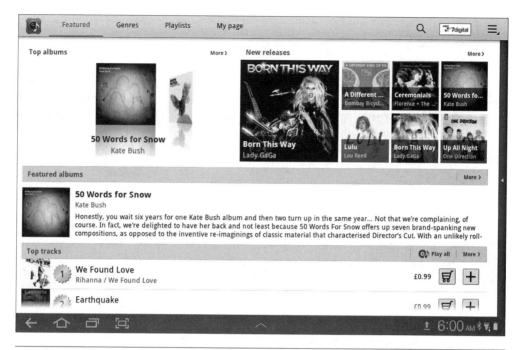

FIGURE 4-1   Depending on your Galaxy Tab model and carrier, you may have the Music Hub app for buying music online.

Digital Rights Management (DRM) Removes Value from Music You Buy Online

Before you buy any music or other media files via the Music Hub app or Media Hub app, make sure you understand what you're getting if you do choose to pay.

First, find out whether the files you intend to buy are protected with digital rights management (DRM) that prevents you from transferring them to other devices and playing them there. MP3 files such as those from Amazon.com do not have DRM, but files in other formats (such as Windows Media Audio, WMA) may have DRM.

Second, find out whether the Galaxy Tab or other playback device must be connected to the Internet in order for you to play back music or other media.

Either of these restrictions is a deal-breaker. DRM is a set of technologies that music companies like to use to restrict what you and I can do with the music we buy. While DRM is mainly meant to prevent piracy, it tends to make playing music and media so much less flexible for honest buyers that it's hardly worth buying music protected with DRM—especially as you can buy unprotected files elsewhere (as discussed later in this section).

Of the many online music stores at this writing, these are arguably the best three to start with:

- **Amazon.com** Amazon.com sells files in the widely used MP3 format without DRM. Prices tend to be competitive with buying new CDs. If you've bought books or other items from Amazon.com before, you may find this a good place to start.
- **iTunes Store** Apple's iTunes Store sells music in the Advanced Audio Coding (AAC) format, which the Galaxy Tab can't play, but you can create MP3 versions of the songs by using iTunes. To access the iTunes Store, you need to download and install iTunes from Apple's web site (www.apple.com/itunes/download/). Apple is aggressively pushing the record companies to allow 90-second previews of songs that are longer than a couple of minutes, which is a great help in deciding whether you like the songs.

 The advantage of Rhapsody and other online music services is that you can listen to a wide variety of music and buy only those songs you're sure you want, rather than judging songs by 30-second, 60-second, or 90-second previews. The disadvantage is that you have to pay the subscription fees.

- **Rhapsody** Rhapsody (www.rhapsody.com) is an online music service with subscription plans that also let you buy songs. At this writing, Rhapsody claims to have 13 million songs, but not all of them are available for purchase. Rhapsody has bought Napster (www.napster.com), another subscription service with sales, and integrated it into Rhapsody.

 Beware of sites that offer large amounts of songs for suspiciously small sums. Many of these sites are hosted in lightly policed countries by companies you'd likely prefer not to give your credit-card details to.

Find Free Music Online

Instead of buying music at all, you can get increasing amounts of it for free online—legally. These days, more and more artists either offer sample tracks online or give away most of their songs online to encourage fans to attend their concerts, buy merchandise, and contribute to the artists' upkeep in other ways than by buying CDs.

You can find free music online by entering terms such as **free music download** into your favorite search engine, but the results are likely to contain a high proportion of dangerous sites. Generally, you're better off checking the web site of the artist you're interested in; the artist's presence on Facebook, MySpace, or other social-networking sites; or the artist's record company's web site (if the artist is beholden to a record company).

 You can also download just about any music online illegally by using file-sharing networks. Before you choose to use a file-sharing network, do some research on copyright law, and make sure you understand how your computer's IP address identifies your actions online.

Play Music with the Music Player App

After you've added music files to the Galaxy Tab, you can play them using the Music Player app. This app is easy to use, but it has various hidden features, as you'll see in this section.

Open the Music Player App

To open the Music Player app, follow these steps:

1. From the home screen, tap the Apps button to display the Apps screen.
2. Tap the Music Player icon.

 When you open the Music Player app after copying music files to the Galaxy Tab, the Galaxy Tab doesn't actually launch the Music Player—instead, it runs the Media Scanner to update your music library with the latest files. When you see the message that media scanning is complete, tap the Music Player icon on the Apps screen again to start the Music Player app.

Browse to Find the Songs You Want

To find the songs you want to play, you can browse your music library in five different ways by tapping the eight tabs on the left of the Music Player screen:

- **Songs** Tap this tab to display an alphabetical list of the songs on the Galaxy Tab, as shown in Figure 4-2.
- **Playlists** Tap this tab to display the Galaxy Tab's built-in playlists and the playlists you've created manually, as shown in Figure 4-3. Tap the playlist you want to play, and then tap the song at which you want to start playing.

 The Music Player app displays a CD cover image when the song file contains one. When there's no CD cover image, the Music Player app displays multicolored soft-focus graphics to represent the CDs and songs.

- **Albums** Tap this tab to display an alphabetical list of albums, as shown in Figure 4-4. When you find the album you want, tap its icon to display the album's songs. Tap the song you want to play.
- **Artists** Tap this tab to display an alphabetical list of artists. Tap the artist whose songs you want to see. You can then tap the song you want to play.
- **Genres** Tap this tab to display an alphabetical list of musical genres, as shown in Figure 4-5. You can then tap a genre to display the list of songs in that genre. Tap the song you want to play.

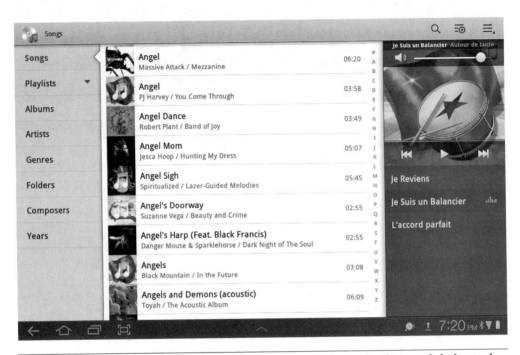

FIGURE 4-2 Tap the Songs tab in the Music Player app to display an alphabetical list of the songs on the Galaxy Tab.

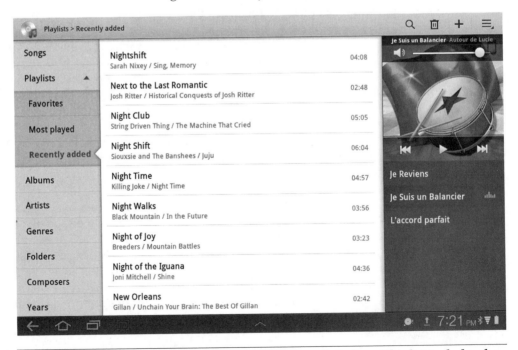

FIGURE 4-3 Tap the Playlists tab to expand the list of playlists. This list includes the Music Player app's built-in playlists and any playlists you've created.

FIGURE 4-4   Tap the Albums tab in the Music Player app to browse through an alphabetical list of albums.

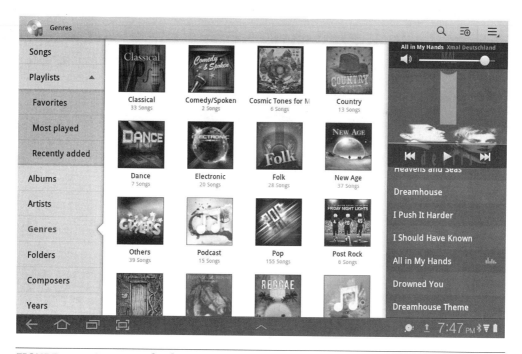

FIGURE 4-5   You can also browse by genre in the Music Player app.

- **Folders** If your songs are stored in different folders, you can tap the Folders tab to browse by folders. If your songs are all in the Media folder, there's not much point in browsing by folders.
- **Composers** To browse by composers, tap the Composers tab, and then tap the composer whose songs you want to view. For browsing by composers to work well, you need to make sure that your music files contain an entry in the Composer tag. Many music files don't contain an entry in the Composer tag.
- **Years** To browse your songs by years, tap the Years tab, and then tap the year you want to see. A list of the songs appears. For browsing by years to work properly, you need to make sure that each music file contains the correct year in the Year tag. Many music files don't contain such an entry.

Use the Play Controls

When you tap a song to play it, the Music Player app displays the song's cover image (or its colorful stand-in) next to the play controls:

- When the Galaxy Tab is in portrait orientation, the play controls appear at the bottom of the screen, with the cover to their left.
- When the Galaxy Tab is in landscape orientation, the play controls appear on the right side of the screen, with the cover near the top. Figure 4-6 shows this arrangement.

FIGURE 4-6 You can control playback from the panel on the right side of the Music Player app in landscape mode.

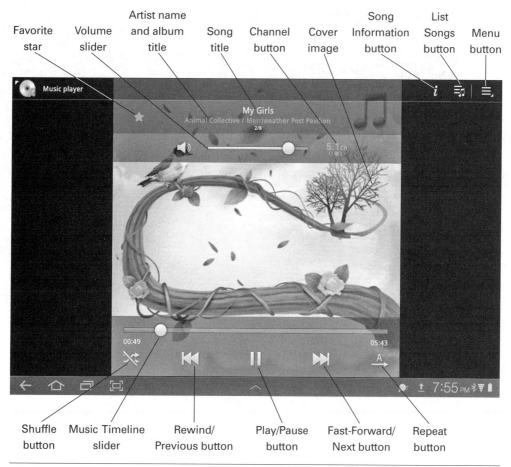

FIGURE 4-7   The Now Playing screen displays an overlay of controls for playing the music.

Whichever orientation you're using, tap the cover image to display the Now Playing screen with its overlay of controls. Figure 4-7 shows the Now Playing screen with the controls labeled. The Galaxy Tab displays the overlay for a few seconds; if you don't tap a button, it hides the overlay until you tap the screen to display it again.

The controls are straightforward to use:

• **Song Information button**   Tap the *i* button to display the Media Info screen (shown in Figure 4-8).
• **Favorite star**   Tap this star to turn it gold and mark the song as a favorite. If the song is already a favorite, and you want to stop it being one, tap the gold star to turn it gray.
• **Volume slider**   Tap and drag this slider to set the volume. You can also press the volume rocker button on the top edge of the Galaxy Tab.

FIGURE 4-8 Tap the Song Information button to display the Media Info screen. Tap the *i* button, or the cover picture that replaces the *i* button, when you want to hide the Media Info screen.

- **Artist name and album title** This readout shows the artist name, a forward slash, and the album title.
- **Song title** This readout shows the song title.
- **Channel button** Tap this button to switch between regular stereo (with the 5.1Ch button grayed out) and 5.1 surround sound (with the 5.1Ch button white). Normally, you'll want to use regular stereo when listening through headphones or a pair of speakers, and 5.1 surround sound only when you've connected the Galaxy Tab to a speaker system with five satellite speakers and one subwoofer.
- **Cover image** This area shows the CD's cover image or the picture that the Galaxy Tab has substituted for it.
- **List Songs button** Tap this button to return to the screen from which you went to the Now Playing screen.
- **Menu button** Tap this button to display the menu, which contains extra commands—for example, for displaying the Settings screen.
- **Music Timeline slider** Tap and drag this slider to move quickly to a different point in the song.
- **Shuffle button** Tap this button to turn shuffling on or off. When shuffling is off, a diagonal line appears through the shuffle arrows.
- **Rewind/Previous button** Tap and hold this button to move back through the song a few seconds at a time; release the button when you reach the part you

want to hear. Tap the button once to go back to the start of the song; tap it again to go to the previous song.

- **Play/Pause button**   Tap this button to start playback or to pause playback.
- **Fast-Forward/Next button**   Tap and hold this button to move forward through the song a few seconds at a time; release the button when you reach the part you want to play. Tap the button once to go to the start of the next song.
- **Repeat button**   At first, when repeat is off, the icon shows A with an arrow under it pointing to the right, indicating that the album, playlist, or other song grouping is playing in sequence. Tap this button once to turn on repeat for the album or group of songs you're playing; the icon shows A surrounded by counterclockwise arrows. Tap this button again to turn on repeat for a single song; the icon shows 1 with arrows going counterclockwise around it. Tap again to turn repeat off.

Create a Playlist

Playing music by artist or by album can be great, but what you'll often want to do is play a sequence of songs in exactly the order you want to hear them, no matter which artist or album they come from. To do this, you create a playlist and add songs to it.

To create a playlist, follow these steps:

1. Open the Music Player app if it's not already open.
2. Tap the Playlists tab to display it.
3. Tap the Menu button to display the menu panel.
4. Tap the New Playlist (+) button to display the New Playlist dialog box (shown here).

5. Type the name for the new playlist, and then tap the Done button. The Music Player app displays the list of songs in the middle of the screen, and displays on the right a pane containing the playlist with no songs in it, as you can see in Figure 4-9.
6. Tap the Add (+) button for each song you want to add to the playlist.
7. After you finish adding songs to the playlist, tap the Done button above the playlist. The Music Player app displays the playlist with the songs added to it.
8. To change the order of the songs in the playlist, tap the Change Order button, the button that shows three lines with an up arrow and a down arrow, on the toolbar at the top of the screen. The Music Player app displays a movement handle (a grid of nine squares) to the right of each song.
9. Tap and hold a song's movement handle so that a blue outline appears around the song's button. Then drag the song up or down the playlist, as shown in Figure 4-10.

FIGURE 4-9 After you create a new playlist, the Music Player app displays the list of songs and a pane on the right containing the empty playlist. Tap the Add (+) button for each song you want to add.

FIGURE 4-10 After adding songs to the playlist, you can leave the songs in their default order. But normally you'll want to tap the Change Order button and then drag the songs into your preferred order.

10. After you finish rearranging the songs, tap the Done button to return to the Playlists screen.

You can now play the playlist and see how well the songs go together.

 To delete a playlist, tap it in the list on the Playlists screen, and then tap the Delete button on the toolbar at the top of the screen. Tap the check box on the playlist's name in the left column, and then tap the Delete button. In the Delete dialog box that appears, tap the Done button.

Choose Settings for Playing Music

To make music sound the way you want it to, you can apply an equalization or a sound effect. You can also change which items the Music Player app includes on the Music menu.

To choose settings, follow these steps:

1. In the Music Player app, tap the Menu button to display the menu panel (shown here).

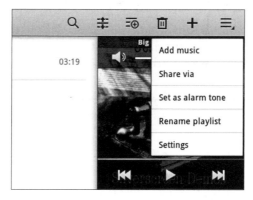

2. Tap the Settings button to display the Settings screen (shown here).

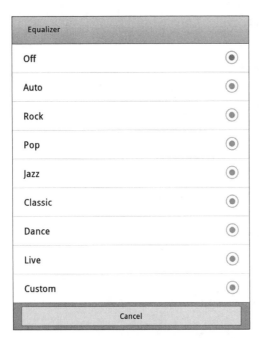
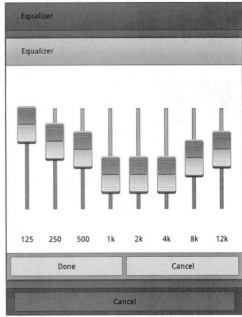

FIGURE 4-11   In the Equalizer dialog box (left), tap the equalization you want. To create a custom equalization, tap the Custom option button, and then work in the smaller Equalizer dialog box that appears (right).

3. Tap the Equalizer button to display the Equalizer dialog box (shown on the left in Figure 4-11).
4. Tap the option button for the equalization you want. To create a custom equalization, tap the Custom option button, drag the sliders in the smaller Equalizer dialog box that appears (see the right screen in Figure 4-11), and then tap the Done button.

 You can create a custom equalization only when 5.1 stereo is turned off.

5. Tap the Back button to return to the Settings screen.

6. Tap the Sound Effects button to display the Sound Effects screen (shown here).

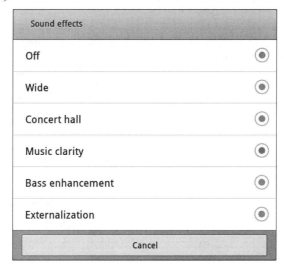

7. Tap the option button for the effect you want—for example, Concert Hall or Musical Clarity.
8. Tap the Back button to return to the Settings screen.
9. Tap the Music Menu button to display the Music Menu screen (shown here).

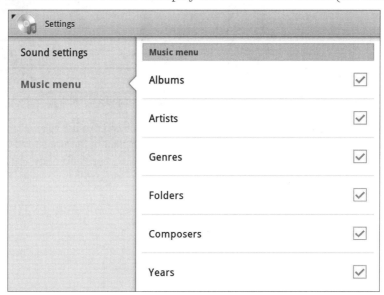

10. Select the check boxes for the items you want to display in the Music menu.
11. Tap the Back button to return to the Settings screen, and then tap it again to go back to your music.

How to...

Set a Song as an Alarm Tone

When you're listening to a song, you may realize you'd like to use it as an alarm tone. You don't need to go into Settings to use the song this way—you can do it right from the Music Player app.

To set a song as an alarm tone, follow these steps:

1. From the Now Playing screen, tap the Menu button to display the menu panel.
2. Tap the Set As Alarm Tone button. The Galaxy Tab displays an option button to the right of each song in whatever you're playing, as shown here.

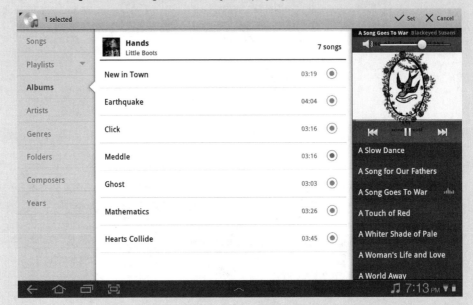

3. Tap the option button for the song you want to use as an alarm.
4. Tap the Set button in the upper-right corner of the screen. The Galaxy Tab displays the Alarm screen, from which you can set the details of the alarm.

5

Watch Movies and Videos on the Galaxy Tab

HOW TO...

- Watch movies and videos on the Galaxy Tab
- Play movies and videos from the Galaxy Tab on your TV
- Watch movies with the YouTube app
- Watch movies with the Google Videos app

In this chapter, we'll look at how you can enjoy movies and videos on the Galaxy Tab. The Galaxy Tab includes a Video app that makes it easy to play movie and video files that you load on the Galaxy Tab using Kies.

You can also use the YouTube app to watch videos on the popular YouTube web site. And if you create a YouTube account, you can upload your own videos to YouTube straight from the Galaxy Tab.

Your Galaxy Tab also gives you access to Google Videos, which provides videos for rental and purchase.

Watch Movies and Videos on the Galaxy Tab

After you've put movies and video files on the Galaxy Tab as described in Chapter 3, you're ready to watch them, either on the Galaxy Tab's screen or on a TV to which you connect the Galaxy Tab.

How to... Play Movies and Videos from the Galaxy Tab on Your TV

The Galaxy Tab's screen is great for viewing videos on your own, but if you want to watch them with others, you can connect the Galaxy Tab to a TV and play the videos at a good size.

To make the connection, buy a suitable cable:

- **Samsung Galaxy Tab TV Out Cable** Use this cable (around $20) or an equivalent cable—one with a Samsung connector at the Galaxy Tab's end and three composite connectors at the TV's end—to connect the Galaxy Tab to a TV that offers composite connectors.
- **Galaxy Tab HDTV Adapter** Use this adapter (around $40) to connect the Galaxy Tab to an HDTV.

When choosing a cable, double-check that it will work with your Galaxy Tab model. Samsung has made this complicated by giving the various Galaxy Tab models different capabilities and using similar names for different accessories.

Once you've connected the cable, what you see on the Galaxy Tab's screen is replicated on the TV. So if you start a movie or video playing, it appears on the TV's screen as well.

Open the Video App

To open the Video app, follow these steps:

1. From the home screen, tap the Apps button to display the Apps screen.
2. Scroll to the home screen panel that contains the Video icon.
3. Tap the Video icon.

Browse to Find the Videos or Movies You Want

To find the videos or movies you want to play, you can browse the videos and movies on the Galaxy Tab by tapping the three tabs at the top of the Video screen:

- **Thumbnails** Tap the Thumbnails tab to display thumbnail pictures of the videos and movies on the Galaxy Tab, as shown in Figure 5-1.
- **List** Tap this tab to display the List screen (shown in Figure 5-2), which shows the videos and movies on the Galaxy Tab as a list. You may find the list easier for navigating by name when you have many videos and movies.

FIGURE 5-1   The Thumbnails screen shows thumbnail pictures of the movies and videos on the Galaxy Tab.

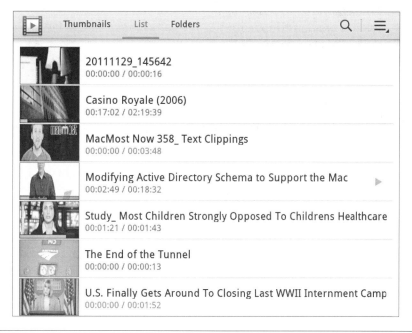

FIGURE 5-2   List view shows your videos and movies as a list.

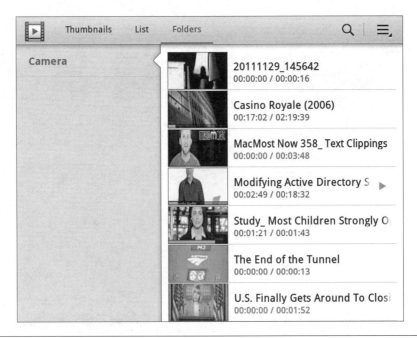

FIGURE 5-3   If you keep your videos and movies in different folders, you can use Folders view to examine the contents of a particular folder.

- **Folders**   Tap this tab to display a list of all the videos and movies separated into folders, as shown in Figure 5-3. You can tap the Camera tab to view the list of videos you've taken with the Galaxy Tab's camera. This tab is good for getting an overview of all the video content available.

Play a Video

When you've found the video or movie file you want to play, tap its button to set it playing.

The Galaxy Tab can play videos and movies in either portrait orientation or landscape orientation. Normally, you'll want to watch the video or movie in the orientation for which it was designed. For example, if you take a video with the Galaxy Tab in portrait orientation, use portrait orientation to watch the video; if you're watching a movie made in conventional landscape orientation, use the Galaxy Tab in landscape orientation. If you hold the Galaxy Tab in the wrong orientation for the video or movie, the Video app squashes or stretches the image to make it fit on the screen.

After you start playback, you can simply watch. If you need to control playback, tap the screen to display the playback controls shown in Figure 5-4, which you can use as follows:

- **Change the volume**   Tap and drag the Volume slider.
- **Switch between full-screen and window views**   Tap the Full Screen button or the Window button (these buttons replace each other).

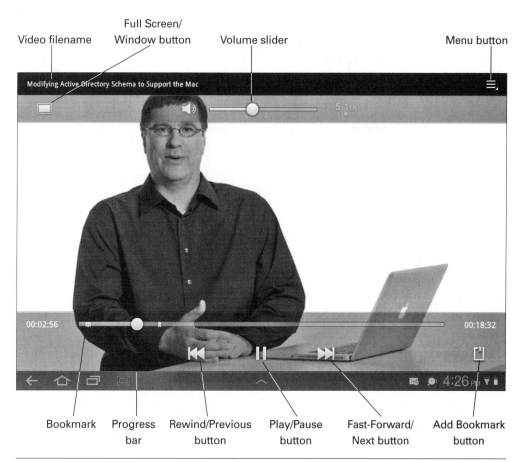

Video filename Full Screen/
Window button Volume slider Menu button

Bookmark Progress bar Rewind/Previous button Play/Pause button Fast-Forward/Next button Add Bookmark button

FIGURE 5-4   When playing back a video, you can tap the screen to display the playback controls shown here.

- **Pause and resume playback**   Tap the Pause button to pause playback; tap the Play button to start playback again.
- **Fast-forward or rewind playback**   Tap the Fast-Forward button or the Rewind button.
- **Add a bookmark**   Play the video until the point where you want the bookmark, and then tap the Add Bookmark button. You can then go to a bookmark by tapping the Menu button, tapping the Bookmark button on the menu panel, and then tapping the bookmark you want.

Note   To return from playing a video or movie to the list of videos, tap the Back button.

Set the Video App to Play the Next File Automatically

If you want to watch videos in sequence, turn on the Auto Play Next feature. Follow these steps:

1. Tap the Menu button to display the menu panel.
2. Tap the Auto Play Next button to display the Auto Play Next dialog box (shown here).

3. Tap the On option button. The dialog box closes when you tap the option button.

Watch Videos with the YouTube App

YouTube is the biggest video site on the Web, and most Galaxy Tab models include a YouTube app that gives you easy access to the videos YouTube hosts. In this section, we'll look at both how to watch videos on YouTube and how to upload your own videos to YouTube directly from the Galaxy Tab.

Launch the YouTube App

To get started with the YouTube app, launch it. Follow these steps:

1. From the home screen, tap the Apps button to display the Apps screen.

 If the YouTube icon appears on the home screen, tap it there.

2. Scroll left or right to display the home screen panel that contains the YouTube icon.
3. Tap the YouTube icon. The home screen of the YouTube app appears (see Figure 5-5).

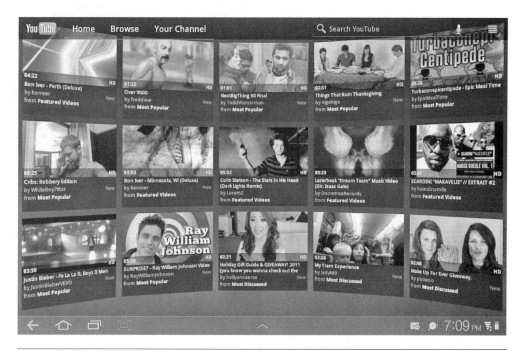

FIGURE 5-5   From the home screen of the YouTube app, you can tap a video
to view it, tap the Browse button to browse by category, or tap the
Search YouTube button to search using keywords.

Find a Video to Watch

From the home screen of the YouTube app, you can find videos in several ways:

- **Play one of the videos on the home screen**   Tap the button for the video.

Tap at the right of the screen and drag your finger to the left to display more
videos on the home screen.

- **Browse videos by categories**   Tap the Browse button to display the Browse
screen (see Figure 5-6). You can then browse the videos that appear directly on
the screen, or tap the category you want in the left column—for example, tap
the Comedy button to view videos in the Comedy category. To browse videos
by time, tap the This Week button, and then tap the appropriate period—Today,
This Week, This Month, or All Time—on the drop-down panel (shown on the
left next). To browse videos by popularity, tap the Top Rated button, and then

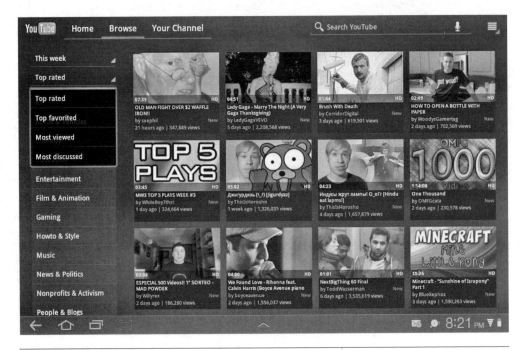

FIGURE 5-6   Use the column on the left of the Browse screen to browse by a period of time (for example, This Week), by Top Rated videos, or by a category.

tap the appropriate category—Top Rated, Top Favorited, Most Viewed, or Most Discussed—on the drop-down panel (shown on the right below).

- **Search for videos** Tap in the Search YouTube box in the upper-right corner of the screen to display the onscreen keyboard. Start typing your search terms,

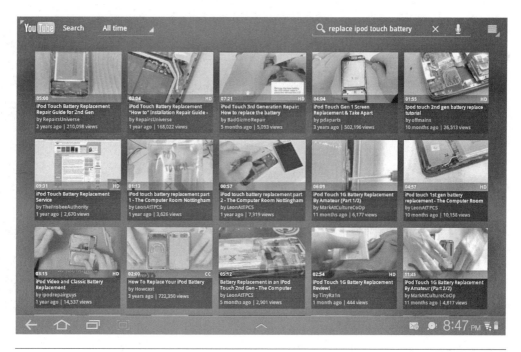

FIGURE 5-7 The Search screen displays the matches for the search result you tapped.

as shown here, and the YouTube app displays matching results. Tap a result to display a list of matches (see Figure 5-7).

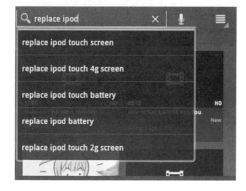

Play a Video

When you've found a video you want to play, tap its button to play it. The YouTube app displays the video's page, which shows three things (see Figure 5-8):

- The video itself in the upper-left corner, starting to play.
- Brief information about the video, in the lower-left corner. You can scroll down to see more information.

Full Screen button

FIGURE 5-8   The page for a YouTube video contains the video itself, the video's details, and related videos. You can tap the Comments button to display a list of comments on the video.

- Related videos and comments. On the right side of the screen, the Related Videos tab displays thumbnails and brief details of related videos. You can tap the Comments button to display the Comments tab, which lists comments that viewers have left about the video.

Tap the Full Screen button (the button with the four arrows pointing outward) at the lower-right corner of the video area to switch the video to playing full-screen. You can tap anywhere on the screen to bring up the playback controls (see Figure 5-9). You can then use the controls to pause playback, move through the song, or switch back to the video's page.

Note   If the HD button appears, you can tap it to switch to a high-definition version of the video. This version needs more bandwidth, so it works best if you have a fast Internet connection.

The playback controls are straightforward to use:

- **Pause**   Tap this button to pause playback. Tap the Play button (which replaces the Pause button) to resume playback.

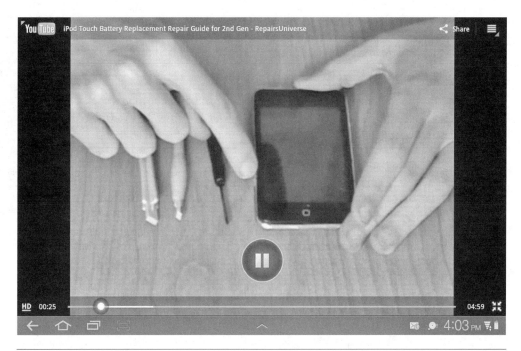

FIGURE 5-9   Tap the screen to display the playback controls.

- **Timeline bar**   Tap and drag the slider to move quickly back or forward through the video. The red part of the bar shows how much of the video you've played; the white part shows how much the Galaxy Tab has downloaded; and the gray part shows how much of the video is left to download.
- **HD**   Tap this button to switch between standard-quality and high-quality versions of the video. Some videos don't have high-quality versions.

While playing a video, you can tap the Share button to display the Share This Video Via dialog box (shown here). Tap the button for the way you want to share the video, and then follow through the steps for establishing the connection or sending the message.

Tap the Menu button to display the menu panel (shown here), which provides these commands:

- **Captions** Tap this button to turn captions on. Many videos don't have captions.

 The first time you use a feature that involves a YouTube account, such as adding a video to your favorites, the YouTube app prompts you to sign in. You can either sign in using an existing account or create a new account and start using it immediately.

- **Favorite** Tap this button to add the video to your favorites.

 To display the list of your favorites, go back to the main YouTube screen, and then tap the Your Channel button at the top of the screen. On the left side of the screen that appears, tap the Favorites button.

- **Save To** Tap this button to save the video to a playlist in your YouTube account.
- **Copy URL** Tap this button to copy the video's URL to the Clipboard so that you can paste it into a document, a text message, or an e-mail message. A small notice saying "URL copied" appears briefly onscreen as confirmation.
- **Flag** Tap this button to sign in to YouTube using your web browser. You can then flag the video as being inappropriate (for example, because it contains violent or repulsive content).
- **Settings** Tap this button to display the YouTube Settings screen. We'll look at choosing settings in the section "Choose Settings for the YouTube App," later in this chapter.
- **Help** Tap this button to display YouTube help in your web browser.
- **Feedback** Tap this button to open a form that you can fill in to give feedback on the YouTube app.

Set Up Your YouTube Account

You can watch YouTube videos by simply firing up the YouTube app, but if you want to rate the videos or flag them as inappropriate, you need to add a YouTube account to the Galaxy Tab. You also need an account if you want to upload your own videos to YouTube.

If you try to take an action that requires a YouTube account, the YouTube app prompts you to sign in. You can also sign in preemptively by tapping the Menu button and then tapping Sign In.

 If you don't already have a YouTube account, tap the Add Account button, and then follow through the process of creating a new account.

FIGURE 5-10 The Your Channel screen gives quick access to your uploaded videos, favorites, playlists, and subscriptions.

Once you sign in, the YouTube app displays the Your Channel screen (shown in Figure 5-10). From here, you can access the videos you've uploaded, your favorites, your playlists, and your subscriptions.

Choose Settings for the YouTube App

To choose settings for the YouTube app, follow these steps:

1. From the home screen of the YouTube app, tap the Menu button to display the menu panel.
2. Tap the Settings button to display the Settings screen.
3. Tap the General Settings tab to display the General Settings screen (shown in the upper part of Figure 5-11), and then choose settings:
   - **High Quality On Mobile**   Select this check box if you want to make the Galaxy Tab always download high-quality versions of the videos from YouTube. High-quality versions look better onscreen, but they take longer to start downloading and longer to download overall—and they may make playback stop because not enough data has downloaded to continue. Experiment with playing back high-quality videos over your typical connection and decide whether this setting brings you more good than ill.

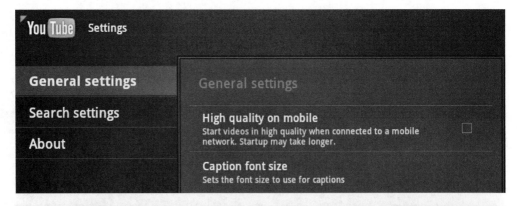

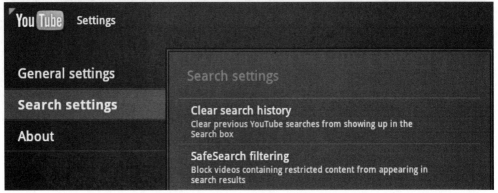

FIGURE 5-11   On the Settings screen, you can choose whether to play high-quality video by default (top) and choose settings for searches (bottom).

- **Caption Font Size**   To set the font size in which the YouTube app displays captions, tap this button. In the Caption Font Size dialog box, tap the Small option button, the Medium option button, the Large option button, or the Extra Large option button.

4. Tap the Search Settings tab to display the Search Settings screen (shown in the lower part of Figure 5-11), and then choose settings:
   - **Clear Search History**   Tap this button to clear the YouTube search history and prevent items you've previously searched for from appearing in the Search box. You may want to clear the search history after you've performed a search—however innocently—that returned filthier results than you expected.
   - **SafeSearch Filtering**   If you want to adjust YouTube's SafeSearch feature, tap this button to display the SafeSearch dialog box (shown here), and then tap the appropriate option button: Tap the Don't Filter option button

to receive raw search results, tap the Moderate option button to receive lightly processed search results, or tap the Strict option button to apply full discipline to the search results.

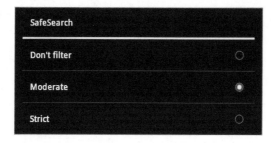

 Applying the Moderate setting or the Strict setting in YouTube's SafeSearch feature doesn't guarantee smut-free videos.

5. Tap the About button if you want to get help, provide your feedback, or read the Google Mobile Terms of Service, the YouTube Terms of Service, the Google Mobile Privacy Policy, or the YouTube Privacy Policy. On the About screen, you can also see the version number of the YouTube app; you may occasionally need this piece of information to troubleshoot problems.

Tap the Back button when you've finished choosing settings and are ready to leave the Settings screen.

Upload Your Own Videos to YouTube

To upload your own videos to YouTube, you must create a YouTube account and set the Galaxy Tab to use it. You can then upload videos from the Image Viewer app or from the Gallery app.

 Tap the Upload button in the upper-right corner of the home screen in the YouTube app to switch quickly to the Gallery app so that you can pick a video to upload.

To upload a video to YouTube, follow these steps:

1. Navigate to the video you want to upload.
2. Tap the Menu button to display the menu panel, and then tap the Share button. A panel of sharing choices appears, as shown here.

3. Tap the YouTube button to display the Upload Video screen (shown here).

4. Tap the More Details button to display the More Details area (see Figure 5-12).
5. Type the title for the video in the text box at the top.
6. If you have set up multiple YouTube accounts on the Galaxy Tab, open the Account drop-down menu and tap the account you want to use.
7. Type a description of the video in the Description text box.

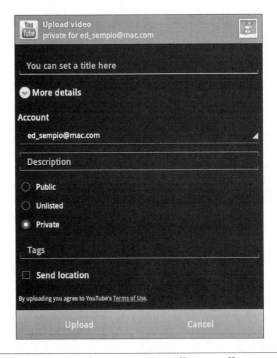

FIGURE 5-12   On the Upload Video screen, you'll normally want to display the More Details area so that you can fill in the tags and decide whether to make the video public or private.

8. Tap the Public option button if you want to make the video available to everyone. If you prefer to keep it to yourself, tap the Private option button. Tap the Unlisted option button if you don't want the video to be listed.

9. In the Tags text box, type the tags for the video. The tags help YouTube categorize the video and identify it in searches.

10. Select the Send Location check box if you want to include information on your location—for example, if it's relevant because you're posting a news report.

11. Tap the Upload button. The Galaxy Tab uploads the video to YouTube and briefly displays a message onscreen telling you it has done so. The Galaxy Tab then returns you to your video.

If you want to watch the video you've uploaded, go back to the YouTube home screen, and then tap the Your Channel button at the top of the screen. Tap the Uploads button on the left to display the videos you've uploaded. You can then tap the button for the video to start it playing. Be aware that videos you post usually take an hour or so to show up on YouTube.

Watch Videos with the Google Videos App

You can also watch videos using the Google Videos app, which gives you access to the videos that Google Videos offers for rental or purchase. Google Videos provides a handy way to get new video content to watch on your Galaxy Tab.

If your Galaxy Tab didn't include the Google Videos app, you can go to Android Market, download the app, and install it. This app is free.

Launch Google Videos and Choose Your Account

To launch Google Videos, simply tap the Videos icon if it appears on the home screen. If it does not, tap the Apps button to display the Apps screen, and then tap the Videos icon.

If Google Videos displays the Show Videos From Which Account? dialog box (shown here), tap the account you want to use. If the account isn't listed, tap the Add Account button, and then follow through the process of adding it.

If Google Videos displays the Access Request dialog box requesting permission to access your account, as shown here, tap the Allow button.

Browse, Rent, and Buy Videos

Once you've sorted out your account, you see the Welcome screen (see Figure 5-13).

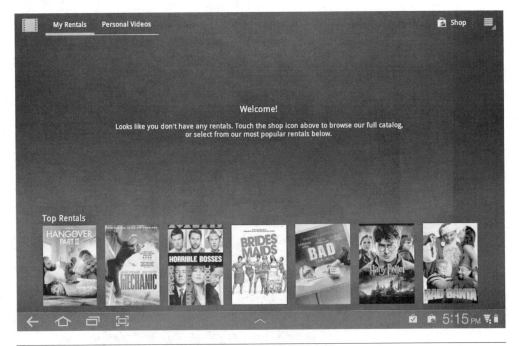

FIGURE 5-13 From the Welcome screen, tap the Shop icon to browse for videos.

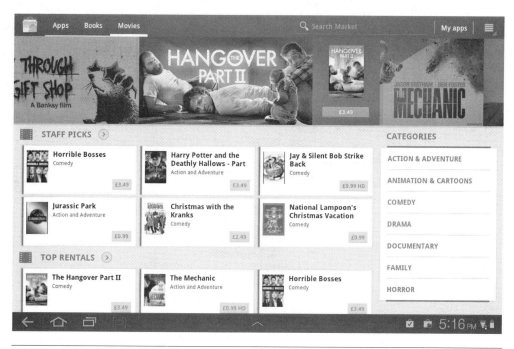

FIGURE 5-14   From the main screen, you can browse by category, search for videos, or simply scroll down to see more videos.

Tap the Shop icon to display the main screen (see Figure 5-14). From here you can browse in the usual ways:

- Tap a presentation category, such as Staff Picks or Top Rentals, to see more videos in that category.
- Tap a category in the Categories list box on the right to browse by that category—for example, Comedy or Horror.
- Scroll down to see more videos.
- Tap in the Search box at the top of the screen, type your search terms, and then tap Enter.

To see the details of a video, tap its button. The screen that appears (see Figure 5-15) contains a synopsis, usually a preview, a listing of cast and credits, and a Users Also Viewed list.

To watch a video's preview or trailer, tap the button. You'll see the video at full screen, as shown in Figure 5-16. Tap the screen to display the playback controls when you need them, and tap the Back button when you finish watching the video.

To rent a movie, tap its Rent button. To buy a movie, tap its Buy button.

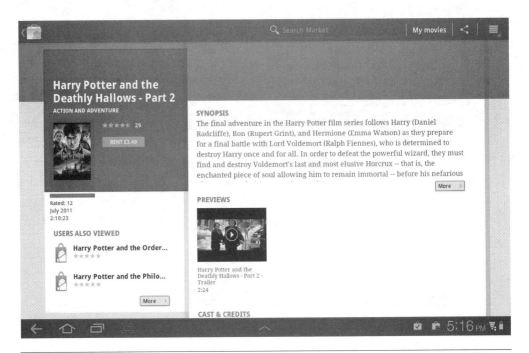

FIGURE 5-15 On a video's page, you can read its synopsis. Most videos also offer a preview you can watch.

FIGURE 5-16 You can watch a preview or trailer to help decide whether to rent or buy the movie. Tap the screen to bring up the playback controls.

6

Use the Camera and Make the Most of Photos and Videos

HOW TO...

- Open the Camera app and meet the controls
- Take photos and videos with the default settings
- Configure the Camera app to take photos or videos the way you want
- Take panorama photos and action photos
- Review your photos and videos
- Take pictures of what's on the Galaxy Tab's screen
- Share your photos and videos with other people

Armed with a 3-megapixel camera on its back, the Galaxy Tab is fully equipped to act as both a camera and a camcorder. And for when you need to capture your own mug shot, the Galaxy Tab has a 2-megapixel camera atop the screen, pointing straight at you.

This chapter shows you how to use the Galaxy Tab's camera and camcorder features. You'll learn how to open the Camera app so that you can start snapping photos and shooting videos with the default settings. We'll then look at how you can configure the Camera app to take photos and videos the way you want them, how to review the photos and videos you take, and how to share the results online with other people.

Open the Camera App and Meet the Controls

To get started taking photos or videos, open the Camera app like this:

1. Tap the Home button to display the home screen.
2. If a Camera icon appears on the home screen, tap that icon. If not, follow these substeps:
   a. Tap the Apps button to display the apps screen.
   b. If necessary, scroll to the home screen panel that contains the Camera icon.
   c. Tap the Camera icon.

When the Camera app opens, you see whatever the lens is pointing at, with an overlay of controls. Figure 6-1 shows these controls with labels.

You'll learn how to use all these controls later in this chapter.

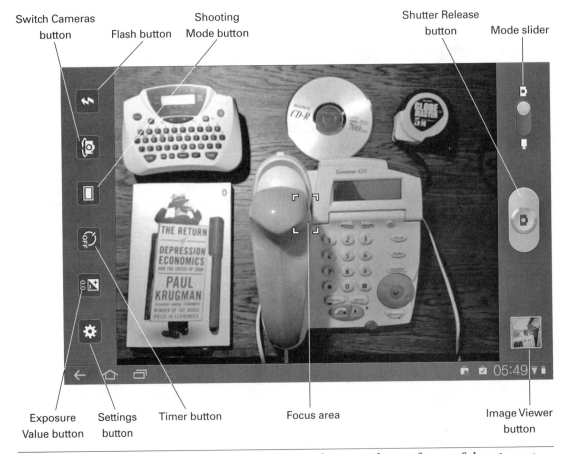

FIGURE 6-1 The Camera app is easy to use, but it also puts plenty of powerful options at your fingertips.

Take Photos and Videos with the Default Settings

The Camera app comes set with default settings for taking standard photos and videos, so you can start snapping and shooting without changing any settings. These are the basic moves you'll need:

- **Take a photo**   With the Mode slider moved up to the Photo position, aim the Galaxy Tab's camera at your subject so that the subject appears in the focus area, and then tap the Shutter Release button. By default, the Galaxy Tab plays a shutter noise when you take a picture, so you can easily tell that you've taken one.
- **Focus on an object that isn't in the middle of the picture**   If you need to focus on an object that isn't in the middle of the picture, tap the area you want to focus on. The Camera app moves the focus area to where you tapped. When you're ready, tap the Shutter Release button to take the photo.
- **Take a video**   Tap the Mode slider and drag it down to the Video position. You then see the video controls, which appear labeled in Figure 6-2. Tap the Record button to start recording; tap the Stop Recording button (which replaces the Record button) when you want to stop.

FIGURE 6-2   You can quickly shoot video by dragging the Mode slider to the Video position, and then using the default video settings.

The Camera app's auto-focus feature takes up lots of processing power. To help you avoid running the battery down, if you leave the Camera app running without tapping the screen for several minutes, the Galaxy Tab automatically switches from the Camera app back to whichever app or screen was displayed previously—for example, the home screen.

Configure the Camera App to Take Photos or Videos the Way You Want

As you saw in the previous section, you can start taking photos and videos using the Camera app's default settings. But to get the best photos and videos possible, you'll need to change the settings at some point—so it's a good idea to know which options the Camera app offers and what you can do with them.

This section shows you how to choose settings for taking photos and shooting videos with the Camera app.

Choose Settings for Taking Photos

To make your photos look the way you want them to, you can change various aspects of the Camera app, including the flash, the shooting mode, the scene mode, the exposure value, the resolution, and the white balance. This section gives you the details.

Set the Flash Mode

To control whether the Camera app uses the Galaxy Tab's flash, tap the Flash button, and then tap the appropriate option button on the Flash pop-up menu (shown here). These are your choices:

- **Auto Flash** The Camera app uses the flash when it detects lighting conditions poor enough to need more light. This is the default setting and is a good choice for general use.

 The Galaxy Tab's flash is pretty anemic compared to the flash on a full-powered camera—but it's still much better than not having a flash at all. To get good results with the flash, shoot only when you can see the whites of your subjects' eyes.

- **On** Choose this setting to force the Camera app to use the flash for each shot. The normal reason for doing this is to provide extra light on the subjects against a bright background that may otherwise trick the light sensor into thinking there's plenty of light.

- **Off**   Choose this setting to turn the flash off, no matter how dark the conditions. The normal reason for turning the flash off is discretion—for example, when taking photos you're not supposed to be taking or when photos are allowed but flash would be disruptive.

Take a Photo of Yourself

To take a photo of yourself, tap the Switch Cameras button to switch from the rear camera to the camera positioned above the Galaxy Tab's screen so that you see yourself on the screen. Grimace appealingly or appallingly, and then tap the Shutter Release button as usual.

Tap the Switch Cameras button again when you want to switch back to the rear camera.

Change the Shooting Mode

To change the shooting mode, tap the Shooting Mode button, and then tap the appropriate option button in the Shooting Mode pop-up menu (shown here).

These are your choices:

- **Single Shot**   Use this mode to take a single standard photo at a time. This is the default setting.
- **Smile Shot**   Use this mode to set the Camera app to automatically capture a photo when the subject smiles. You tap the Shutter Release button, and the Camera app then waits to take the shot until it detects that the subject is smiling. This doesn't always work, but it's an interesting feature that's worth trying.

 The Galaxy Tab uses lower resolution for photos you shoot in Panorama mode and Action Shot mode. This resolution is too low for much use, but it's required for the Galaxy Tab to be able to shoot a stream of photos. To get high-quality photos, make sure you switch back to Single Shot mode when you finish using Continuous mode or Panorama mode.

- **Panorama**   Use this mode to shoot a panorama of a stationary object, such as a landscape. The panorama consists of up to eight images that the Camera app automatically assembles into a single long image for you. See the section "Take a Panorama Photo," later in this chapter, for details.
- **Action Shot**   Use this mode to take a panorama photo of a moving object—for example, a child running past you or a car zooming by. Like the stationary panorama, the action shot consists of a series of photos that the Camera app merges into a single long image for you.

Use the Timer

When you need to take group shots that include you, or when you need to pose in front of a landscape, use the Timer feature. Follow these steps:

1. Set up the Galaxy Tab on a tripod or another support.

 You can find various holders and rigs for mounting the Galaxy Tab on a tripod. Search sites such as Amazon or eBay with terms such as **galaxy tab tripod mount**, and you'll turn up various possibilities.

2. Compose the photo as usual.
3. Tap the Timer button to display the Timer pop-up menu, as shown here.
4. Tap the appropriate option button: 2 Sec, 5 Sec, or 10 Sec. (Tap the Off option button when you want to turn the Timer off.)
5. Tap the Shutter Release button to start the countdown. If you need to get in the shot, do so.

 You can also use the Timer to make sure you don't shake the Galaxy Tab by tapping the Shutter Release button when you're using a tripod.

Set the Exposure Value

Normally, the Camera app consults the Galaxy Tab's light sensor, calculates the appropriate exposure for the photo, and lets fly. But sometimes you may need to set the exposure value manually—for example, when you're shooting photos with a bright background (such as snow), you may need to boost the exposure to avoid getting underexposed pictures.

To change the exposure value, tap the Exposure Value button, and then drag the Exposure Value slider (shown here) to the left or right as needed.

FIGURE 6-3   Open the Settings pop-up menu when you want to change the focus mode (shown on top here), the scene mode, the white balance, the effect used, the resolution, the metering, or the GPS tagging.

Set the Focus Mode

To set the focus mode, first tap the Settings button to display the Settings pop-up menu (shown in Figure 6-3 with the Focus Mode pop-up menu from the next step displayed in front of it). Then tap the Focus Mode button to display the Focus Mode pop-up menu, and tap the focus type you want:

- **Auto Focus**   Tap this option button to have the Camera app focus automatically for you. This is what you'll want most of the time. You can tap the screen to indicate the area you want to focus on.
- **Macro**   Tap this option button when you need to use Macro mode for close-up photos.

Set the Scene Mode

To control the settings the Camera app uses for taking a photo, you can change the scene mode. To do so, tap the Settings button to display the Settings pop-up menu, tap the Scene Mode button to display the Scene Mode pop-up menu (shown here), and then tap the appropriate option button:

- **None** Select this mode when you don't want any special effects applied to the photo.

 When you choose Landscape mode, Night mode, Sports mode, or Candlelight mode, the Camera app turns off the flash, white balance, effects, and metering, making their buttons unavailable so that you can't adjust them. For Sports mode and Text mode, the Camera app turns off the white balance, effects, and metering, but leaves the flash under your control.

- **Landscape** Select this mode when you're taking a picture of scenery.
- **Night** Select this mode when you're taking a photo in dark conditions.
- **Sports** Select this mode when you're taking a photo of moving subjects.
- **Party/Indoor** Select this mode when you're taking a photo of people indoors.
- **Sunset** Select this mode when you're shooting a sunset.
- **Dawn** Select this mode when you're shooting a sunrise.
- **Text** Select this mode when you're taking a photo of text (for example, a newspaper article).
- **Candlelight** Select this mode when you're taking a photo by candlelight.

FIGURE 6-4   On the White Balance pop-up menu, tap the option button for the type of light you're using. AWB stands for automatic white balance, which gives the best results for general photography.

Adjust the White Balance

To adjust the white balance for the photo, tap the Settings button to display the Settings pop-up menu, then tap the White Balance button to display the White Balance pop-up menu (shown in Figure 6-4). You can then tap the option button for the white balance you want:

- **Auto**   Tap this option button to use automatic white balance (AWB) for general use.
- **Daylight**   Tap this option button if you're shooting outdoors in sunshine.
- **Incandescent**   Tap this option button if you're shooting under old-style bulbs.
- **Fluorescent**   Tap this option button if you're shooting under fluorescent lights.
- **Cloudy**   Tap this option button if you're shooting outdoors with cloud cover.

Apply an Effect to the Photo

To apply an effect to the photo, tap the Settings button to display the Settings pop-up menu, then tap the Effects button to display the Effects pop-up menu (see Figure 6-5). You can then tap the option button for the effect you want:

- **None**   Tap this option button to remove whichever other effect is applied.
- **Grayscale**   Tap this option button to convert the colors to grayscale.
- **Sepia**   Tap this option button to apply an antiquing touch of brown.
- **Negative**   Tap this option button to reverse the colors.

FIGURE 6-5 Use the Effects pop-up menu to apply a Grayscale effect, a Sepia effect, or a Negative effect—or to remove whichever effect is currently applied.

Change the Resolution for the Photo

Normally, you'll want to stick with the camera's full resolution—2048 × 1536 pixels, which gives 3.2 megapixels. If you need lower-resolution versions of the photos, you can down-resolve them using software on your computer.

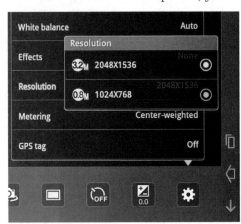

But if you want to shoot photos at the camera's lower resolution, 1024 × 768 pixels (which gives 0.8 megapixels), follow these steps:

1. Tap the Settings button to display the Settings pop-up menu.
2. Tap the Resolution button to display the Resolution pop-up menu (shown here).
3. Tap the 1024×768 option button.

Change the Metering

To control how the camera meters the light for the exposure, tap the Settings button to display the Settings pop-up menu, then tap the Metering button. In the Metering pop-up menu (shown here), tap the appropriate option button:

- **Matrix**   Tap this option button to use matrix metering, which takes measurements from various points in the picture.
- **Center-Weighted**   Tap this option button to have the camera give more importance to the light conditions in the middle of the picture than around the edges.
- **Spot**   Tap this option button to base the light metering on the middle of the picture.

Turn GPS Tagging On or Off

The Camera app can automatically add GPS information to the photos you take. Adding GPS information is great if you want to be able to sort your photos by where you took them.

 If you post your photos to sites on the Internet, other people may be able to learn your location from the GPS information (if you let the Galaxy Tab add it to the photos).

To control whether the Camera app automatically adds GPS information, follow these steps:

1. Tap the Settings button to display the Settings pop-up menu.
2. Tap the GPS Tag button to display the GPS Tag pop-up menu (shown here).
3. Tap the On option button or the Off option button, as needed.

When GPS tagging is on, the Camera app displays the GPS symbol that you see to the left of the On option button in the GPS Tag pop-up menu.

Choose Settings for Shooting Videos

To get your videos to turn out as you intend, you'll probably want to set the camcorder settings the Camera app offers. First, move the Mode slider to the Video position to make the Camera app display the video controls. You can then choose settings by using the line of buttons that appears on the left of the screen when you're holding the Galaxy Tab in landscape orientation or on the bottom of the screen when you're holding the Galaxy Tab in portrait orientation. Figure 6-2, earlier in this chapter, shows these buttons with labels.

Turn the Flash On or Off

To control whether the Camera app uses the flash when recording video, tap the Flash button, and then tap the On option button or the Off option button on the Flash pop-up menu, shown here. Normally, you'll want to leave the flash off when recording video unless conditions are dark.

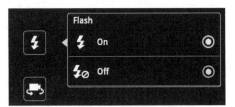

Take a Video of Yourself

To take a video of yourself (or of whatever is in front of the Galaxy Tab's screenside camera), tap the Switch Cameras button. You'll see whatever the camera's lens is seeing, so you can compose your features into a suitable expression before tapping the Record button.

Tap the Switch Cameras button again when you've taken enough footage of your features.

Choose the Recording Mode

To choose the recording mode, tap the Recording Mode button, and then tap the appropriate option button in the Recording Mode pop-up menu (shown here). These are your choices:

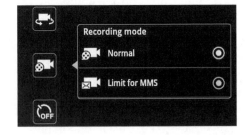

- **Normal** Tap this option button to record video normally, as you'll usually want to do. The Camera app uses the 1280 × 720 resolution, which gives results good enough to play full screen on a computer or a large TV.
- **Limit For MMS** Tap this option button to shoot video for sending in an MMS message. The Camera app uses the 176 × 144 resolution to keep file size down. This size is suitable only for viewing at a very small size.

Use the Timer

If you need to set the Camera app's timer to start the video capture running, tap the Timer button, and then tap the appropriate option button on the Timer pop-up menu (shown here). Your choices are Off (for recording to start when you tap the Record button), 2 Sec, 5 Sec, and 10 Sec.

After setting the timer, tap the Record button to start the timer running. When the time elapses, recording starts.

Control the Exposure Value

To control the exposure value, tap the Exposure Value button, and then drag the slider, shown here in its vertical orientation, up (or right in horizontal orientation) to increase the exposure or down (or left) to decrease it.

Control the White Balance

To control the white balance for the video, follow these steps:

1. Tap the Settings button to display the Settings pop-up menu (see Figure 6-6).

FIGURE 6-6 The Settings pop-up menu for video gives you access to the White Balance settings, the Effects settings, and the Resolution settings.

2. Tap the White Balance button to display the White Balance pop-up menu (shown here).

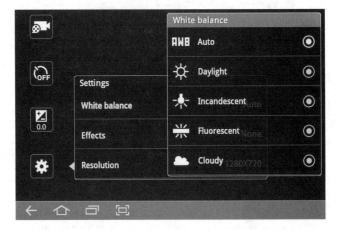

3. Tap the option button for the white balance you want:
   - **Auto** Tap this option button to use automatic white balance (AWB) for general use.
   - **Daylight** Tap this option button if you're shooting outdoors in sunshine.
   - **Incandescent** Tap this option button if you're shooting under old-style bulbs.
   - **Fluorescent** Tap this option button if you're shooting under fluorescent lights.
   - **Cloudy** Tap this option button if you're shooting outdoors with cloud cover.

Apply an Effect to the Video

To apply an effect to the video, tap the Settings button to display the Settings pop-up menu, then tap the Effects button to display the Effects pop-up menu (shown here). You can then tap the option button for the effect you want to apply:

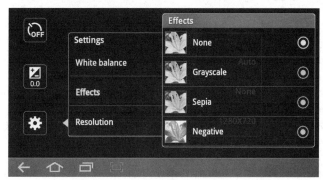

- **None**   Tap this option button to remove whichever other effect is applied.
- **Grayscale**   Tap this option button to convert the colors to grayscale.
- **Sepia**   Tap this option button to apply an antiquing touch of brown.
- **Negative**   Tap this option button to reverse the colors.

Change the Video Resolution

Normally, you'll want to shoot your video at the full quality that the Galaxy Tab's Camera app supports—1280 × 720 resolution. If you need to produce a lower-resolution version of a video clip, you can make the change on your computer using an application such as Windows Live Movie Maker (on Windows) or iMovie (on the Mac).

But the Camera app can also record at 640 × 480 resolution (standard VGA resolution) if necessary. To change the resolution, follow these steps:

1. Tap the Settings button to display the Settings pop-up menu.
2. Tap the Resolution button to display the Resolution pop-up menu (shown here).

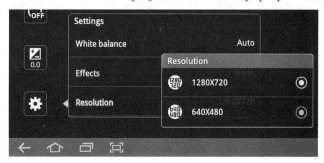

3. Tap the 640×480 option button (or tap the 1280×720 option button if you're switching back).

Take Panorama Photos and Action Photos

As you saw in the earlier section, the Camera app provides features for taking panorama photos and action photos. This section explains how to use these features.

Take a Panorama Photo

If you want to take a photo of a landscape or other panorama, follow these steps:

1. In the Camera app, tap the Shooting Mode button to display the Shooting Mode pop-up menu, and then tap the Panorama option button.
2. Line up the first frame of the panorama, and then tap the Shutter Release button. The Galaxy Tab takes the first shot and then displays a green frame with yellow directional arrows, a message telling you to move the camera slowly in one direction, and a progress readout showing the number of photos it has taken.
3. Move the camera in the direction you want. The Camera app then continues to display the green frame, but displays only a single yellow directional arrow indicating the direction of movement, as you can see in Figure 6-7.

Press the camera key and move device slowly in one direction

1 / 8

FIGURE 6-7 To guide you through the process of taking a panorama photo, the Galaxy Tab displays a green frame, a yellow directional arrow that shows you which way to move the Galaxy Tab, and a progress readout.

4. Pan the Galaxy Tab in the direction of the yellow directional arrow. When the lens is pointing in the correct direction, the Camera app automatically takes the next shot.

5. Keep following the directional arrow as the Camera app takes the remaining shots.

 If you want to stop the panorama before taking all eight photos, tap the Shutter Release button.

6. When you have taken all the photos for the panorama photo, the Camera app sews the photos together into a single strip and displays it for you to view. From here, you can share the picture (as discussed later in this chapter), set it as the wallpaper or as a contact's icon (likewise), or delete it by tapping the Delete button.

Take an Action Photo

When you want to take a sequence of photos of a moving subject, switch to Action Shot mode. To switch, tap the Shooting Mode button, and then tap the Action Shot option button in the Shooting Mode pop-up menu.

You can then tap the Shutter Release button to start shooting up to eight pictures in rapid sequence. The Camera app displays a green tracking rectangle to help you keep your subject aligned, as you see in Figure 6-8. A progress indicator near the bottom of the screen shows how many shots you've taken.

FIGURE 6-8   In Action Shot mode, use the green rectangle (the upper rectangle here) to track your moving subject.

When you finish taking the action photo, the Camera app puts the photos together into a single strip.

If you want to stop the action photo before taking all eight photos, tap the Shutter Release button.

Review Your Photos and Videos

After taking your photos or videos, you can review them by using the Image Viewer app. Tap the Image Viewer button in the lower-right corner of the Camera app's screen to fire up the Image Viewer app, which displays the last photo or video you took.

Figure 6-9 shows the Image Viewer app with a photo open; the controls for a video are similar, except that the menu has fewer items and an extra Play button appears in the middle of the frame.

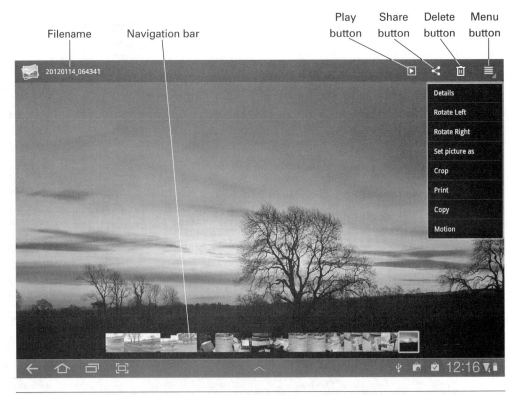

FIGURE 6-9 When reviewing your photos with the Image Viewer app, you can play a slideshow, share a photo, set it as wallpaper or a contact's icon, or delete it.

From this screen, you can take the following actions:

- **Play a slideshow**   Tap the Play button to start a slideshow playing at the current photo. The Image Viewer app uses a Ken Burns effect, zooming and panning a little over the photo, to add interest to the show.
- **Play a video**   Tap the Play button to start the video playing. You can then tap the screen again to display the playback controls shown in Figure 6-10, which enable you to do the following:
  - **Switch to Outdoor Visibility mode**   If you're watching out of doors, switch to Outdoor Visibility mode to make the screen more viewable in bright light. Tap the Menu button to display the menu panel, then tap the Outdoor Visibility item to display the Outdoor Visibility dialog box. Tap the On option button to turn Outdoor Visibility mode on.
  - **Change the volume**   Tap and drag the Volume slider.
  - **Switch to 5.1 Channel Mode**   Tap the 5.1 Channel Mode button.
  - **Switch between full-screen and window views**   Tap the Full Screen button or the Window button (these buttons replace each other).

FIGURE 6-10   When playing back a video, you can tap the screen to display the playback controls shown here.

- **Pause and resume playback** Tap the Pause button to pause playback; tap the Play button to start playback again.
- **Fast-forward or rewind playback** Tap the Fast-Forward button or the Rewind button.
- **Add a bookmark** Play the video until the point where you want the bookmark, then tap the Add Bookmark button. You can then go to a bookmark by tapping the Menu button, tapping the Bookmarks button on the menu panel, and then tapping the bookmark you want.
- **Zoom in or out on a photo** Double-tap to zoom in by a set amount on a particular area of the photo. Double-tap again to zoom back out by the same set amount. You can also zoom in by placing your thumb and finger (or two fingers) together on the screen and then pinching apart, and zoom back by placing your thumb and finger apart and then pinching them together.
- **Display the next item or the previous item** Swipe your finger from right to left to display the next photo or video. Swipe your finger from left to right to display the previous photo or video.
- **Crop the photo** Tap the Menu button to display the menu panel, and then tap the Crop item. On the Crop Picture screen (see Figure 6-11), tap the blue outline and drag it to encompass the part of the photo you want to keep. Tap the OK button to apply the cropping.

FIGURE 6-11 You can quickly crop a photo by moving the blue outline to encompass the appropriate part, and then tapping the OK button.

- **Share the photo** Tap the Share button to display the Share pop-up menu (shown here), and then choose the means of sharing—for example, Email. See the section "Share Your Photos and Videos with Other People," later in this chapter, for details on sharing.

- **Set the photo as wallpaper** Tap the Menu button to display the menu panel, tap the Set Picture As button to display the Set As dialog box (shown next), and then tap the Wallpaper button. To set the photo as the lock screen picture, tap the Lock Screen button.

- **Use the photo as a contact's picture** Tap the Menu button to display the menu panel, tap the Set Picture As button to display the Set As dialog box, tap the Contact Photo button to display the Contacts list, and then tap the contact's name. The Galaxy Tab displays the photo and a square. Resize and reposition the square until it shows the correct part of the photo, and then tap the OK button.
- **Rotate the photo** Tap the Menu button to display the menu panel, and then tap the Rotate Left item or the Rotate Right item, as needed.
- **Delete the photo** Tap the Delete button, and then tap the OK button in the Delete dialog box the Galaxy Tab displays.
- **View the photo's details** Tap the Menu button to display the menu panel, then tap the Details button to display the Details dialog box, which shows all the photo's details—its date and time, width and height, file size, aperture, exposure time, and so on. Tap the × button when you're ready to close the Details dialog box.
- **Print the photo** If you have a Samsung printer, tap the Menu button to display the menu panel, then tap the Print button. Follow the prompts to choose the printer and how you want to print the photo.
- **Copy the photo** If you want to use the photo in a document, tap the Menu button to display the menu panel, then tap the Copy button. The Galaxy Tab copies the photo to the Clipboard. You can then paste it into a document.
- **Motion** If you want to use the Galaxy Tab's Tilt motions to zoom in and out on photos, tap the Menu button to display the menu panel, then tap the Motion button. The Galaxy Tab displays the Motion Settings screen in the Settings app. On this screen, you can tap the Tilt button to choose settings for the Tilt feature.

How to... **Take Pictures of What's on the Galaxy Tab's Screen**

Sometimes it's useful to take a picture of what's on the Galaxy Tab's screen—for example, so that you can record and share a peculiar error you run into.

To capture the screen, simply tap the Screen Capture button at the lower-left corner of the screen—the button to the right of the Recent Apps button. The Galaxy Tab captures the screen's contents as a JPG file and stores the file in the ScreenCapture folder. You can access the file by opening the Gallery app and then tapping the ScreenCapture collection or by connecting the Galaxy Tab to your PC or Mac and then opening the ScreenCapture folder.

Share Your Photos and Videos with Other People

Some photos or videos you'll probably prefer to enjoy on your own, but others you'll likely want to share with others. The Galaxy Tab makes sharing as easy as possible.

To share a photo or video, open it in the Image Viewer app as discussed earlier in this chapter. Tap the Share button to display the Share menu, and then tap the menu item for the sharing service you want to use:

- **Social Hub** Tap this menu item to share the photo to the account you've set up in the Social Hub app.
- **Messaging** Tap this menu item to start a new instant message with the photo or video attached. Choose the recipient, type any explanatory text, and then tap the Send button to set the message winging its way through the ether.
- **Picasa** For a photo, tap this menu item to add the photo to your Picasa account.
- **Bluetooth** Tap this menu item to send the picture or video to another device or computer via Bluetooth. On the Bluetooth Device Picker screen that appears, tap the button for the device to which you want to send the file. You can tap the Scan Devices button to scan for devices that haven't yet been added to the list.
- **Google Mail** Tap this menu item to start a new e-mail message in your Gmail account with the photo or video attached. You then address the message, type a subject and message body, and send the message as normal.
- **Email** Tap this menu item to start a new e-mail message with the photo or video attached. You then address the message, give it a subject, write any explanatory text, and send it as usual.
- **YouTube** For a video, tap this menu item to start the process of signing into YouTube so that you can upload a video to your account. See Chapter 5 for further coverage of using YouTube on the Galaxy Tab.

You can also share your photos and videos with other people using social networks such as Facebook and Flickr, as described in Chapter 9.

7

Browse the Web

HOW TO...

- Launch the Browser app
- Scroll, zoom, and navigate from page to page
- Enjoy full Flash features on the Galaxy Tab
- Open multiple web pages at once
- Surf secretly with Incognito tabs
- Create and use bookmarks
- Go back to a web page in your history or a most-visited page
- Search for information
- Download files
- Choose custom settings for the Browser
- Use other web browsers

The Galaxy Tab's screen is a good size for browsing the Web and reading web pages—especially when you turn the Galaxy Tab sideways and view the screen in landscape mode. In this chapter, I'll show you how to browse the Web on the Galaxy Tab using the built-in Browser app.

If you've used a web browser on any kind of computer (desktop, laptop, tablet, or smartphone), you'll grasp the basics of the Browser app in no time: Opening web pages, following hyperlinks, and moving back and forward along the list of pages you've visited works in much the same way as in most other web browsers. You'll also quickly learn how to open multiple web pages at the same time and move among them, mark pages you want to return to with bookmarks, and navigate through your browsing history.

The Browser app comes with default settings that work pretty well when you're getting started—but soon enough you'll likely want to change some of them. So in the second half of the chapter, I take you through the settings the Browser offers, tell you what each setting does, and recommend choices for the most important settings.

Dip into this section of the chapter when you're ready to improve your browsing experience. At the very least, you'll almost certainly want to change your home page from the page the Browser comes set to access each time you launch it. You may also want to protect your privacy by deleting your browsing history, preventing web sites from learning your location, or even tossing all your cookies if some of them seem to have gone bad.

At the end of the chapter, I'll mention four other web browsers that you may want to use to supplement or replace the Browser app.

Launch the Browser App

To start browsing the Web, launch the Browser by tapping the Browser button at the bottom of the home screen. Assuming the Galaxy Tab has an Internet connection, the Browser displays your Most Visited page, which is shown in Figure 7-1 with the Browser's toolbar buttons and other items labeled.

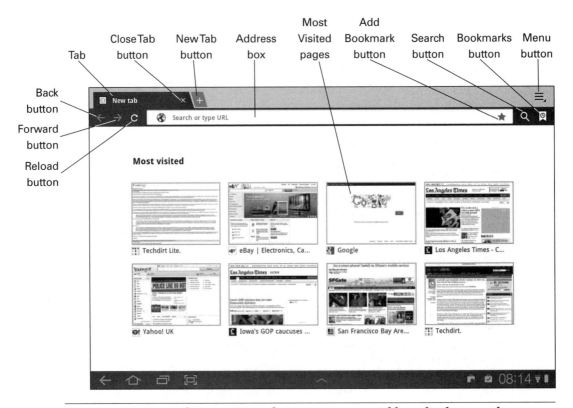

FIGURE 7-1 From the Most Visited page, you can quickly go back to a web page you've visited before.

Two quick things here. First, some localizations of the Galaxy Tab call the Browser button the Web button—so look for a Web button on the home screen if you don't see a Browser button. Second, the Most Visited page comes with some default web sites at first. The sites you visit most frequently replace these default sites as you use the Browser.

 Instead of using the Most Visited page, you can make the Browser app display a single home page if you prefer. And you can change that home page to any web page you want to see. See the sections "Set Your Home Page" and "Choose Labs Settings," both later in this chapter, for details.

To go to one of your most-visited web pages, tap its icon on the Most Visited screen. Tap one of the icons now to go to a page, even if the Most Visited page is still showing its default pages rather than pages you're actually interested in.

Scroll, Zoom, and Navigate from Page to Page

With the Browser open, you're ready to start browsing. In this section, you'll learn how to scroll around a web page, zoom in and out, and navigate from one page to another.

Scroll Around a Web Page

Most web pages are larger than the Galaxy Tab's screen can display at a readable size, so you'll need to scroll around to see the parts you want. To scroll, drag your finger up, down, or across the screen. The Browser scrolls in the direction you drag.

Zoom In and Out

You can zoom in as needed to display part of a web page at a larger size, or zoom out so that you can see more of a page at once:

- **Zoom in**   Place your thumb and finger (or two fingers) on the screen, and then move them apart—"pinching out," as it were.
- **Zoom out**   Place your thumb and finger (or two fingers) apart on the screen, and then move them together.

 You can also zoom in by double-tapping the screen, and zoom out by double-tapping again. The Browser zooms automatically to a degree of zoom that seems to fit; you may need to adjust the zoom manually by placing two fingers on the screen and pinching them together or moving them apart.

Navigate from Page to Page

The easiest way to move from one web page to another is by following a hyperlink on the current page. Tap the hyperlink to open the linked web page in place of the current page.

A hyperlink may appear as text in a different color, underlined text (in the same color or a different color), as an icon (such as an arrow), or as a picture.

After you've moved to another page, you can tap the Back button on the toolbar to move back to the previous page. Tap the Back button again to go further back if you've browsed more than two pages. And after tapping the Back button one or more times, you can tap the Forward button to move forward again.

You can also go back to the previous page by tapping the Back button below the display. This works as long as there are previous pages to go back to. After that, you'll find yourself back at the home screen.

Enter a URL in the Address Box

When you know the web address, or Uniform Resource Locator (URL), for the web site you want to go to, you can enter it in the Address box. Tap the Address box to place the insertion point there, and then start typing the address. If the suggestions list that appears below the Address box (see Figure 7-2) shows the URL you want to visit, tap it to go to the site.

If you end up typing in the whole URL, tap the .com button to quickly enter the .com domain, or tap and hold down the .com button to display a pop-up panel of other domains (as shown here), then tap the domain you want.

To paste a URL into the Address box, tap and hold in the Address box. Then tap the Paste button on the Text Selection toolbar that appears at the top of the screen.

When you're free to announce your web destinations aloud, you can speak a URL or search term. Follow these steps:

1. Tap the Address box to select it. The Browser automatically selects the URL in the Address box and displays the onscreen keyboard.

FIGURE 7-2 The suggestions list below the Address box shows possible URLs and search terms as you type.

2. Tap the Microphone button to display the Speak Now dialog box (shown here). The location of the microphone button varies depending on which onscreen keyboard you're using.

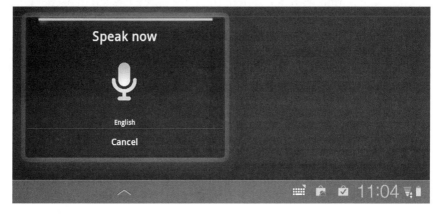

3. Speak the search term or the URL, and then wait while the Galaxy Tab thinks about it.

4. If one of the search results is what you want, tap it to open that web page.

How to... **Enjoy Full Flash Features on the Galaxy Tab**

One of the Browser's strengths is that it supports Adobe Systems' Flash technology, which many web sites use to present active content. (By contrast, Apple's iPad doesn't support Flash at this writing, and so cannot fully display many web pages.)

To make the Browser capable of running all Flash features, you may need to install the Flash Player app on your Galaxy Tab. From the home screen, tap the Apps button, and then see if the Flash Player icon appears on the Apps screen. If so, Flash Player is installed, and you're all set to view Flash content.

If the Flash Player app doesn't appear on the Apps screen, tap the Market icon to launch the Market app. Search Android Market for "flash player," and then follow through the steps for downloading and installing the latest version of the Flash Player app.

Open Multiple Web Pages at Once Using Tabs

Opening a single web page at a time is fine for lightweight browsing, but often you'll want to keep one web page open while you open another page. You can do this easily by using the Browser app's tabs.

At first, the Browser app starts you off with a single tab, as you saw in Figure 7-1, earlier in this chapter. You can open another tab at any time by tapping the New Tab button, the button with a + sign to the right of the last tab that's open (see Figure 7-3).

When you open a new tab, the Browser app shows your Most Visited page in it. You can tap one of the icons on that page to open the corresponding web page in the new tab, or tap in the Address box and enter the URL for another page.

You can also open a new tab from a hyperlink on a page that's already open. Instead of tapping the link to open it in the same page, tap and hold the link to display the dialog box shown here, then tap the Open In New Tab button.

http://srx.main.ebayrtm.com/ clk?RtmClk&u=1H4sIAAAAAAAAB2PzYqDMBRG94LvIAztL
Open
Open in new tab
Save link
Copy link URL
Select text

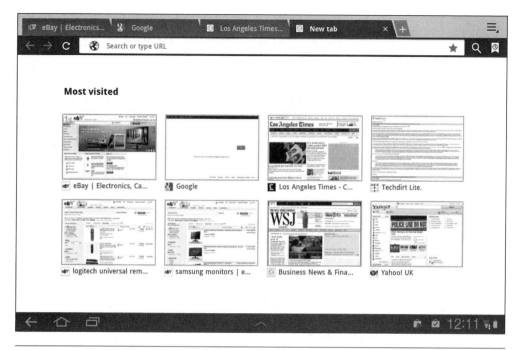

FIGURE 7-3   Tap the + button to the right of the rightmost tab to open a new tab. Tap the Close Tab button (the × button) on the current tab to close the tab.

You can also go to a page on the new tab by using a bookmark, as discussed later in this chapter.

To display a different tab, tap it.

To close the current tab, tap the Close Tab button (the × button) at the right side of the tab.

After you open a handful of tabs, the leftmost tabs disappear off the left edge of the Galaxy Tab's screen. To display them again, tap your finger on whichever tab is displayed on the left side of the screen and drag it to the right, scrolling the tab bar across.

How to... **Surf Secretly with Incognito Tabs**

When you don't want a particular web page to show up in your history, you can use the Browser app's Incognito feature. By opening a page in an Incognito tab, you prevent it from appearing in your history. You also prevent the page from leaving permanent cookies on the Galaxy Tab.

To open an Incognito tab, tap the Menu button, and then tap the New Incognito Tab item on the menu panel. The tab opens with a screen of information about Incognito browsing and an extra Incognito symbol on the tab itself to enable you to identify your Incognito tabs easily. Once the tab is open, you can go to a web site by using the usual techniques discussed in the main text.

Create and Use Bookmarks

When you find a web page that you want to be able to return to, create a bookmark for it. You can then go back to it easily at any point without having to remember or type the address. To keep your bookmarks in order and make them easy to find, you can organize them into different folders.

Create a Bookmark to Mark a Web Page

To create a bookmark, follow these steps:

1. Go to the web page you want to bookmark.
2. Tap the Add Bookmark (star icon) button to display the Add Bookmark dialog box (see Figure 7-4).

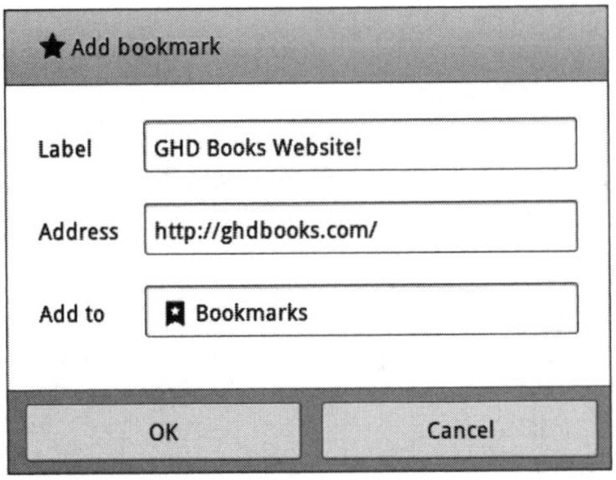

FIGURE 7-4 Use the Add Bookmark dialog box to create a bookmark for a web page you want to be able to access again quickly.

3. In the Label text box, type the name you want to give the bookmark. The Galaxy Tab suggests the page's title, but you'll often want to type something shorter, more descriptive, or both.

4. If you want to put the bookmark in the folder currently shown in the Add To drop-down list, skip this step. Otherwise, tap the Add To drop-down button to display the drop-down list, and then tap one of the items:

   - **Home Screen**   Tap this item to put the bookmark on the home screen. You can then open the bookmarked web page by tapping the icon on the home screen. This is great for sites you visit frequently.

   - **Bookmarks**   Tap this item to put the bookmark at the top level. This gives you quick access to the bookmark, but you'll want to put only your most important bookmarks here—otherwise, it gets crowded.

   - **Other Folder**   Tap this item to display the list of subfolders in the Bookmarks dialog box, as shown on the left in the next illustration. (To create a new subfolder, tap the New Subfolder button, the + button in the upper-right corner. Then type the subfolder name in the text box that appears, as shown on the right in the next illustration, and tap the OK button.) Tap the subfolder you want to put the bookmark in, and if necessary tap another subfolder within that subfolder. When you've opened the right subfolder, tap the OK button.

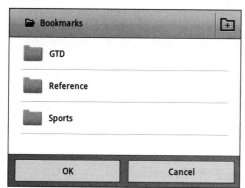 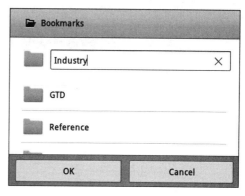

5. Tap the OK button to close the Add Bookmark dialog box.

Go to a Bookmark

To go to a bookmark, follow these steps:

1. In the Browser, tap the Bookmarks button to display the Bookmarks screen (see Figure 7-5).

2. If the bookmark appears directly on the screen, tap it. If not, tap the folder that contains it, then tap the bookmark in the folder. The Browser hides the Bookmarks screen and displays the web page associated with the bookmark.

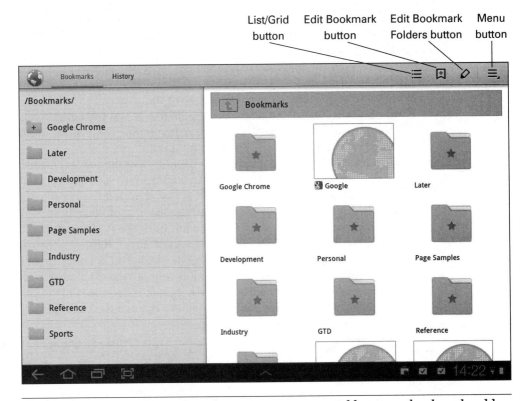

FIGURE 7-5 From the Bookmarks screen, you can quickly go to a bookmark, add a new bookmark, or edit an existing bookmark.

Move a Bookmark to a Different Folder

As you collect bookmarks, you'll probably need to organize them into different folders. To do so, follow these steps:

1. In the Browser, tap the Bookmarks button to display the Bookmarks screen.
2. If the bookmark is in a folder rather than directly on the screen, tap the folder to open it.
3. Tap the Edit Bookmark button. The Browser displays a list of the bookmarks in the folder, as shown here.

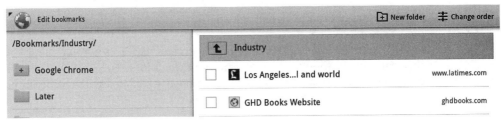

4. Tap the bookmark you want to move. The Browser displays the bookmark's details in the Edit Bookmarks dialog box.
5. Open the Add To drop-down list, and then tap the appropriate item:
   - **Home Screen**   Tap this item to put the bookmark on the home screen.
   - **Bookmarks**   Tap this item to put the bookmark at the top level.
   - **Other Folder**   Tap this item to display the list of subfolders, tap the subfolder to which you want to move the bookmark, and then tap the OK button. You can create a new subfolder by tapping the New Subfolder button (the + button in the upper-right corner), typing the name, and then tapping the OK button.

When you've opened the Edit Bookmarks dialog box, you can also change the bookmark's name if you want.

6. Tap the OK button to close the Edit Bookmark dialog box.

Delete a Bookmark

When you no longer need a bookmark, delete it. Follow these steps:

1. In the Browser, tap the Bookmarks button to display the Bookmarks screen.
2. If the bookmark is in a folder rather than directly on the screen, tap the folder to open it.
3. Tap the Edit Bookmark button. The Browser displays a list of the bookmarks in the folder.
4. Tap to select the check box for each bookmark you want to delete. As soon as you select a check box, a Delete button appears on the toolbar at the top of the screen, as shown here.

5. Tap the Delete button. The Browser displays the Delete dialog box (shown here).

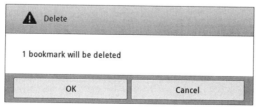

6. Tap the OK button.

Go Back to a Web Page in Your History or a Most-Visited Page

As you browse the Web, the Browser automatically stores the list of web pages you visit. You can use this list, which is called your *history*, to quickly go back to sites you visited before (and perhaps didn't bookmark). The Browser also tracks the web pages you visit most often, adding them to the Most Visited page, which gives you another handy way of identifying and accessing useful or amusing pages.

To go back to a web page in your history, follow these steps:

1. In the Browser, tap the Bookmarks button to display the Bookmarks screen.
2. In the upper-left corner of the screen, tap the History button to display the History screen (shown in Figure 7-6). A gold star to the right of a history item indicates you've bookmarked the page already.
3. In the left column, click the category you want to see: Most Visited, Today, Yesterday, or another category, such as Last 7 Days or Last Month. The History screen displays the list of sites visited.

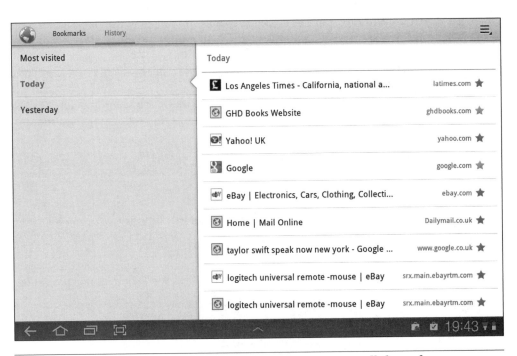

FIGURE 7-6 The History screen gives you instant access to all the web pages you've browsed recently, even if you haven't bookmarked them.

The categories in the left column of the History screen change depending on which history is available. For example, when you're starting out with the Browser app, you won't see the Last 7 Days category or the Last Month category.

4. Tap the button for the web page you want to visit.

To go back to one of the pages you've visited most, display the History screen as described in the previous list, tap the Most Visited button, and then tap the page you want to display. Alternatively, with any web page open in the Browser, tap the New Tab button to open a new tab, which automatically displays the icons for your Most Visited pages, then tap the icon for the page you want to display.

 If you don't want other users of your Galaxy Tab to be able to see which web pages you've visited, you can clear your history by tapping the Menu button and then tapping the Clear History item on the menu panel. In the Clear dialog box that opens, tap the OK button.

Search for Information

To get the most out of the Web, you'll often need to search for information. To find the web pages you want, you usually use a search engine such as Google, Yahoo!, or Bing. To find a particular piece of information on a web page you've opened, you can search within that page.

Search for Information Using Google

To search using Google, you don't need to display the Google web page in the Browser—all you need to do is tap the Address box, and then type in your search terms. The Browser searches Google and displays results, as shown in Figure 7-7. Tap the result you want to display.

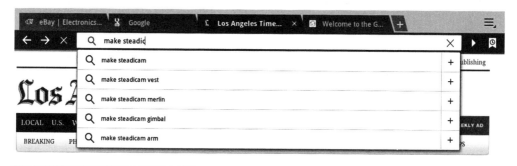

FIGURE 7-7   To find pages on the Web, search directly from the Address box.

Search for Information Using Another Search Engine

To search for information using a search engine other than Google, display that search engine's web page in the Browser app. For example, to use Yahoo!, go to the www .yahoo.com web page. You can then enter your search terms and get the results.

 You can also change the Browser app's default search engine from Google to Yahoo! or Bing. I'll show you how to do this later in this chapter.

Find a Word or Phrase on the Current Web Page

To find a particular word or phrase on the current web page, follow these steps:

1. Tap the Menu button to display the menu panel.
2. Tap the Find On Page item to display the Find On Page controls, shown here.

3. Type (or paste) the search term in the text box. The Browser shows the number of matches and scrolls the page (if necessary) enough to highlight the first match.
4. Tap the Forward button or Back button to move among the matches. When you tap one of these buttons, the Browser hides the keyboard and selects the next match or previous match.
5. Tap the × Cancel button in the upper-left corner of the screen when you've finished using the Find On Page controls.

Download Files

When you tap the link to start downloading a file, the Browser briefly displays a Starting Download message onscreen. If you want to control or stop the download, tap the Menu button to display the menu panel, and then tap the Downloads button to display the Downloads dialog box (shown here).

Downloads - Sorted by date		
⊘ **Today**		
☐	TextWrangler_User_Manual-1.pdf pine.barebones.com Complete 4.76MB	06:24
☐	TextWrangler_3.5.3.dmg pine.barebones.com Complete 12.38MB	06:23
⊙ **Yesterday**		
	Sort by size	

From the Downloads dialog box, you can take the following actions:

- **Open the downloaded file**   Once the download finishes, tap the file's button to open it in a suitable app. If the Complete Action Using dialog box opens, as shown here, tap the button for the app you want to use. (If you always want to use this app, tap to select the Use By Default For This Action check box before tapping the app's button.)

 If the Galaxy Tab doesn't have a suitable app to open the downloaded file, you'll get no reaction when you tap the file to try to open it.

- **Cancel the download**   Tap to select the check box to the left of the file's listing, and then tap the Cancel button in the upper-left corner of the screen.
- **Remove the listing of the downloaded file**   Tap to select the check box to the left of the file's listing, and then tap the Delete button in the upper-right corner of the screen.
- **Sort the files by size or by date**   To switch to sorting by size, tap the Sort By Size button at the bottom of the Downloads dialog box. To switch back to sorting by date, tap the Sort By Date button that replaces the Sort By Size button.
- **Close the Downloads dialog box**   Tap the Back button, or simply tap in the Browser window outside the Downloads dialog box.

Choose Custom Settings for the Browser

If you use the Browser a lot, spend a few minutes choosing custom settings to make the Browser work your way. The Browser has a large number of settings that let you make major adjustments to the way it works. In particular, you may want to change the default zoom level and switch the home page to a page of your choosing rather than your carrier's choosing.

Open the Browser Settings Screen

To start configuring settings for the Browser, open the Browser's Settings screen. Follow these steps:

1. Launch the Browser if it's not running, or switch to it if it is running.
2. Tap the Menu button to display the menu panel.
3. Tap the Settings item to display the Settings screen.

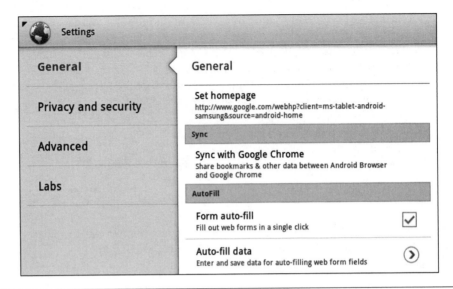

FIGURE 7-8 In the General category of the Settings screen for the Browser, you can set your home page, choose sync options, and control AutoFill.

The Settings screen contains four separate categories—General, Privacy and Security, Advanced, and Labs—which you navigate among by tapping the categories in the list on the left. Figure 7-8 shows the General category of settings.

Choose General Settings

Start by tapping the General category to display its contents, and then choose settings as described in the following sections.

Set Your Home Page

To set your home page, follow these steps:

1. Tap the Set Homepage button at the top of the General category in Settings to display the Set Homepage dialog box (shown here).

2. Enter the URL of the web page in the text box in one of these ways:
   - Type the URL.
   - If you've navigated to the page you want in the Browser, tap the Current Page button.
   - If you've copied the page's URL, tap in the text box, and then tap the Paste button that appears on the toolbar.
   - If you want to go back to the Browser app's default page, tap the Default Page button.
3. Tap the OK button. The Set Homepage dialog box closes, and the Set Homepage readout in the General category shows the page you chose.

Sync Your Bookmarks and Other Data with Google Chrome

If you use the Google Chrome web browser on your computer, you can set the Browser app on the Galaxy Tab to sync your bookmarks and other data with Google Chrome. This is a handy way of getting your bookmarks from your computer to the Galaxy Tab.

To set up sync with Google Chrome, tap the Sync With Google Chrome button in the General category in Settings, and then follow the prompts for selecting the account (as shown here) and performing the sync.

 If you've created bookmarks on the Galaxy Tab, the Browser prompts you to choose between adding them to your Google Account and deleting them. Normally, you'll want to select the Add Bookmarks To Google Account option button, but if the bookmarks are duplicates of ones your Google Account already contains, select the Delete Bookmarks option button instead.

Control the Form AutoFill Feature

The Browser app's AutoFill feature can automatically fill in standard data, such as your name and address, in forms for you. Once you've set it up with the right information, AutoFill can save you plenty of time and typing.

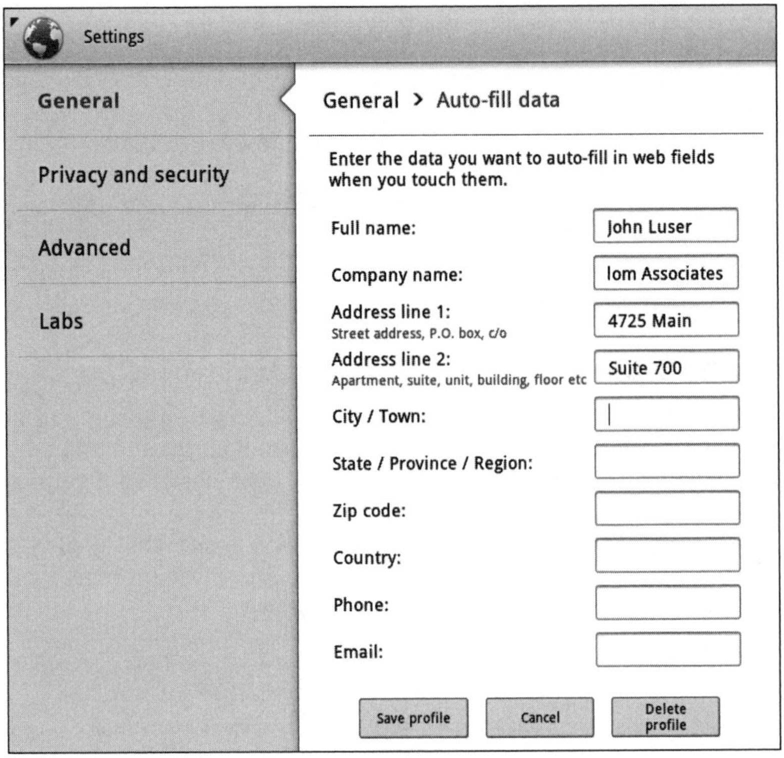

FIGURE 7-9 On the Auto-Fill Data screen, enter the name and address data you want the Browser app to automatically enter in web forms for you, and then tap the Save Profile button.

If you want to use AutoFill, select the Form Auto-Fill check box in the AutoFill area of the General category in Settings. Then tap the Auto-Fill Data button to display the Auto-Fill Data screen (see Figure 7-9), type the data you want to use, and then tap the Save Profile button.

Choose Privacy and Security Settings

Next, tap the Privacy And Security category on the left of the Settings screen to display its settings (see Figure 7-10).

Choose Settings for Cache, History, and Security Warnings

At the top of the Privacy And Security category, you can choose these three settings:

- **Clear Cache** To clear the information that the Galaxy Tab has stored in its cache, tap this button, and then tap the OK button in the Clear dialog box that opens (shown on the left in the next illustration). The *cache* is an area of memory in which the Browser app stores information that it may need to access quickly

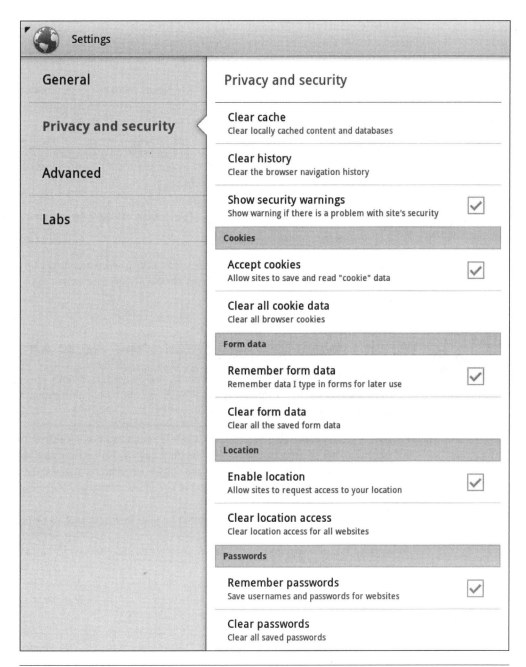

FIGURE 7-10   In the Privacy And Security category, choose which data you will let the Browser app store about you. From here, you can clear the cache, history, cookies, form data, location access, and saved passwords.

in the future. Caching information helps speed up web browsing, so it's usually a good idea to leave the cache information on your Galaxy Tab. But the cache may contain confidential or otherwise sensitive information—which is why you may want to clear it for safety.

- **Clear History** When you want to get rid of the details of the web sites you've visited, tap the Clear History button. In the Clear dialog box that opens (shown on the right in the next illustration), tap the OK button.

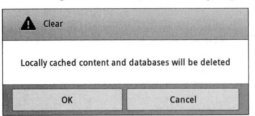

- **Show Security Warnings** Select this check box if you want the Browser to display a warning if it detects a problem with the security of a web site you're visiting. This is almost always a good idea.

Which Privacy Settings Should You Worry About?

The Web is wonderful, but when you browse it, you leave traces both on the sites you visit and on the Galaxy Tab. These are the three main types of information you need to worry about:

- **History** Like most web browsers, the Galaxy Tab's Browser keeps a list of the web pages you visit so as to help you return to them quickly. This list is called your *history*. You can clear your history when you don't want someone else who uses your Galaxy Tab to be able to see the sites you've visited—for example, because you accidentally visited an embarrassing site.
- **Cookies** A *cookie* is a small text file stored on your computer (in this case, the Galaxy Tab) that helps a site track the pages you visit—for example, so that it can maintain for you a shopping cart or a list of products you've browsed. You can clear cookie data when you want all web sites to forget who you are—for example, because you've accessed some sites that you want to forget you. If you clear cookies, next time you visit any site on which you have an account (for example, Amazon.com or eBay), you'll need to enter your login details again.
- **Location** As you learned in Chapter 2, the Galaxy Tab can determine its location either by consulting the Global Positioning System satellites or by feeling out known wireless networks around you. If you choose, the Galaxy Tab can make your location available to web sites—for example, so that a search engine can give you results that are geographically close to you. Giving your location to web sites raises privacy concerns, so you may prefer to set the Browser to not provide location information automatically; you can then provide the location information manually only when you need location-specific search results.

Choose Cookies Settings

In the Cookies section of the Privacy And Security category, choose settings to control how the Browser app handles cookies:

- **Accept Cookies**   Select this check box if you want sites to be able to save cookies on the Galaxy Tab. Cookies can infringe your privacy, but many sites don't work correctly without cookies, so you'll probably want the Browser to accept them.
- **Clear All Cookie Data**   When you want to get rid of the details of the cookies stored on the Galaxy Tab, tap this button, and then tap the OK button in the Clear dialog box that opens.

Choose Form Data Settings

In the Form Data section of the Privacy And Security category, choose settings to control how the Browser app handles form data:

- **Remember Form Data**   Select this check box if you want the Browser to store data you enter in forms on web pages so that it can provide that data for you automatically next time you visit that site. For example, the Browser can offer to store your address so that it can fill it in automatically for you in the future.
- **Clear Form Data**   If you want to get rid of form data the Browser has stored, tap this button, and then tap the OK button in the Clear dialog box that opens. Next time you visit any site for which the Browser had stored form data, you'll need to enter the data again.

Choose Location Settings

In the Location section of the Privacy And Security category, choose settings to control how the Browser app handles requests from apps for your location:

- **Enable Location**   Select this check box if you want web sites to be able to request your location from the Browser app. By giving web sites access to your location, you can get more targeted search results. But you may prefer to turn off this feature and provide your location manually only when it is necessary (for example, when you need to find the best Chinese restaurant in your ZIP code).
- **Clear Location Access**   If you want to prevent web sites you've previously allowed to request your location from requesting it again automatically, tap this button, and then tap the OK button in the Clear dialog box that opens.

Choose Passwords Settings

In the Passwords section of the Privacy And Security category, choose settings to control whether the Browser app stores your user names and passwords:

- **Remember Passwords**   Select this check box if you want the Browser to remember user names and passwords you enter for sites so that it can provide them automatically next time you visit. Saving the user names and passwords like this saves time and effort, but it means that anyone who commandeers your Galaxy Tab can masquerade as you.

- **Clear Passwords**   To make the Browser get rid of all the passwords it has saved, tap this button, and then tap the OK button in the Clear dialog box that opens.

Choose Advanced Settings

Next, tap the Advanced category on the left of the Settings screen to display its settings (see Figure 7-11). You can then choose settings as discussed in the following subsections.

Choose Settings in the Upper Part of the Advanced Category

The upper part of the Advanced category contains these five settings:

- **Select Search Engine**   The Galaxy Tab typically comes set to use Google as its search engine. If you prefer to use Yahoo! or Bing instead, tap the Select Search Engine button, and then tap the appropriate option button in the Select Search Engine dialog box (shown here).

- **Open In Background**   Select this check box if you want each new tab to open behind the current page rather than in front of it. This setting is good for going to a news site, opening a bunch of other pages from its links, and then reading them in turn.
- **Enable JavaScript**   Select this check box if you want the Browser to be able to run scripts written in the JavaScript scripting language. Many web pages use JavaScript to implement functionality, such as showing updated information, so normally you want to use JavaScript. The downside to running JavaScript is that a malicious web site can use a script to attack your computer. Because the Galaxy Tab runs the Android operating system rather than Windows (which is the main target of malicious hackers), you're fairly safe enabling JavaScript—but not entirely safe.

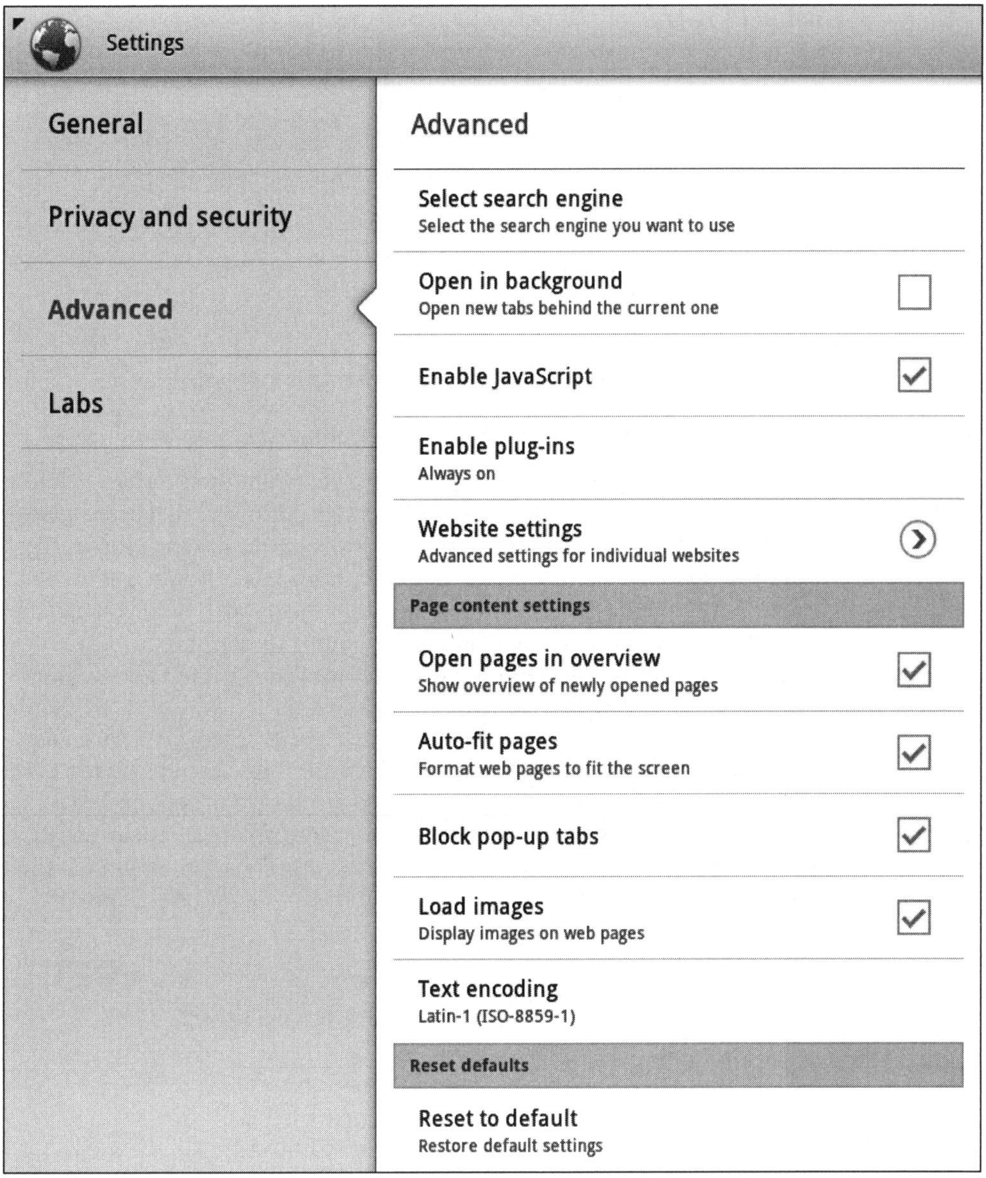

Settings

General	**Advanced**	
Privacy and security	**Select search engine** Select the search engine you want to use	
Advanced	**Open in background** Open new tabs behind the current one	☐
Labs	**Enable JavaScript**	☑
	Enable plug-ins Always on	
	Website settings Advanced settings for individual websites	⊙

Page content settings

Open pages in overview
Show overview of newly opened pages ☑

Auto-fit pages
Format web pages to fit the screen ☑

Block pop-up tabs ☑

Load images
Display images on web pages ☑

Text encoding
Latin-1 (ISO-8859-1)

Reset defaults

Reset to default
Restore default settings

FIGURE 7-11 In the Advanced category of the Settings screen, you can choose your search engine and other assorted settings, select page content settings, or reset the Browser app to its default settings.

- **Enable Plug-Ins** To change which plug-ins the Browser runs, tap this button. In the Enable Plug-Ins dialog box (shown here), tap the appropriate option button:
  - **Always On** Tap this option button if you want to enable every plug-in.

  - **On Demand** Tap this option button if you want the Browser to block plug-ins but allow you to run the ones you want. The Browser displays a placeholder—a box containing a downward-pointing arrow—to indicate a plug-in. Tap this button to enable all the plug-ins on the page. This setting enables you to check out a web page without running its plug-ins, so it can help you avoid plug-ins that are malicious or that take huge amounts of memory.
  - **Off** Tap this option button when you want to turn plug-ins off and not have the option of turning them on for a page.
- **Website Settings** When you need to change the settings for a particular web site, tap this button, and then work on the Website Settings screen (the top part of which is shown here). From here, tap a web site to display your options for configuring it, and then tap the appropriate button. For example, tap the Clear Location Access button to prevent the web site from accessing your location, or tap the Clear Stored Data button to delete the data the web site has stored on the Galaxy Tab.

Choose Page Content Settings

In the Page Content Settings area of the Advanced category, you can choose the following settings:

- **Open Pages In Overview** Select this check box if you want the Browser to open a page in Overview mode, in which it fits the web page to the screen, rather than zooming in. Overview mode is usually useful, because it lets you see more of the page at once and choose the part you want to focus on.

- **Auto-Fit Pages**   Select this check box if you want the Browser to automatically resize web pages to fit the screen. Web pages come in all shapes and sizes, and this feature doesn't always work as well as you'd want it to, but it's well worth trying. If Auto-Fit Pages doesn't get the page to a suitable size, you can change the zoom by pinching in or out or by double-tapping.
- **Block Pop-Up Tabs**   Select this check box to try to prevent web sites from displaying pop-up windows. Pop-up windows are often used for displaying content most people wouldn't normally summon up (such as discount medications, mail order brides, and specialist publications), so suppressing them is usually a good idea. But if you go to a bona fide web site that uses pop-up windows to display extra information about products, you may need to clear the Block Pop-Up Tabs check box to allow the site to work correctly.
- **Load Images**   Select this check box if you want the Browser to load pictures automatically when it displays a web page. Normally, you'll want to do this, but if you have a really slow Internet connection, you may want to turn pictures off to make pages display more quickly.
- **Text Encoding**   If a page appears to have weird characters, you may be able to fix the problem by tapping this button, and then tapping the option button for the appropriate character set in the Text Encoding dialog box. But usually you'll find that the default settings work well.

Reset the Browser App to Its Default Settings

At the bottom of the Advanced category is the Reset Defaults section, which contains just one control—the Reset To Default button.

If you want to return the Browser to its default settings, tap the Reset To Default button, and then tap the OK button in the Reset To Default dialog box (shown here). You may want to do this if you've changed settings and gotten unsatisfactory results, but you're not sure which setting is causing the problem.

Choose Labs Settings

Finally, tap the Labs category to display the settings it contains. These settings may vary depending on which build of Android your Galaxy Tab is using, but you will typically find settings such as those shown in Figure 7-12:

- **Quick Controls**   Select this check box to turn on the Quick Controls feature, which lets you swipe your thumb to hide the Browser's toolbar and URL bar and instead navigate with pop-up controls that appear on the screen. You can see these pop-up controls on the right side of the screen in Figure 7-13.

Settings	
General	**Labs**
Privacy and security	**Quick controls** Swipe thumb from left or right edge to access quick controls and hide Application and URL bars ☐
Advanced	**Most Visited Homepage** Sets your homepage to show the most visited pages ☑
Labs	**Google Instant** Use Google Instant when you use Google Search, to show results as you type (this can increase data use). ☐

FIGURE 7-12 In the Labs category on the Settings screen, you can turn various experimental settings on or off.

FIGURE 7-13 The Quick Controls feature removes the Browser's toolbar and URL bar and provides pop-up controls for navigation.

How to... Use Other Web Browsers

The Galaxy Tab's Browser app works well for standard web browsing, but you may want to try other browsers as well or instead. You can find a good selection of browsers on Android Market for free. At this writing, these are the four best browsers—but if none of these suits you, try searching for others:

- **Skyfire**   Skyfire is a neatly built browser that features strong integration with Facebook. Skyfire can grab much of its data from a proxy server, which can help you reduce the rate at which you munch your way through a limited data plan.
- **Firefox**   Firefox is the Android version of the web browser that is currently challenging Internet Explorer. Among other tricks, Firefox can synchronize bookmarks and other information with your desktop computer, which helps make the Galaxy Tab behave more like an extension of your desktop computer rather than a separate computer.
- **Dolphin Browser HD**   Dolphin Browser HD features a tabbed interface, in which you can open multiple pages, each on a different tab. You may find tabs easier to navigate than the separate windows that the Browser uses.
- **Opera Mobile**   Opera Mobile is a powerful browser that includes Facebook integration. If you've used and liked the PC or Mac version of Opera, you'll want to try Opera Mobile.

- **Most Visited Homepage**   Select this check box to make the Browser app show your Most Visited page in place of the home page you've set in General settings.
- **Google Instant**   Select this check box to have Google Search deliver results as you type. This feature can save you time, but on a 3G Galaxy Tab it may increase your usage of wireless data—so keep an eye on your plan.

When you finish choosing settings on the Settings screen, tap the Back button to return to the Browser window and resume browsing.

8

Set Up and Use E-mail

Being able to read and write e-mail—wherever you happen to be, and on a decent-size screen—is one of the great bonuses of having a Galaxy Tab.

If you set up the Galaxy Tab as described in Chapter 1, you probably have one e-mail account set up already. In this chapter, I'll show you how to set up however many other e-mail accounts you need and how to configure them so that they behave the way you want them to. You'll also learn how to send and receive both e-mail messages and attachments, and how to set up the built-in Email app so that folders and messages appear the way you find easiest to view.

If you have a Gmail account, you can use the Email app if you want, but you'll probably want to try the Gmail app instead—this app is designed to work solely with Gmail, so it gives better performance. We'll look at how to use the Gmail app toward the end of the chapter.

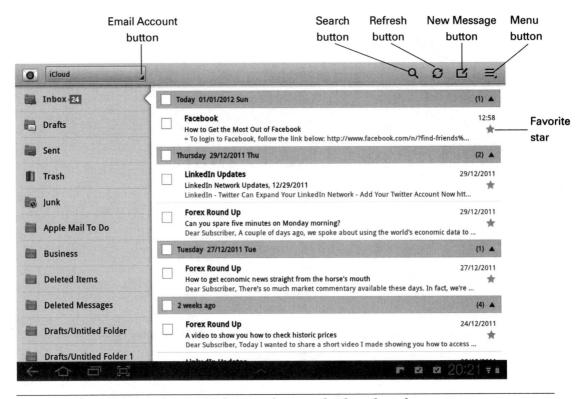

FIGURE 8-1 When you first open the Email app, it displays the Inbox.

Open the Email App

To start working with e-mail, open the Email app in one of these ways:

- **Home screen** Tap the Email button at the bottom of any home screen panel.
- **Apps screen** Tap the Email button.

You'll see the messages in your Inbox, as in Figure 8-1.

We'll look at how to read your e-mail later in this chapter. Before that, we'll look at how to set up and configure your e-mail accounts.

Set Up and Configure E-mail Accounts

Most likely you added an e-mail account to the Galaxy Tab during setup—but these days, many (if not most) people use two or more e-mail accounts. For example, you may use separate accounts for business use and home use. Or you may use a secondary e-mail address for public activities such as commenting online or subscribing to e-mail newsletters, so that if the account gets onto a spammer's list, you can dispose of the account without interrupting your regular e-mail addresses.

Whatever the reason, you can easily add another e-mail account to the Galaxy Tab. And if you no longer need an account on the Galaxy Tab, you can delete the account from the device.

Add an E-mail Account

To add an e-mail account to the Galaxy Tab, follow these steps:

1. From the Inbox for an e-mail account, tap the Menu button to display the menu panel.
2. Tap the Settings button to display the Settings screen (see Figure 8-2).
3. Tap the Add Account button to display the first Set Up Email screen (shown in Figure 8-3).
4. Type your e-mail address in the upper text box.
5. Type your password in the lower text box.

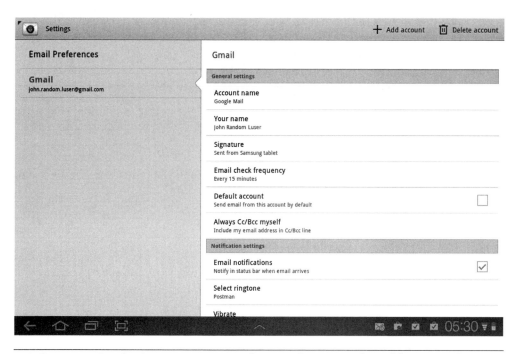

FIGURE 8-2   On the Settings screen in the Email app, tap the Add Account button to start adding a new e-mail account to the Galaxy Tab.

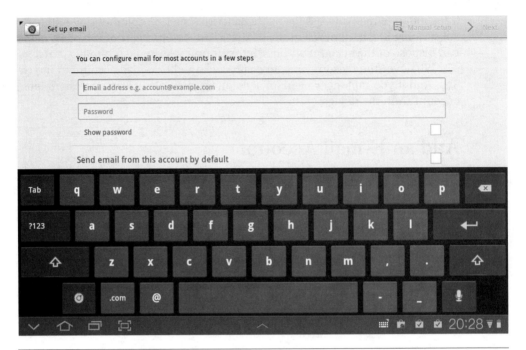

FIGURE 8-3 On the first Set Up Email screen, enter your e-mail address and password, and decide whether to use this account as your default e-mail account.

6. Select the Send Email From This Account By Default check box if you want to use this account as the default account for sending e-mail messages. If you're setting up a second account at this point, clear this check box if you want to keep on using the account you've been using so far as the default account.

7. Tap the Next button. The Email app checks the incoming server settings and the outgoing server settings, and then displays the Account Options screen (shown here).

8. Tap the Email Check Frequency drop-down menu, and then tap the frequency with which you want to check for new messages: Never, Every 5 Minutes, Every 10 Minutes, Every 15 Minutes, Every 30 Minutes, Every Hour, Every 4 Hours, or Once A Day.

If the Email app can't work out the incoming server and outgoing server settings from the e-mail address you enter, you'll need to set up the e-mail account manually. See the next section, "Set Up an E-mail Account Manually," for details.

9. Select the Send Email From This Account By Default check box if you want to use this account as your default account. (This setting appears on the Account Options screen as well as on the first Set Up Email screen.)
10. Select the Notify Me When Email Arrives check box if you want the Galaxy Tab to display an alert or play a sound to draw your attention to incoming messages.
11. Tap the Next button. The Email app displays your Inbox and displays the list of messages.

Set Up an E-mail Account Manually

If you want to set up an e-mail account manually—for example, so that you can specify custom mail server settings—tap the Manual Setup button on the Set Up Email screen (shown in Figure 8-3, earlier in this chapter) rather than tapping the Next button. The Email app then displays the Add Email Account: What Type Of Account? screen, shown in Figure 8-4.

 You'll also see the Add Email Account: What Type Of Account? screen if you try to use the automated setup routine but the Email app cannot determine which server settings to use for the account.

You can then start setting up the account manually by tapping the appropriate button. The following subsections give you the details.

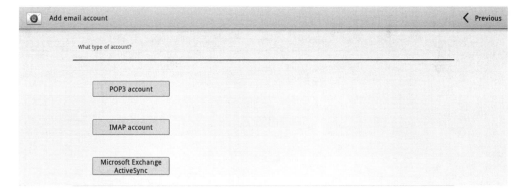

FIGURE 8-4   On the Add Email Account: What Type Of Account? screen, tap the POP3 Account button, the IMAP Account button, or the Microsoft Exchange ActiveSync button, as appropriate.

To set up an e-mail account manually, you will need to know not only the account's user name and password but also the address of the incoming mail server, the address of the outgoing mail server, and the security type used.

Set Up a POP3 E-mail Account

To set up a POP3 e-mail account, follow these steps:

1. On the Add Email Account: What Type Of Account? screen, tap the POP3 Account button to display the Incoming Server Settings screen for a POP3 server. Figure 8-5 shows this screen with the onscreen keyboard hidden so that you can see all the fields.
2. Make sure the user name in the Username text box is correct. This is the user name you entered earlier in the setup process.
3. Reenter the password in the Password text box if necessary. This is the password you entered earlier, but because it appears as security-conscious dots, you can't tell if it's correct.

 If you need to see the password when setting up an account, open the Settings app, tap the Location And Security button in the left column, and then select the Visible Passwords check box in the Passwords area of the Location And Security screen.

4. In the POP3 Server text box, type or paste the name of the incoming mail server.
5. Open the Security Type drop-down list (see Figure 8-6) and choose the appropriate security type: None, SSL, SSL (Accept All Certificates), TLS, or TLS (Accept All Certificates). See the sidebar "Choose the Right Security Types for Your E-mail Servers" for advice.

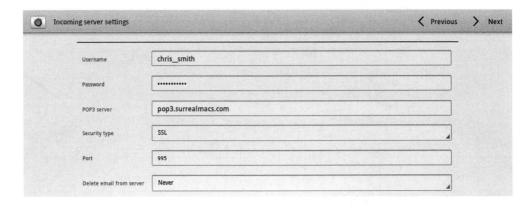

FIGURE 8-5 On the Incoming Server Settings screen for a POP3 account, fill in the server details.

Security type	None	
	None	
Port	SSL	
Delete email from server	SSL (Accept all certificates)	
	TLS	
	TLS (Accept all certificates)	

FIGURE 8-6 In the Security Type drop-down list, choose the type of security for the e-mail account you're setting up.

How to... **Choose the Right Security Types for Your E-mail Servers**

The Security Type drop-down list gives you five security choices for connecting to mail servers. It's vital you get the right security type—otherwise, the Email app won't be able to connect to the servers, and you won't be able to send or receive e-mail.

These are the five security types to choose from:

- **None** Select this security type (or rather, lack of security) to use neither Secure Sockets Layer (SSL) nor Transport Level Security (TLS) for connecting to the mail server. Many regular e-mail accounts need this setting.
- **SSL** Select this security type to secure the connection between the Galaxy Tab and the mail server with SSL security. SSL establishes an encrypted "tunnel" (a secure connection) between the Galaxy Tab and the mail server. SSL uses digital certificates (see the paragraph after the list) to create this secure connection.
- **SSL (Accept All Certificates)** Select this security type to secure the connection between the Galaxy Tab and the mail server with SSL security, but to allow SSL to use self-signed digital certificates as well as certificates issued by certificate authorities (CAs). Normally, you won't want to use this setting, because self-signed certificates deserve no trust. (That said, some organizations and colleges do use self-signed certificates.)
- **TLS** Select this security type to secure the connection between the Galaxy Tab and the mail server with Transport Level Security. You may need to use this setting to connect to corporate mail servers.
- **TLS (Accept All Certificates)** Select this security type to secure the connection between the Galaxy Tab and the mail server with TLS security, but to allow TLS to use self-signed digital certificates instead of the CA-issued digital certificates it usually requires. Under normal circumstances, you won't want to use this setting.

(Continued)

SSL and TLS connections require digital certificates to create the connection. A *digital certificate* is a chunk of encrypted code that uniquely identifies a person or entity (for example, a company or a department). Normally, digital certificates are issued by certificate authorities, supposedly (and usually) trustworthy bodies. You can also use programs to create your own digital certificates, but these are normally valid only for testing and so appear not to be trustworthy. This is why you won't normally want to use the SSL (Accept All Certificates) setting or the TLS (Accept All Certificates) setting.

If you don't know which security type to use, ask your e-mail provider—and ask them which to use for both the incoming mail server and the outgoing mail server, because some providers use different security types for different servers.

There's another complication here—because of the way the Galaxy Tab's Email app implements security, you may need to specify TLS as the security type for the outgoing mail server instead of the SSL security type that you would use in another e-mail app. For example, to connect to Microsoft's Windows Live Hotmail or Apple's iCloud Mail using the Galaxy Tab's Email app, you need to use SSL for the incoming mail server but TLS for the outgoing mail server. Normally, you would use SSL for the outgoing mail server as well.

6. After setting the security type, verify the port in the Port text box. The Email app sets the port number automatically to the default port for the security type you chose. If your administrator or ISP has told you to use a different port number, enter it now.

7. Open the Delete Email From Server drop-down list and then tap the appropriate button:
   - **Never** Tap this button to leave the messages on the server. This setting is useful if you are using another computer to manage your e-mail and don't want the Galaxy Tab to delete the messages.
   - **When I Delete From Inbox** Tap this button to delete messages from the server when you delete them from your Inbox.

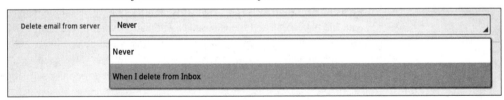

8. Tap the Next button. The Galaxy Tab checks your incoming server settings, and then displays the Outgoing Server Settings screen (shown in Figure 8-7).

9. In the SMTP Server text box, type or paste the name of the outgoing mail server.

SMTP is the abbreviation for Simple Mail Transport Protocol, the protocol that most e-mail servers use for sending outgoing mail.

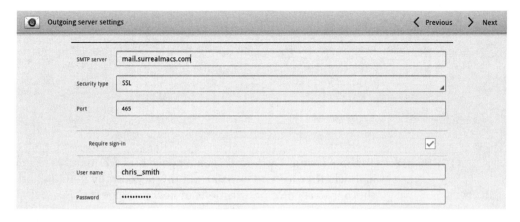

FIGURE 8-7   On the Outgoing Server Settings screen for a POP3 account, specify the details of the SMTP server, the security type, and any authentication needed.

10. Open the Security Type drop-down list (shown in Figure 8-6, earlier in this chapter), and then tap the security type you need for outgoing messages: None, SSL, SSL (Accept All Certificates), TLS, or TLS (Accept All Certificates). See the earlier sidebar "Choose the Right Security Types for Your E-mail Servers" for advice.
11. Verify the port in the Port text box. The Email app sets the port number automatically to the default port for the security type you chose. If your administrator or ISP has given you a different port number, type it in now.

 SSL connections for SMTP servers normally use ports 587, 465, and 25, in that order of preference. If the Email app says it can't contact the server, try those ports in that order. If none of those ports works, change the security type to TLS, and then try those ports in that order again.

12. If the e-mail provider requires you to sign in when sending outgoing mail, select the Require Sign-In check box, and then type your user name in the User Name text box and your password in the Password text box.
13. Tap the Next button. The Email app checks the outgoing server settings and then displays the Account Options screen (shown in Figure 8-8).
14. Tap the Email Check Frequency drop-down button, and then tap the interval you want to use: Never, Every 5 Minutes, Every 10 Minutes, Every 15 Minutes, Every 30 Minutes, Every Hour, Every 4 Hours, or Once A Day. (You can also check for messages manually whenever you need to.)
15. Select the Send Email From This Account By Default check box if you want to use this e-mail account for new outgoing messages.
16. Select the Notify Me When Email Arrives check box if you want the Email app to display an alert or play a sound when you receive a message.
17. Tap the Next button. The Email app displays your Inbox for this e-mail account.

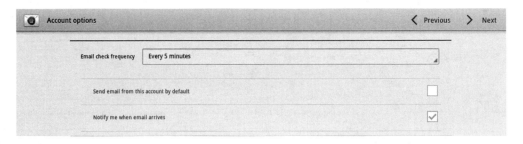

FIGURE 8-8 On the Account Options screen, choose how frequently to check mail, whether to send e-mail from this account by default, and whether to receive notifications of new messages.

Set Up an IMAP E-mail Account

To set up an IMAP e-mail account, follow these steps:

1. On the Add Email Account: What Type Of Account? screen (shown in Figure 8-4, earlier in this chapter), tap the IMAP Account button to display the Incoming Server Settings screen for an IMAP server. Figure 8-9 shows this screen with the onscreen keyboard hidden so that you can see all the fields.
2. Make sure the user name in the Username text box is correct. This is the user name you entered earlier in the setup process, so it should be right.
3. Reenter the password in the Password text box if necessary. This is the password you entered earlier, so you shouldn't need to reenter it unless you got it wrong—but because the password appears as dots by default, it's hard to tell. If you need to see the password, open the Settings app, tap the Location And Security button to display the Location And Security screen, and then select the Visible Passwords check box.

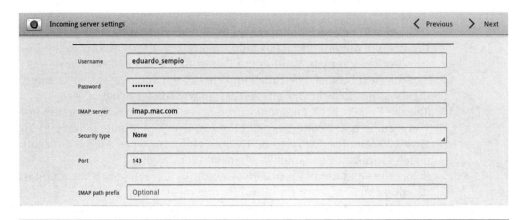

FIGURE 8-9 Enter the details of your IMAP account on the Incoming Server Settings screen.

4. In the IMAP Server text box, type or paste the name of the incoming IMAP server.
5. Open the Security Type drop-down list (shown in Figure 8-6, earlier in this chapter), and then choose the appropriate security type: None, SSL, SSL (Accept All Certificates), TLS, or TLS (Accept All Certificates). See the sidebar "Choose the Right Security Types for Your E-mail Servers," earlier in this chapter, for advice.
6. Verify the port in the Port text box. The Email app sets the port number automatically to the default port for the security type you chose. If your administrator or ISP has given you a different port number, type it in now.
7. In the IMAP Path Prefix text box, type any path prefix the administrator or ISP has told you to enter. This path prefix tells the Email app where to find your mail folders. For many IMAP accounts, you don't need to enter a path.
8. Tap the Next button. The Email app checks your incoming server settings, and then displays the Outgoing Server Settings screen (shown in Figure 8-10).
9. In the SMTP Server text box, type or paste the name of the outgoing mail server.
10. Open the Security Type drop-down list (shown in Figure 8-6, earlier in this chapter), and then tap the security type you need for outgoing messages: None, SSL, SSL (Accept All Certificates), TLS, or TLS (Accept All Certificates). See the earlier sidebar "Choose the Right Security Types for Your E-mail Servers" for advice.
11. Verify the port in the Port text box. The Email app sets the port number automatically to the default port for the security type you chose. If your administrator or ISP has given you a different port number, type it in now.
12. If the e-mail provider requires you to sign in when sending outgoing mail, select the Require Sign-In check box, and then type your user name in the User Name text box and your password in the Password text box.
13. Tap the Next button. The Email app checks the outgoing server settings and then displays the Account Options screen (shown in Figure 8-8, earlier in this chapter).

FIGURE 8-10   On the Outgoing Server Settings screen for an IMAP account, specify the details of the SMTP server, the security type, and any authentication needed.

14. Tap the Email Check Frequency drop-down button, and then tap the interval you want to use: Never, Every 5 Minutes, Every 10 Minutes, Every 15 Minutes, Every 30 Minutes, Every Hour, Every 4 Hours, or Once A Day. (You can also check for messages manually whenever you need to.)
15. Select the Send Email From This Account By Default check box if you want to use this e-mail account for new outgoing messages.
16. Select the Notify Me When Email Arrives check box if you want the Email app to display an alert or play a sound when you receive a message.
17. Tap the Next button. The Email app displays your Inbox for this email account.

Set Up an Exchange E-mail Account

To set up an e-mail account that uses Microsoft's Exchange Server, follow these steps:

1. On the Add Email Account: What Type Of Account? screen (shown in Figure 8-4, earlier in this chapter), tap the Microsoft Exchange ActiveSync button to display the Exchange Server Settings screen (see Figure 8-11).
2. In the Domain\User Name text box, type your Windows domain, a backslash (\), and your user name—for example, **CORP\aconnor**. If you're not sure of any of these items of information, ask your Exchange administrator for them.
3. In the Password text box, type your password.
4. In the Exchange Server box, type the Exchange server's hostname—for example, **exchange.surrealpcs.com**.
5. Select the Use Secure Connection (SSL) check box if you need to use SSL to connect to the Exchange server.
6. Select the Accept All SSL Certificates check box if you've been told to do so. Otherwise, clear this check box.

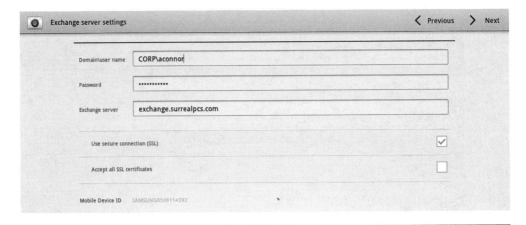

FIGURE 8-11 On the Exchange Server Settings screen, enter your domain, user name, password, and Exchange server name. You can also choose whether to use SSL and accept all SSL certificates.

7. Tap the Next button. The Email app makes sure the Exchange server settings work, and then displays the Exchange Account screen.

8. If you want to use Exchange for e-mail, contacts, and calendars (as is likely), leave the Email slider, Contacts slider, and Calendar slider set to the On position. If you want to turn off one or more items, move the appropriate slider or sliders to the Off position.

9. Tap the Next button. The Email app displays the Set Up Email screen.

 When you tap the Next button to move on from the Exchange Server Settings screen, you may see a dialog box warning you that Samsung will store your mobile phone's IMEI (its identification number) and model name for licensing purposes and asking if you want to continue. Normally, you'll want to tap the OK button here—otherwise, you can't finish setting up the Exchange account.

10. In the Give This Account A Name text box, type a descriptive name for the e-mail account—for example, Exchange Mail.

11. In the Your Name (Displayed On Outgoing Messages) text box, make sure your name appears the way you want it to in outgoing messages. Correct it if necessary.

12. Tap the Done button. The Email app displays your Inbox for the Exchange account.

Switch Among E-mail Accounts

When you have only a single e-mail account on the Galaxy Tab, you simply work with that account all the time in the Email app. But when you've set up two or more e-mail accounts, you switch among them by tapping the button at the top of the screen (as shown here) and then tapping the name of the account you want. To see all the e-mail accounts together, tap the Combined View item.

Choose Settings for an E-mail Account

Apart from the details you specified and the options you chose while setting up the account, each e-mail account has various settings that you can configure at any point. For example, you can change the account's name, the version of your name that goes on messages, the account's default signature, or the frequency with which the account checks for new messages. You can also set a ringtone or turn on vibration for the account.

You may not want (or need) to make any changes immediately, so skip ahead to the "Send and Receive E-mail" section if you want. Come back to this section when you want to change the signature or the way the account behaves.

Open the Settings Screen

To choose settings for an e-mail account, first open the Settings screen for e-mail accounts. Follow these steps:

1. From the Inbox, tap the Menu button to display the menu panel, and then tap the Settings button to display the Settings screen.
2. Tap the account you want to configure. The Settings screen displays the settings for that account (see Figure 8-12).

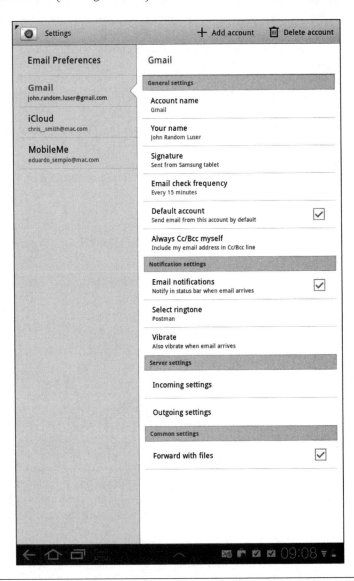

FIGURE 8-12 From the Settings screen, you can customize the way each e-mail account behaves.

Change General Settings

In the General Settings area of the Settings screen, you can choose the following settings:

- **Account Name** This readout shows the name you gave the account when you set it up. To change the name, tap the Account Name button, type the name in the Account Name dialog box, and then tap the OK button.
- **Your Name** This readout shows the name you entered to use on your outgoing messages. To change it, tap the Your Name button, type the new name in the Your Name dialog box, and then tap the OK button.
- **Signature** This readout shows the signature text that the Email app automatically adds to each new message you send from the e-mail account. The default setting is usually "Sent from Samsung tablet," which is neither grammatical nor particularly helpful. To change the signature, tap the Signature button, type something more useful in the Signature dialog box (see Figure 8-13), and then tap the OK button.

 The signature is optional. If you don't want to use a signature, delete the text in the Signature dialog box, then tap the OK button. The readout "Create signature for your outgoing messages" means that the Email app is set to use no signature.

- **Email Check Frequency** This readout shows the frequency you chose when setting up the account—for example, Every 15 Minutes. To change the frequency, tap this button, and then tap the appropriate option button in the Email Check Frequency dialog box.

 For an Exchange e-mail account, you can set the Email Check Frequency to Automatic (Push) to get your messages pushed to you as soon as they become available.

- **Default Account** Select this check box to make the Email app use this account as the default account for sending new messages. Selecting this check box for the current account clears the check box for whichever other account was the default.

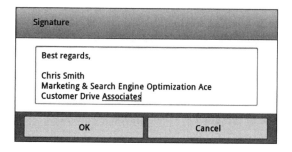

FIGURE 8-13 Type your signature for outgoing messages in the Signature dialog box. Tap the Enter button when you need to start a new paragraph.

- **Always Cc/Bcc Myself** If you need the Email app to Cc or Bcc your e-mail account on every outgoing message, tap this button to display the Always Cc/Bcc Myself dialog box (shown here), and then tap the Cc option button or the Bcc option button, as needed.

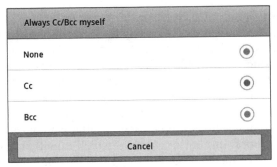

 If your e-mail provider automatically saves a copy of each outgoing message to a Sent folder, as most e-mail providers do, you don't normally need to Cc or Bcc yourself on messages. But if your provider doesn't give you a Sent folder, you may find the Always Cc/Bcc Myself feature useful.

When You Should Use Bcc on Messages You Send

Bcc is the abbreviation for *blind carbon copy*, which used to mean creating a carbon copy (using sheets of carbon paper or other duplicating paper) in a typewriter, then adding an address to the carbon copies that didn't appear on the top copy (hence the "blind" bit).

Adding Bcc recipients to e-mail messages is much easier than winding a stack of carbon copies back into a typewriter, so it's tempting to use Bcc messages more than necessary. But in general, Bcc messages are best kept for these two purposes:

- **Sending a secret copy of a message** In some business circumstances, you may need to send a copy of the message to a recipient you don't want the other recipients to see—for example, a manager or the HR department.
- **Sending change-of-address messages and similar announcements** When you send a message announcing a change of address or similar news, put your own address in the To field and all the other addresses in the Bcc field. That way, each recipient sees only your address (which they get in the From field anyway) and their own address, and you don't hand out all the addresses in your address book to a slew of people who might misuse them (or have them grabbed by malware).

Otherwise, for most business or personal messages, it's normally better to let all the recipients see all the other recipients' addresses. This keeps the messages straightforward and avoids surprises.

Choose Notification Settings

In the Notification Settings area of the Settings screen, you can set these three options:

- **Email Notifications**   Select this check box to have this account display notifications in the notifications area when new messages arrive. For secondary accounts, you may want to clear this check box so that you don't receive notifications for routine messages, newsletters, and supposedly special offers.
- **Select Ringtone**   If you want this account to notify you of new messages using a ringtone, tap this button to display the Select Ringtone dialog box (shown here). You can then either tap the Sounds button to display the Sounds dialog box, tap the option button for a sound such as Bubbles or Harmonics, and then tap the OK button; or tap the Go To My Files button to display a My Files window, select the file you want, and then tap the Done button at the top of the screen.

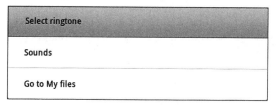

- **Vibrate**   If you want the Galaxy Tab to vibrate when you receive a message to this account, tap this button to display the Vibrate dialog box (shown here). Tap the Always option button or the Only In Silent Mode option button, as appropriate. (If you want to turn off the tingling, tap the Never option button.)

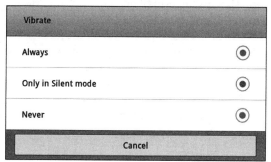

Change Your Incoming Server Settings or Outgoing Server Settings

When you set up your e-mail account, you specified the details of the incoming mail server and the outgoing mail server. If your e-mail account is working, you got the details right.

Normally, you won't need to change the details if the e-mail account is working. But if you do need to, tap the Incoming Settings button or the Outgoing Settings button in the Server Settings section, and then work on the Incoming Server Settings screen or the Outgoing Server Settings screen, just as described earlier in this chapter. Tap the Done button when you finish.

 For an Exchange account, you can toggle synchronization for Contacts and Calendar in the Server Settings area.

Choose Whether to Forward Files with a Message

The Common Settings section at the bottom of the Settings screen contains just one setting—the Forward With Files check box. Select this check box if you want to include attached files with messages you forward, as is often useful. Clear this check box if you want to send only the text of a message you're forwarding.

 The Forward With Files setting applies to all your e-mail accounts—you can't set it differently for different accounts. (That's why the section is called Common Settings.)

Delete an E-mail Account

When you no longer need to use a particular e-mail account on the Galaxy Tab, delete the account. Follow these steps:

1. From the Inbox for an e-mail account, tap the Menu button to display the menu panel.
2. Tap the Settings item to display the Settings screen.
3. Tap the Delete Account button in the upper-right corner. The Settings screen displays a check box to the left of each account.
4. Select the check box for the account you want to delete.
5. Tap the OK button at the top of the screen. The Galaxy Tab displays the Delete dialog box, shown here, to make clear that you'll remove all the account's messages, contacts, and other data (such as attached files) from the Galaxy Tab.

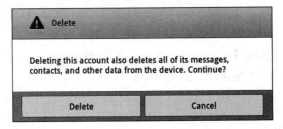

6. Tap the Delete button if you're sure you want to remove the account.
7. From the Settings screen, tap the Back button to return to your Inbox.

Send and Receive E-mail

When you've set up however many e-mail accounts you need on the Galaxy Tab, you'll be ready to send and receive e-mail. This section shows you how to do both.

Send a Message

To send a message, follow these steps:

1. Tap the New Mail button in the upper-right corner of the Inbox to display the New Email screen.
2. Tap the To area, and then either type the e-mail address or (usually better) add it from your Contacts list like this:
   a. Tap the Contacts button on the right side of the To area to display your Contacts list. The Contacts button is the icon that shows a card file.
   b. On the Contacts tab, the Favorites tab, or the Groups tab, select the check box for each recipient you want to add.
   c. Tap the Done button at the top of the screen. The Email app adds the recipient or recipients and returns you to the New Email screen. Each recipient's address appears as a button.

 To remove a recipient from a message, tap and hold the recipient's button until the Email app displays a dialog box. Then tap the Delete button.

3. Tap the Subject area, and then type the subject line for the message. Make it concise and descriptive so that the recipient can easily see in her Inbox what the message is about without opening it.
4. Tap in the body area, and then type the body of the message.
5. If you want to attach a file or other item to the message, attach it as described in the section "Add an Attachment to a Message You're Sending," later in this chapter.
6. When you're ready to send the message, tap the Send button. The Email app sends the message, and then displays your Inbox again.

Read Your Incoming Messages

To read an incoming message, go to your Inbox (if you're not already there), and then tap the message to open it. Figure 8-14 shows an open message with the toolbar buttons labeled.

 If you hold the Galaxy Tab in portrait orientation, the Email app hides the list of messages. At the bottom of the screen are a < button you can tap to display the previous message and a > button you can tap to display the next message.

How to... Cancel a Message You're Writing, or Save It as a Draft for Later

If you decide to stop writing a message, tap the Cancel button that appears at the upper-right corner of the screen. The Email app displays the Sending Cancelled dialog box (shown here), which prompts you to save the message in your Drafts folder.

If you want to save the message so you can resume writing it later, tap the OK button. If you want to discard the message completely, tap the Cancel button.

If you save the message as a draft, you can open it again at any time by tapping the Drafts folder in the left column of the screen for the e-mail account, and then tapping the message in the list that appears.

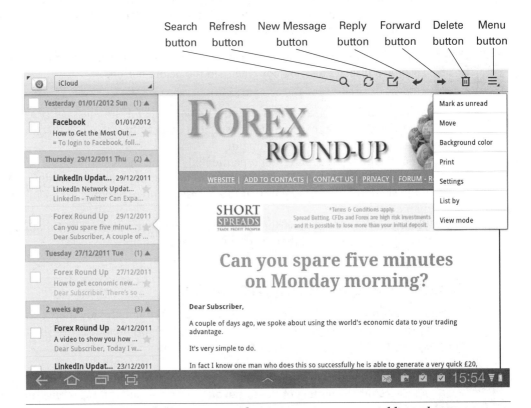

FIGURE 8-14   From the message-reading screen, you can quickly reply to a message, put it in a folder, or delete it.

Holding the Galaxy Tab in portrait orientation lets you see more of a message at once, but when you're reviewing the messages in your Inbox (or another folder), you may prefer to hold the Galaxy Tab in landscape orientation. This way, you can see the Inbox as well as the message, so you can move quickly among messages by tapping the message you want to see next. Tap the < < button if you want to close the folder list to see more of the message; tap the resulting > > button when you want to display the folder list again.

You can zoom in on the message by pinching out with two fingers or by double-tapping, or zoom out by pinching in with two fingers or double-tapping again.

From the message-reading screen, you can take the following actions:

- **Display another message**   In landscape orientation, tap the message in the message list. In portrait orientation, tap the < button or the > button.
- **Search the mailbox**   Tap the Search button on the toolbar to display the Search box, then tap in it and type your search term. You can restrict the search to Title, Sender, or Date instead of All by tapping the triangular button and then tapping the appropriate word on the pop-up menu.
- **Move the message to a folder**   Tap the Menu button to display the menu panel, then tap the Move item to display the Move To dialog box (see Figure 8-15). Tap the folder you want to put the message in.
- **Delete the message**   Tap the Delete button. The Email app moves the message to the Trash folder.

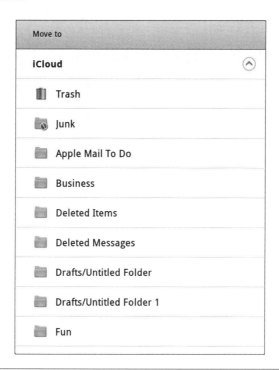

FIGURE 8-15   To move the current message to a folder, choose Menu | Move, then tap the destination folder in the Move To dialog box.

If you delete a message by mistake, you may be able to recover it. Tap the Folders button in the upper-left corner of the screen to display the list of folders, and then tap the Trash button to display the Trash folder. Tap the message you want to recover, choose Menu | Move, and then tap the folder you want to put the message in—for example, Inbox.

- **Reply to the message**   Tap the Reply button on the toolbar. The Email app starts a reply to the message's sender and gives it the subject line **Re:** and the message's original title (for example, Re: Project Meeting). Write the reply, and then tap the Send button.
- **Forward a message to someone else**   Tap the Forward button on the toolbar. The Email app starts a forwarded message, giving it the subject line **Fwd:** and the message's original title (for example, Fwd: Cookie Recipe). Address the message, write any explanation needed of why you're forwarding it, and then tap the Send button.
- **Write a new message**   Tap the New Message button as usual.

 To mark a message as a Favorite, tap the star button on the right of its button. The Email app changes the empty star to a gold star. If you need to stop the message from being a Favorite, tap the gold star to turn it back to an empty star.

How to... Move Multiple Messages to a Folder at Once

When you're working through your e-mail, moving one message at a time to a folder using the Move command and the Move To dialog box works well. But other times, you may need to move multiple messages to the same folder at once.

To move multiple messages at once, follow these steps:

1. In the list of messages, select the check box for each message you want to affect. The Email app changes the toolbar to display the icons shown in the next illustration.

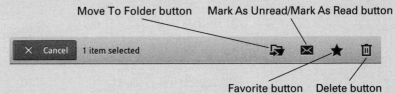

2. Tap the Move To Folder button to display the Move To dialog box.
3. Tap the mailbox you want to move the selected messages to.

After selecting multiple messages, you can also delete them by tapping the Delete button, mark them as favorites by tapping the Favorite button, or switch their status between Read and Unread by tapping the Mark As Unread button or Mark As Read button (these buttons replace each other on the toolbar).

Send and Receive Attachments

E-mail is a great way of communicating via the Internet, but you can also use it to transfer files. To do so, you attach the files to messages you're sending, or receive files that others have attached to messages sent to you.

Add an Attachment to a Message You're Sending

To attach a file to a message you're sending, follow these steps:

1. Create and address the message as described earlier in this chapter. Or reply to a message, or forward a message, as needed.
2. On the New Email screen, tap the Attach button (the button that shows a paperclip) to display the Attach dialog box (shown here).
3. Tap the My Files item to display the My Files app, which shows the Select Items screen.
4. Tap the folder that contains the file or files you want to attach.
5. Select the check box for each file you want to attach.
6. Tap the Done button. The Email app adds the file as an attachment, as shown here.

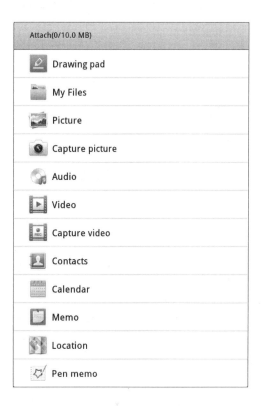

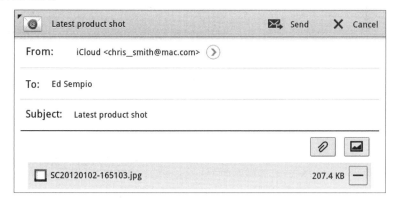

7. Finish the message, and then tap the Send button to send it.

To remove an attachment from a message, tap the Remove (–) icon that appears at the right end of the attachment's shaded bar.

Receive an Attachment

When you receive an attachment, the message title shows a paperclip next to it, and the message is divided into a Message tab and an Attachments tab. The Attachments tab shows the number of attachments. Tap the Attachments tab to view the list of attachments, as shown in Figure 8-16.

 If the Email app hasn't yet downloaded the attachment, it appears as just a gray bar. When the Email app has downloaded the attachment, a blue bar appears below the filename.

Tap the shaded bar to display the attachment in a viewer. Tap the Save button (the floppy disk icon) to save the attachment to the Download folder in your My Files folder and then open it for viewing. In either case, the Email app downloads any parts of the file that it has not yet downloaded; if the file is large and your Internet connection is slow, this may take a few minutes.

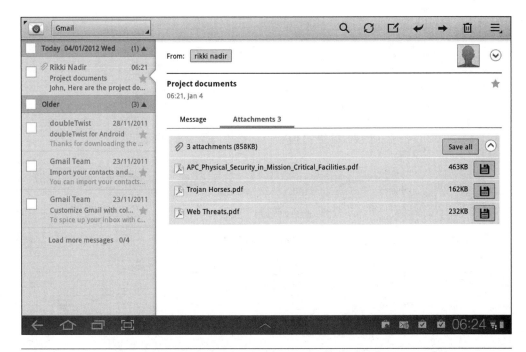

FIGURE 8-16 To view a message's attachments, tap the Attachments tab. You can then open an attached file by tapping its shaded bar or save it by tapping the Save button. Tap the Save All button to save all the files.

Make the Email App Easier to View

To work through your messages quickly, you'll probably want to make your folders and the messages themselves easy to view. For a folder, you can choose a different view and decide how to list the messages (for example, by date). For a message, you can change the font size and the background color.

Choose Your View Mode

The Email app's folders can display messages either in Standard view or in Conversation view:

- **Standard view**   This view shows each message as an unrelated item, as in the left screen in Figure 8-17.
- **Conversation view**   This view groups related messages into conversations (also called *threads*), as in the middle screen in Figure 8-17. You then tap the down-arrow button at the right end of a conversation's entry to display the messages the conversation contains, as in the right screen in Figure 8-17. If you tend to have discussions via e-mail, using Conversation view can make your Inbox much easier to navigate.

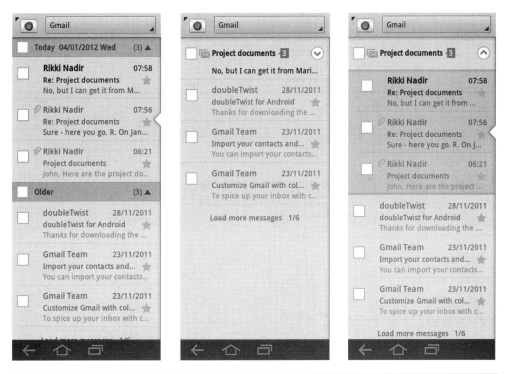

FIGURE 8-17   Standard view (left) shows each message, while Conversation view (middle) groups related messages under a heading that you can expand (right).

To switch between Standard view and Conversation view, follow these steps:

1. Tap the Menu button to display the menu panel.
2. Tap the View Mode item to display the View Mode dialog box (shown here).

3. Tap the Standard View option button or the Conversation View option button, as needed.

Change How the Email App Lists Your Messages

In Standard view, you can also control how the Email app lists your messages. (In Conversation view, you can't change the listing.)

To change the listing, follow these steps:

1. Tap the Menu button to display the menu panel.
2. Tap the List By button to display the List By dialog box (see Figure 8-18).
3. Tap the option button for the sort order you want:
   - **Date (Most Recent)**   Tap this option button to put the most recent messages first. If your mailbox is full, this is a good way of making the newest messages easy to see.

FIGURE 8-18   You can list a folder's messages by date, by sender, by whether they're read or unread, or by favorites.

- **Date (Oldest)**   Tap this option button to put the oldest messages first and the newest messages last. This sort order may make for a long list of messages, but it's good when you want to start at the most recent message and then work your way back up the list.
- **Sender (A to Z)**   Tap this option button to put the messages into alphabetical order by the sender's name. This sort order is good when you need to locate a message by the sender.
- **Sender (Z to A)**   Tap this option button to put the messages into reverse alphabetical order by the sender's name. This sort order is occasionally useful.
- **Read/Unread**   Tap this option button to sort the messages into an Unread category and a Read category. This sort order is good for identifying (and preferably plowing through) the messages you haven't yet read.
- **Favorites**   Tap this option button to sort the messages into a Favorites category and an Other category. If you use Favorites to identify high-interest messages, this sort order is good for identifying the messages you want to concentrate on (or the messages you're less interested in and so may want to delete).

Change the Background Color for Messages

To change the background color for messages, follow these steps:

1. Tap the Menu button to display the menu panel.
2. Tap the Background Color item to display the Background Color dialog box (shown here).

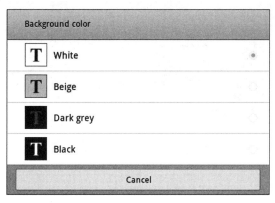

3. Tap the White option button, the Beige option button, the Dark Grey option button, or the Black option button, as needed.

Use the Gmail App

If you have a Gmail account, you can set it up in the Email app and use it there with your other accounts. But you may prefer to use the Gmail app, which is tailored to make Gmail easy to use.

If you chose to set up your Gmail account when going through the Galaxy Tab's initial setup routine, you're good to go with the Gmail app. If not, you'll need to add your Gmail account to the Galaxy Tab the first time you launch the Gmail app.

 In some localizations, the Gmail app is named Google Mail.

Launch the Gmail App

To launch the Gmail app, follow these steps:

1. Tap the Home button to display the home screen.
2. Tap the Apps button to display the Apps screen.
3. Tap the Gmail icon.

Set Up Your Gmail Account

If you haven't yet set up a Gmail account on the Galaxy Tab, the Gmail app displays the Sign In With Your Google Account screen (the top part of which is shown here).

If you don't have a Gmail account, you can tap the Create Account button to start creating a Google account. Otherwise, type your user name and password, and then tap the Sign In button.

After the Gmail app contacts the Google servers and confirms your credentials, the app displays the Backup And Restore screen (shown in Figure 8-19).

Select the Keep This Device Backed Up With My Google Account check box if you want to back up essential data to Google's servers. This is usually a good idea, because you can then restore the data easily if you lose the Galaxy Tab or need to restore it to factory settings (which wipes out your custom settings). The disadvantage is the

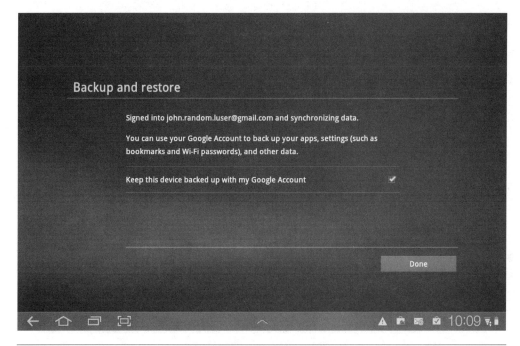

FIGURE 8-19   On the Backup And Restore screen, choose whether to back up essential data to the Google servers.

potential cost to your privacy of storing your information on Google's servers—but this is a cost you will normally have weighed before creating a Gmail account.

Tap the Done button to finish the setup process. You'll see the Waiting For Sync screen while the Gmail app gets your data, and then the contents of your Inbox appear.

Read and Send E-mail with the Gmail App

From your Inbox (shown in Figure 8-20), you can quickly take standard e-mail actions:

- **Get any new messages**   Tap the Refresh button on the toolbar.
- **Read a message**   Tap the message to open it full screen, as shown in Figure 8-21. You can then take the following actions:
    - **Archive the message**   Tap the Archive button on the toolbar.
    - **Delete the message**   Tap the Delete button on the toolbar.
    - **Star the message**   Tap the star button to turn it from gray to gold.
    - **Reply to the message**   Tap the Reply button.
    - **Reply to all recipients of the message**   Tap the Reply All button.
    - **Forward the message**   Tap the Forward button.
    - **Display another message**   Tap the message in the message list.

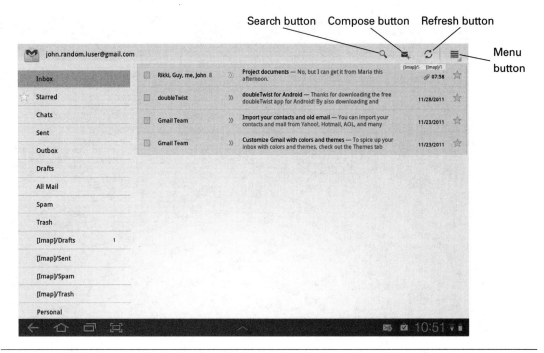

FIGURE 8-20 The Gmail app's Inbox is designed to help you get through your messages quickly.

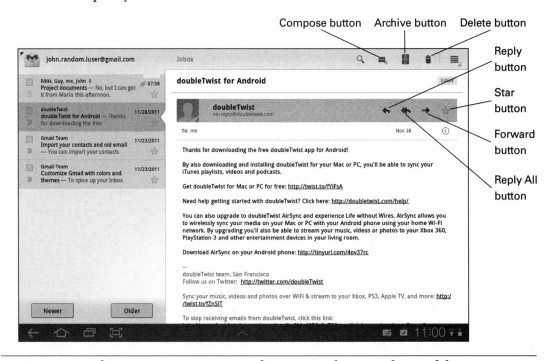

FIGURE 8-21 After opening a message to read, you can reply to it, archive it, delete it, or star it.

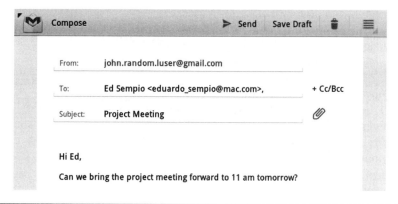

FIGURE 8-22   Compose your e-mail message as usual on the Compose screen.

- **Start a new message**   Tap the Compose button. On the Compose screen (shown in Figure 8-22), address the message, type its subject and body text, and then tap the Send button to send it.

To attach a file to a message, tap the Menu button, and then tap the Attach button on the menu panel. To add a Cc or Bcc recipient, tap the Cc/Bcc button to the right of the To field.

- **Search for messages**   Tap the Search button on the toolbar, type your search term in the Search box, and then tap the Enter button on the keyboard.
- **Switch to a different folder**   To switch to a different folder, tap the button in the upper-left corner of the screen to display the list of folders, and then tap the button for the folder you want to display.

Tap and hold a message in the Inbox to display a dialog box showing actions you can take with the message—for example, open it for reading, mark it as unread, or delete it.

Choose Settings for Your Gmail Account

To make your Gmail account work the way you want it to, take a few minutes to choose settings for it. From the Inbox, tap the Menu button to display the menu panel, and then tap the Settings button to display the Settings screen.

Choose General Settings for a Gmail Account

Start by tapping the General Preferences button in the left column to display the settings in this category (see Figure 8-23). You can then set these settings:

- **Confirm Before Deleting**   Select this check box if you want Gmail to confirm the deletion of each message. Normally, this feature is overkill, but if you find yourself deleting messages by mistake, try turning it on.

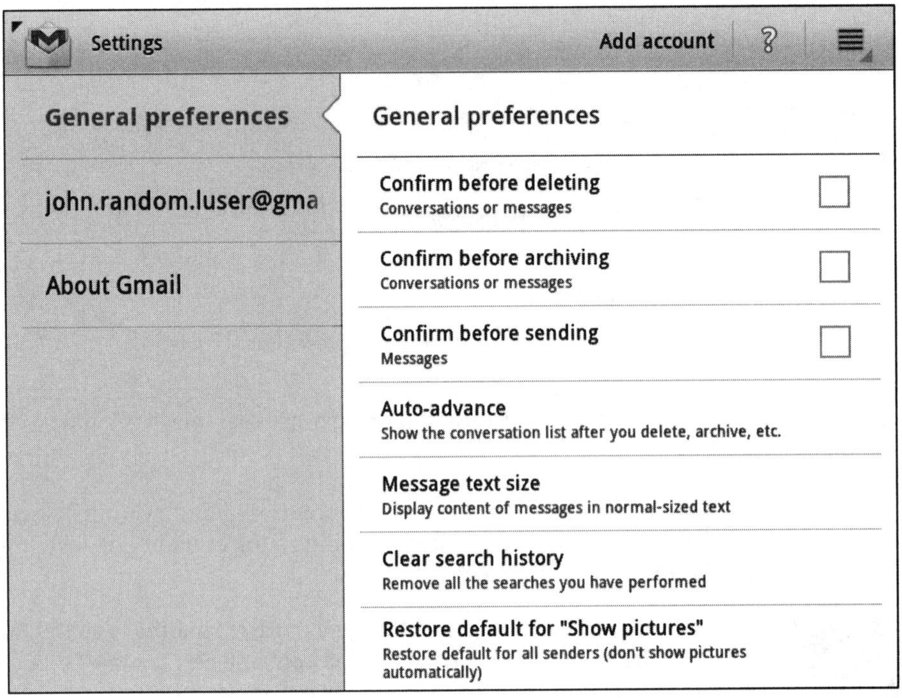

FIGURE 8-23 Settings in the General Preferences category let you control whether Gmail requires confirmations for actions, whether it uses Auto-Advance, and whether it displays pictures automatically.

- **Confirm Before Archiving** Select this check box if you want Gmail to confirm the archiving of any conversation or message.
- **Confirm Before Sending** Select this check box if you want Gmail to confirm the sending of each message. If you find yourself hitting the Send button by accident (for example, while using the Galaxy Tab on public transport), turn this setting on to give yourself a safety net.
- **Auto-Advance** This clever feature lets you specify which screen you want the Gmail app to show after you delete or archive a conversation. Tap the Auto-Advance button to display the Advance To dialog box (shown here), and then tap the Newer Conversation option button, the Older Conversation option button, or the Conversation List option button (the default), as needed.

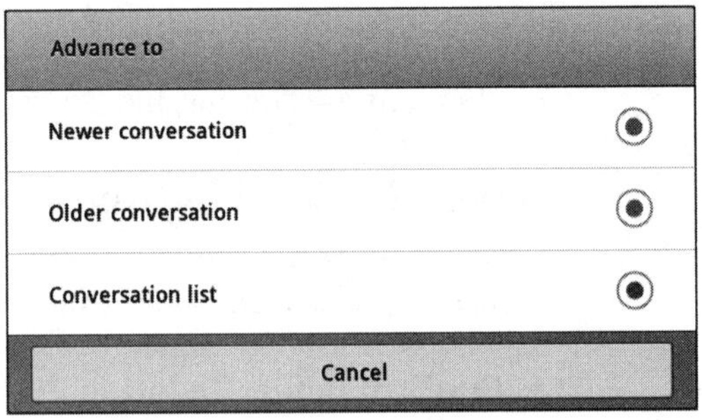

- **Message Text Size**   To choose the size at which the Gmail app displays the message text, tap this button. In the Message Text Size dialog box, tap the appropriate option button—Tiny, Small, Normal, Large, or Huge.
- **Clear Search History**   Tap this button to clear your search history. The Gmail app doesn't confirm the clearance.
- **Restore Default For "Show Pictures"**   Tap this button if you want to restore the default Show Pictures setting, which is not to show pictures for all senders.

Choose Account-Specific Settings for a Gmail Account

When you finish setting the General preferences, tap the account's name in the left column to display the settings for this account (see Figure 8-24). You can then choose settings as described in this section.

In the Sync Options area of the Settings screen for an account, you can configure the following settings:

- **Gmail Sync For This Account Is ON**   This readout shows whether sync is on or off. Normally you'll want to leave it on. To change the setting, tap this button, and then choose settings on the Accounts And Sync screen that appears.

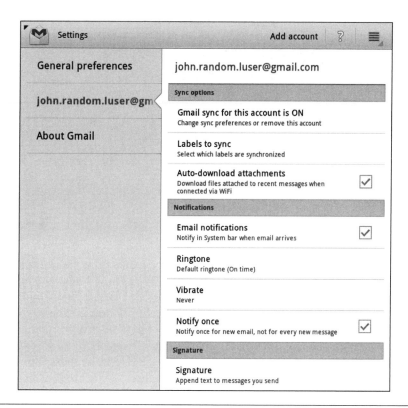

FIGURE 8-24   Choose account-specific settings for your Gmail account.

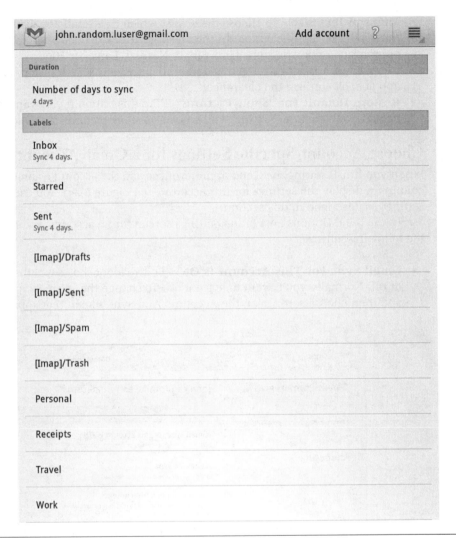

FIGURE 8-25 Choose which labels to sync for your Gmail account.

- **Labels To Sync** To choose which labels the Gmail app synchronizes, tap this button. On the screen shown in Figure 8-25, first tap the Number Of Days To Sync button in the Duration area, set the number of days in the Number Of Days To Sync dialog box (shown on the left in the next illustration), and tap the OK button. Then, in the Labels area, tap the button for the label you want to configure. In the dialog box that opens (for example, the Starred dialog box, shown on the right in the next illustration), tap the Sync None option button, the Sync *N* Days option button, or the Sync All option button, as needed. Tap the Back button when you've finished configuring the labels.

 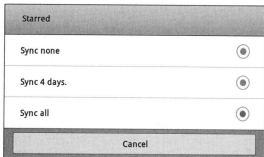

- **Auto-Download Attachments**   Select this check box to have the Gmail app automatically download files attached to messages as long as the Galaxy Tab is connected to Wi-Fi. (If you have a 3G Galaxy Tab, the Gmail app doesn't automatically download attached files so as not to run through your data allowance. But you can force a download at any point by tapping the button for the attached file.)

In the Notifications area of the Settings screen for an account, you can configure the following settings:

- **Email Notifications**   Select this check box if you want the notifications area to display notifications for incoming messages to your Gmail account or accounts.
- **Ringtone**   To choose a ringtone for incoming messages, tap this button. In the Ringtones dialog box, tap the option button for the ringtone you want, and then tap the OK button.
- **Vibrate**   To control whether the Galaxy Tab vibrates to notify you about incoming messages, tap the Vibrate button. In the Vibrate dialog box, tap the Always option button, the Only When Silent option button, or the Never option button, as appropriate.
- **Notify Once**   Select this check box if you want the Galaxy Tab to notify you only once when you've got e-mail rather than notify you for every single message. If you receive lots of messages, turn this setting on to prevent the Galaxy Tab from beating you about the ears with ringtones or about the body with vibrations.

In the Signature area of the Settings screen for an account, you can set up your e-mail signature for the account by tapping the Signature button, typing the text for the signature in the Signature dialog box (shown here), and then taping the OK button. (You can create a multiline signature—just tap the Enter button where you want to create a new line.)

9

Keep Up with Your Social Networks

HOW TO...

- Set up and use Social Hub for integrated social networking
- Upload your photos to Facebook or Twitter via Social Hub
- Keep up with friends on Facebook
- Keep up with business on LinkedIn
- Keep up with news on Twitter

In this chapter, I'll show you how to use the Galaxy Tab to keep up with your social networks.

Many Galaxy Tab models include the Social Hub app, which gives you one-stop access to not only your accounts on social networking services but also your e-mail. We'll start with this app, because it's a great way of handling social networking—as long as your Galaxy Tab offers it.

If your Galaxy Tab has Social Hub, you may want to go no further than that. But if your Galaxy Tab doesn't have Social Hub, you'll need to access your social networks in other ways. So we'll go through the various ways you can access Facebook, LinkedIn, and Twitter on your Galaxy Tab.

Set Up and Use Social Hub for Integrated Social Networking

Many localizations of the Galaxy Tab have the Social Hub app, which gives you an easy way to monitor your e-mail, your Facebook account, your Twitter account, and your LinkedIn account from a single app.

In this section, I'll show you how to launch Social Hub, add your accounts to it, and then use Social Hub to keep up to date with your social networks.

Launch Social Hub

To launch Social Hub, follow these steps:

1. Tap the Home button to display the home screen (unless you're already there).
2. Tap the Apps button to display the Apps screen.
3. Tap the Social Hub icon to launch Social Hub.

 If you've already set up an e-mail account on the Galaxy Tab, it will already be part of Social Hub.

Add Your Accounts to Social Hub

When you first launch Social Hub, it'll probably look like Figure 9-1. In the upper-left corner are a Feeds tab and a Messages tab. At first, the Feeds tab displays a message and button prompting you to add your SNS accounts. SNS is *social network service*—one of those abbreviations that hasn't yet caught on.

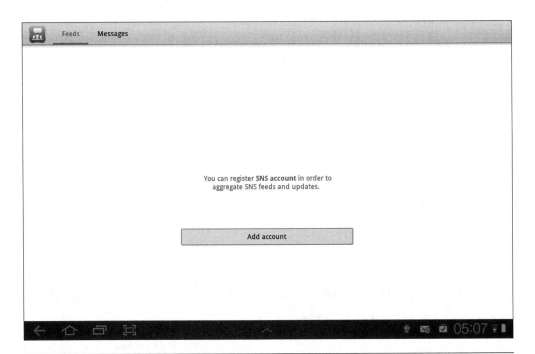

FIGURE 9-1 Social Hub has a Feeds tab and a Messages tab. Until you add one or more social networking accounts, the Feeds tab displays only this message telling you that "you can register SNS account in order to aggregate SNS feeds and updates."

To add an account to Social Hub, follow these steps:

1. If the Feeds tab isn't already displayed, tap the Feeds tab in the upper-left corner of the Social Hub window.
2. Tap the Add Account button on the Feeds tab to display the Add Account screen (shown here).

If you've already added accounts to Social Hub, start adding a new account by choosing Menu | Account, and then tapping the Add Account button at the bottom of the screen.

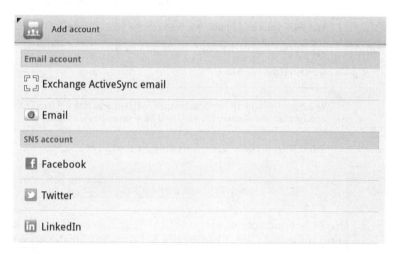

3. Tap the appropriate button to start the process of adding the account:
   - **Exchange ActiveSync Email**   Tap this button to add a Microsoft Exchange account.
   - **Email**   Tap this button to add any e-mail account other than Microsoft Exchange.
   - **Facebook**   Tap this button to add your Facebook account. We'll use Facebook for this example.
   - **Twitter**   Tap this button to add your Twitter account.

Social Hub can handle only one Twitter account. If you have multiple Twitter accounts, you'll need to decide which one to use in Social Hub.

   - **LinkedIn**   Tap this button to add your LinkedIn account.

4. The first time you add an account, Social Hub displays the Samsung Social Hub disclaimer and license agreement. Read as much of the Terms and Conditions, the End User License Agreement, and the Privacy Policy as you can stand. Then, if you want to proceed, select the I Accept All The Terms Above check box, and tap the Agree button.

5. Follow through the process for adding your account. For example, here's what happens with a Facebook account:

a. On the first screen of the Set Up Your Facebook Account wizard (shown here), tap the Next button.

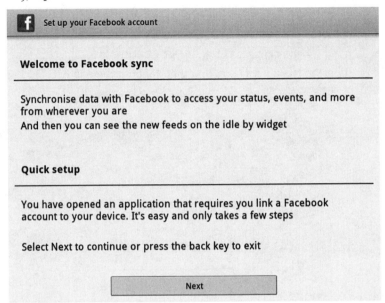

b. On the second screen of the Set Up Your Facebook Account wizard (shown here), type your e-mail address and password for the account, and then tap the Log In button. You can select the Show Password check box if you want to verify which characters you've typed.

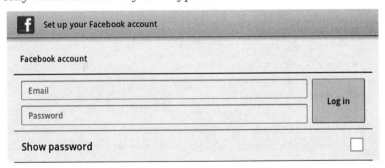

c. On the third screen of the Set Up Your Facebook Account wizard, select the Sync Contacts check box, the Sync Message check box, and the Sync Calendar check box, as needed. Then tap the Done button.

d. Your Facebook account then appears in Social Hub.

FIGURE 9-2   Tap the All Feeds button in the left pane of the Feeds tab to see all your feeds at once.

Track Your Feeds and Messages

After you add your accounts to Social Hub, you can quickly track your feeds and messages.

To track your feeds, tap the Feeds tab, and then either tap the All Feeds button in the left pane (as shown in Figure 9-2) or tap the button for a specific account.

To track your messages, tap the Messages tab. Here, too, you can either tap the All Messages button in the left pane to view all your messages together or tap the button for a specific account (as shown in Figure 9-3).

Send Messages and Updates from Social Hub

To keep others up to date with your news, you can quickly send messages or post updates straight from Social Hub rather than having to switch to an e-mail app or a social networking app. Better yet, you can post an update on all your social networks at once.

Send a Message from Social Hub

To send a message from Social Hub, follow these steps:

1. If the Messages tab isn't already displayed, tap the Messages tab to display it.
2. Tap the Compose button. If the All Messages button is selected in the left column, Social Hub displays the Compose dialog box (shown next); tap the

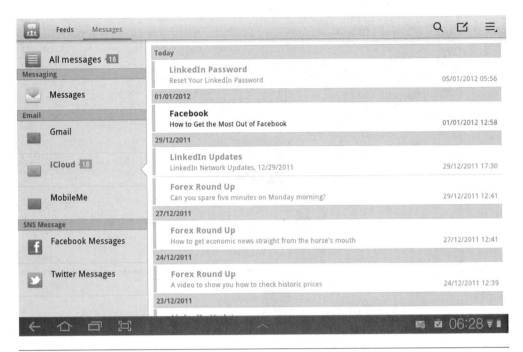

FIGURE 9-3 Tap the button for a specific account in the left pane of the Messages tab to see only the messages from that account.

account you want to use. If the button for a particular account is selected in the left column, Social Hub starts a message using that account.

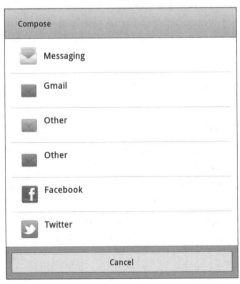

3. Address the message, enter its subject and body text as usual, and then send it.

Post an Update from Social Hub

To post an update from Social Hub, follow these steps:

1. If the Feeds tab isn't already displayed, tap the Feeds tab to display it.
2. Tap the Compose button to display the Status Update window (shown here).

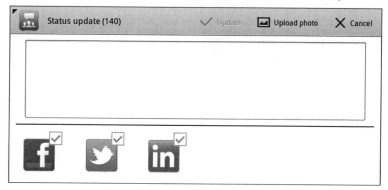

3. Select the check box for each social networking service you want to send the update to.
4. Write your news, and then tap the Update button.

 If you find Social Hub useful, add the Social Hub app to one of your home screens so that you can keep tabs on what's happening.

How to... **Upload Your Photos to Facebook or Twitter via Social Hub**

Once you've set up Social Hub with your Facebook and Twitter accounts, you can quickly upload photos to Facebook or Twitter from the Image Viewer app (which you access from the Camera app) or the Gallery app.

In one of these apps, follow these steps to upload a photo to Facebook or Twitter:

1. Display the photo you want to upload.
2. Tap the photo to display the onscreen controls.
3. Tap the Share button to display the Share menu.

(Continued)

4. Tap the Social Hub button. The Galaxy Tab displays the Upload Photo screen shown here, with the photo already loaded into it.

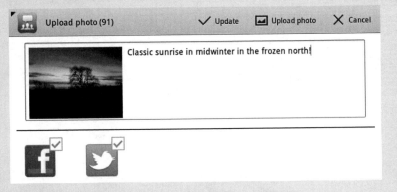

5. Type the text you want to upload with the photo.
6. Clear the Facebook check box or the Twitter check box if you don't want to upload the photo to that account.
7. Tap the Update button. Social Hub uploads the photo to the service you chose.

Keep Up with Friends on Facebook

If you're a member of Facebook, you'll likely want to use the Galaxy Tab to keep up to date with your friends. You can do so in three ways:

- Access Facebook through Social Hub
- Access the Facebook web site in the Browser app (or another browser)
- Install the Facebook app

Access Facebook Through Social Hub

If your Galaxy Tab includes Social Hub, you can add your Facebook account to Social Hub and access Facebook along with your other social networking services. You'll probably find this the easiest and most convenient way of accessing Facebook.

If your Galaxy Tab doesn't have Social Hub, and you can't get it, you'll need to use one of the other two options. Read on.

Access the Facebook Web Site in a Browser

The next most straightforward way to use Facebook on the Galaxy Tab is to access the Facebook web site in the Browser app—or, if you prefer, another browser such as Skyfire or Dolphin. You can then log in and use Facebook just as you would on any other computer. The disadvantage is that the Facebook content isn't optimized for the Galaxy Tab's screen, so you may need to scroll and zoom to see what you want.

Install and Run the Facebook App

If you use Facebook a lot on the Galaxy Tab, and you either can't get Social Hub or don't like it, you can probably save time and effort by installing and running the Facebook app. The advantage of the Facebook app is that it's optimized for Android devices (such as the Galaxy Tab) rather than for browsers in general, so it presents the information in chunks that work on a smaller screen.

The Facebook app is free, and you can uninstall it in moments, so you have nothing to lose but your time by trying it out—but there's one key decision you'll need to make, as you'll see in a moment.

 See Chapter 12 for detailed instructions on installing and uninstalling apps.

Install the Facebook App

To get the Facebook app, launch the Market app from the Apps screen, search for **Facebook**, and then choose the Facebook For Android result. When the download completes, you can run the app either from the notifications panel or from the Apps screen as usual.

When you run the Facebook app for the first time, it displays the Login screen. Type your e-mail address and password, and then tap the Login button.

Choose Whether to Sync Your Facebook Friends with Your Contacts

At this point, the Facebook app gives you a choice that needs careful attention. The Contacts Sync screen (shown here) asks whether you want to add Facebook pictures, status, and contact information to the Galaxy Tab's Contacts:

Contacts Sync	Sync
Add Facebook pictures, status, and contact info to Contacts?	
Sync all Sync data about all friends to Contacts	◉
Sync with existing contacts Sync data only about friends already in Contacts	◉
Don't sync Use information about friends only in Facebook	◉
You can change this later in Facebook Settings.	

- **Sync All** Select this option button to sync data about all your Facebook friends to the Contacts app.

Because syncing your Facebook friends with your contacts in the Galaxy Tab's Contacts list changes your contacts in a way that you can't undo by uninstalling the Facebook app, you may prefer to wait until you've decided that you want to keep using the Facebook app. If so, choose the Don't Sync option button on the Contacts Sync screen. As the screen mentions, you can change this setting later in the Settings area of Facebook—but if you've already synced your contacts with your friends, untangling the information is tricky.

- **Sync With Existing Contacts** Select this option button to have the Facebook app compare your list of friends to your list of contacts, and sync only information for those friends who are in your Contacts list.
- **Don't Sync** Select this option button to keep your Facebook friends separate from your contacts.

Tap the Done button when you've made your choice.

Enjoy Facebook with the Facebook App

Once you get into the Facebook app, it's easy to use. These are the main moves you'll need:

- Tap the Facebook logo at the top of any screen to display the home screen.
- Tap the button in the upper-left corner of the home screen to display a screen of Favorites, Lists, and Apps that you can quickly jump to (see Figure 9-4).
- To choose settings for the Facebook app, tap the Menu button (the button with three lines, fifth from the left) at the bottom of the screen, and then tap the Settings button. On the Settings screen (see Figure 9-5), you can change the refresh interval (from 30 Minutes to 4 Hours—or Never); choose whether to receive notifications and, if so, specify which items to notify you about and which forms of notification to use (vibration, the Galaxy Tab's flash flashing, or a ringtone); and sync your contacts by tapping the Sync Contacts button. Tap the Back button when you finish choosing settings.
- To refresh a screen with the latest data, tap the Menu button at the bottom of the screen, and then tap the Refresh button on the menu panel.

To log out of Facebook *and remove your Facebook data from the Galaxy Tab*, tap the Menu button from the home screen, and then tap the Logout button. Tap the Yes button in the Logout dialog box that appears.

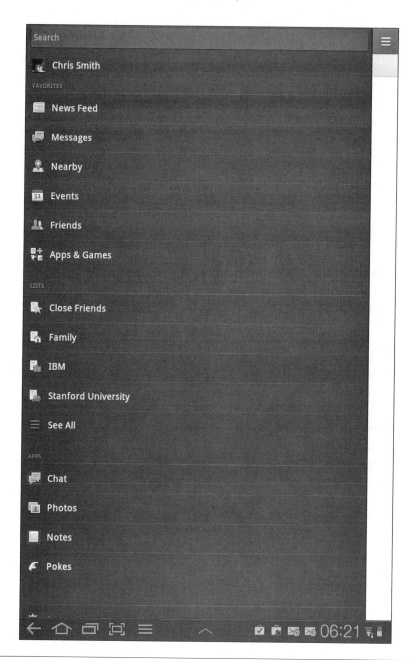

FIGURE 9-4   Tap the button at the upper-left corner of the Facebook app to quickly access any of the main areas of Facebook.

Settings	
General settings	
Refresh interval 1 hour	
Notifications Active	☑
Notification settings	
Messages	☑
Friend requests	☑
Event invites	☑
Vibrate Vibrate on incoming notifications	☐
Phone LED Flash LED on incoming notifications	☐
Notification ringtone Set your notification ringtone	
Other settings	
Sync Contacts Don't sync	

FIGURE 9-5 On the Settings screen for the Facebook app, you can choose which notifications to receive, and even set a ringtone for Facebook notifications.

Keep Up with Business on LinkedIn

Facebook rules the social networking roost at this writing, but the king of the business side of social networking is LinkedIn. If you have a LinkedIn account, you'll likely want to access LinkedIn from the Galaxy Tab to stay in touch with what's happening.

If your Galaxy Tab has Social Hub, you can connect to LinkedIn through it, as discussed at the beginning of this chapter.

If your Galaxy Tab doesn't have Social Hub, you can access LinkedIn by using the Browser app (or another browser), just like you can on most any computer. This is fine for light use, but if you plan to use LinkedIn extensively on the Galaxy Tab, download and install the free LinkedIn Mobile app, which presents LinkedIn data in a Galaxy Tab–friendly format.

Install the LinkedIn App

To get the LinkedIn app, launch the Market app from the Apps screen, search for **LinkedIn**, and then choose the LinkedIn result from LinkedIn. When the download completes, you can run the app either from the notifications panel or from the Apps screen as usual.

Make sure you get the LinkedIn app from LinkedIn—there are other apps with LinkedIn-related names, but this is the one you want.

When you run the LinkedIn app for the first time, it displays the login screen (shown here). Type your e-mail address and password, and then tap the Sign In button.

LinkedIn then displays the Sync LinkedIn Contacts dialog box (shown here), asking if you want to sync your LinkedIn contacts with your existing contacts. Tap the Sync All option button, the Sync With Existing Contacts option button, or the Do Not Sync LinkedIn Contacts option button, as appropriate.

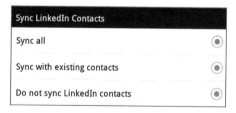

Use the LinkedIn App

After you sign in, LinkedIn displays the home page, the top of which appears in Figure 9-6. From here, you can quickly search using the Search box or access one of the main areas of LinkedIn by tapping its button at the top of the screen. For example, tap the You button to display your profile, or tap the Inbox button to display your inbox.

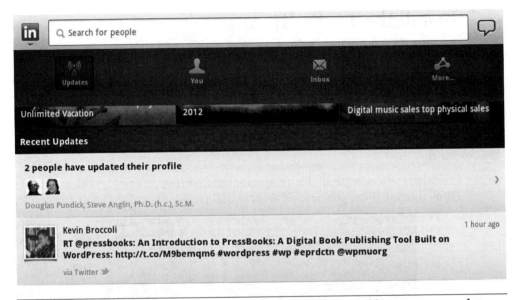

FIGURE 9-6 From the LinkedIn home screen, you can quickly view your updates (shown here), your profile, your inbox, or other items.

Keep Up with News on Twitter

If you want to keep up with the latest happenings, and share your own, you'll almost certainly want to use Twitter on the Galaxy Tab.

If your Galaxy Tab has Social Hub, you can connect to Twitter through it, as discussed at the beginning of this chapter. This is normally the most convenient way to use Twitter, because you can keep up with all your social networking accounts at the same time.

If you don't have Social Hub, you can access the Twitter web site using the Galaxy Tab's built-in Browser, or any other browser you choose to install, but you'll be able to get more out of Twitter by using the free Twitter app for the Android operating system.

Install the Twitter App

To get the Twitter app, launch the Market app from the Apps screen, search for **Twitter**, and then choose the Twitter result. When the download completes, you can run the app either from the notifications panel or from the Apps screen.

Log In and Use Twitter

The first time you run the Twitter app, it displays the Welcome To Twitter screen. Tap the Sign In button to display the Sign In screen (shown here), type your user name (or your e-mail address) and password, and then tap the Sign In button.

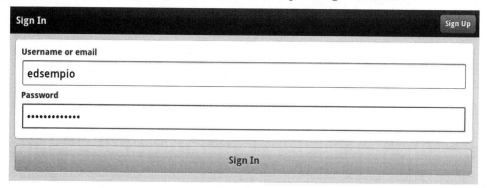

Once you've signed in, the Twitter app displays the home screen (the top part of which is shown in Figure 9-7), on which you can read the latest tweets. From here, you can quickly access the other main areas of Twitter. For example:

FIGURE 9-7   On the Twitter home screen, you can quickly catch up with the latest tweets.

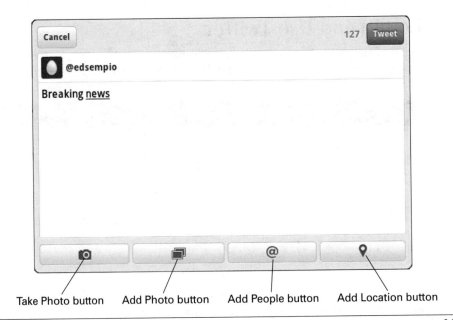

Take Photo button   Add Photo button   Add People button   Add Location button

FIGURE 9-8   In the dialog box for creating a tweet, you can type a text tweet, add an existing photo, take a new photo, add people, or add your location.

- Tap the Compose button in the upper-right corner of the screen at the top of the screen to display the dialog box for creating a tweet (see Figure 9-8). You can then type a text tweet, take a picture by tapping the Take Photo button, add an existing photo by tapping the Add Photo button, add people by tapping the Add People button, or add your location by tapping the Add Location button.
- Tap the Connect button to connect to other people.
- Tap the Discover button to search by a hashtag or keyword.
- Tap the Me button to review or update your profile. To change your profile photo, tap the Edit Profile button, and then tap the Change Profile Photo button on the Edit Profile screen.

Choose Settings for the Twitter App

You can use Twitter with the Twitter app's default settings, but to make Twitter work your way, you'll probably want to tweak the settings. To open the Settings screen (shown in Figure 9-9), follow these steps:

1. Go to the Twitter app's home screen. (You may need to tap the Back button to get to the home screen.)
2. Tap the Menu button to display the menu panel.
3. Tap the Settings button.

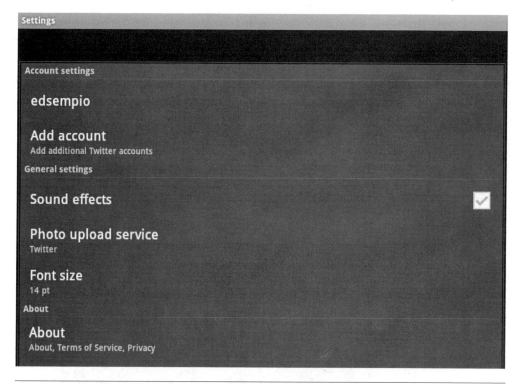

FIGURE 9-9   From the Twitter app's Settings screen, you can choose General
settings such as whether to get sound effects, which photo-upload
service to use, and which font size to display.

You can set the following settings in the General Settings area:

- **Sound Effects**   Select this check box if you want the Twitter app to play sound
  effects at you.
- **Photo Upload Service**   To choose which photo-upload service the Twitter
  app uses, tap this button, and then tap the Twitter option button, the TwitPic
  option button, or the yfrog option button in the Photo Upload Service dialog box
  (shown here).

- **Font Size** To change the font size the Twitter app uses, tap this button, and then tap the appropriate option button in the Font Size dialog box. Your choices run from smallish 13-point font to largish 20-point font.

To choose account-specific settings, tap the account's button in the Account Settings area, and then work on the screen for that account (see Figure 9-10). You can choose four categories of settings:

- **Sync Settings** Select the Sync Data check box if you want to sync data. Then tap the Sync Interval button to display the Sync Interval dialog box, and then tap the option button for the interval you want—anything from 5 Minutes to 4 Hours.
- **Notifications** Select the check box for each type of notification you want—Tweets, Mentions, or Messages.
- **Notification Indicators** Select the Vibrate check box if you want the Galaxy Tab to vibrate when you receive a Twitter notification. Tap the Ringtone button to display the Ringtones dialog box, tap the option button for the ringtone you'd

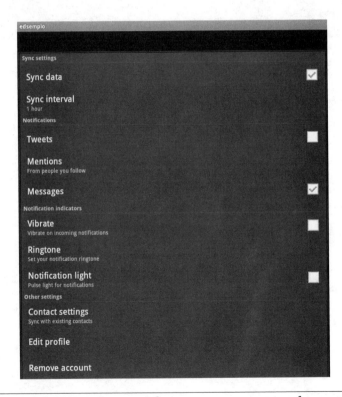

FIGURE 9-10 On the Settings screen for an account, you can choose sync settings, notification settings, notification indicators, and whether to sync with your existing contacts.

like to hear when a notification hits, and then tap the OK button. Select the Notification Light check box if you want the Galaxy Tab's flash to flash in warning.

- **Other Settings**   To choose how the Twitter app syncs your contacts, tap the Contact Settings button, and then tap the appropriate option button in the Contact Settings dialog box (shown here).

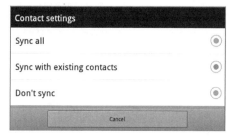

Sign Out of Twitter and Remove Twitter Data from the Galaxy Tab

If you want to sign out of Twitter *and remove the Twitter data from the Galaxy Tab*, tap the Remove Account button in the Other Settings area of the Settings screen for the account. The Twitter app displays the Sign Out dialog box (shown here), warning you that signing out will remove your Twitter data from the Galaxy Tab. Tap the OK button to sign out and remove the data.

10

Stay in Touch with Instant Messaging

HOW TO...

- Open the Messaging app
- Choose settings for instant messaging
- Send instant messages
- Import text into an instant message
- Receive instant messages
- Protect an instant message against deletion
- Forward instant messages
- Delete instant messages

In this chapter, I'll show you how to make the most of the powerful instant-messaging features the Galaxy Tab offers. You'll learn how to send instant messages, receive them, forward them, and delete them when you've had enough of them.

As with many apps, you can start with the default settings for the Messaging app if you like, but most people find it a good idea to customize the settings. We'll cover this topic first—after we open the Messaging app.

Open the Messaging App

To open the Messaging app, go to the home screen, tap the Apps button, and then tap the Messaging icon.

 If you plan to use instant messaging frequently, add the Messaging icon to one of your home screen panels.

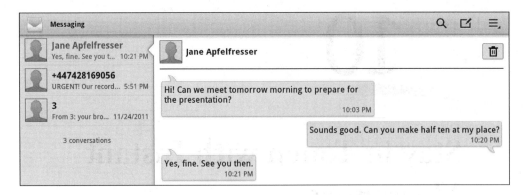

FIGURE 10-1 The Messaging app shows the list of threads (conversations) on the left and the messages in the selected thread on the right.

Figure 10-1 shows the Messaging app open in landscape mode. As you can see, the list of *threads* (conversations) appears on the left, and the messages in the selected thread appear on the right.

Choose Settings for Instant Messaging

To choose settings for instant messaging, open the Settings screen like this:

1. Launch the Messaging app if it's not already open.
2. Tap the Menu button to display the menu panel.
3. Tap the Settings button.

Figure 10-2 shows the upper part of the Settings screen. Figure 10-3 shows the lower part.

Choose Storage Settings for Messaging

In the Storage Settings area of the Settings screen for the Messaging app, you can set these three settings:

- **Delete Old Messages** Select this check box to have the Messaging app automatically delete old messages as soon as you reach the text message limit (see the next paragraph).
- **Text Message Limit** Look at the readout of messages per text thread. If you need to change it, tap the Text Message Limit button, adjust the value in the Text Message Limit dialog box (shown here), and then tap the Set button.

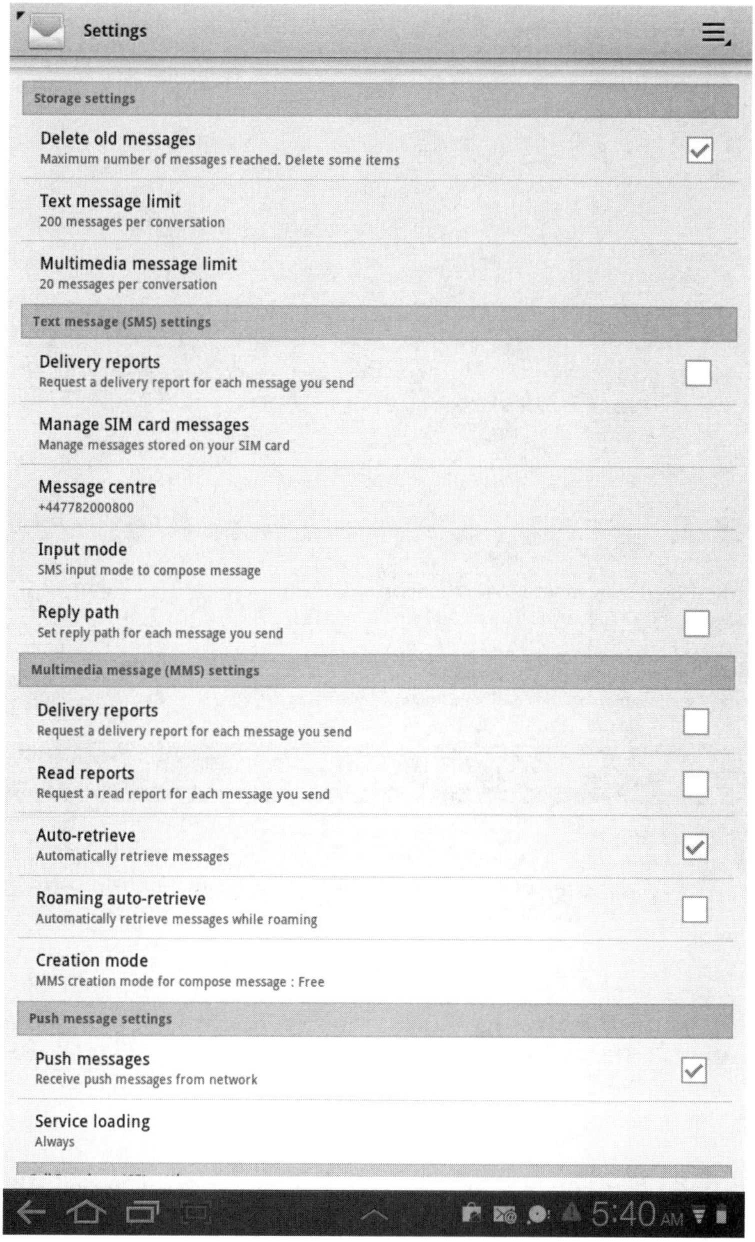

FIGURE 10-2   On the upper part of the Settings screen for the Messaging app, you can set storage settings, text message settings, multimedia message settings, and push message settings.

Cell Broadcast (CB) settings

CB activation
Allows you to receive CB messages

Channel configuration

Language
9 languages allowed

Notification settings

Notifications
Display message notifications in status bar

Select ringtone

Text-to-speech settings

Read out new message notification
New message notifications will be read out automatically

Read out message contents
Message contents will be read out automatically

5:40 AM

FIGURE 10-3 On the lower part of the Settings screen for the Messaging app, you can set Cell Broadcast settings, notification settings, and text-to-speech settings.

- **Multimedia Message Limit** Look at the readout of messages per multimedia thread. If you need to change it, tap the Multimedia Message Limit button, adjust the value in the Multimedia Message Limit dialog box, and then tap the Set button.

 Because text messages are small, you can set a large number (for example, several hundred messages) for the Text Message Limit without taking up much space on the Galaxy Tab. But because multimedia messages can be large, it's a good idea to set a much smaller number for the Multimedia Message Limit—for example, 10 messages.

Choose Text Message (SMS) Settings

In the Text Message (SMS) Settings area of the Settings screen for the Messaging app, you can set the following settings:

- **Delivery Reports**   Select this check box if you want to get a delivery report confirming that each text message you send has arrived. Normally, delivery reports are overkill, especially if your targets tend to text you back. But you may sometimes find this feature useful.

A delivery report appears as a notification titled "Delivery report:" in the notifications area. If you open the notifications panel, you see the delivery report—for example, "Delivery report: Peter Piper: Delivered 9:20 AM." You can tap the delivery report's button in the notifications panel to jump to the thread in the Messaging app.

- **Manage SIM Card Messages**   If your SIM card has messages stored on it, you can tap this button to display a screen for managing them.
- **Message Center**   To change the phone number used for the Message Center, tap this button, type the number in the Set Message Center dialog box, and then tap the OK button.
- **Input Mode**   To change the input mode the Messaging app uses, tap this button to display the Select Input Mode dialog box (shown here), and then select the GSM Alphabet option button, the Unicode option button, or the Automatic option button, as needed. (If this is gibberish to you, see the next Note.)

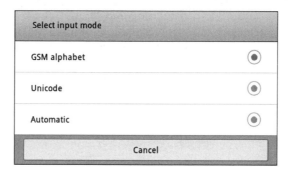

GSM is the abbreviation for Global System for Mobile Communications, a series of standards that includes a standard for SMS. For the input mode, GSM means using a 7-bit alphabet, which provides enough characters for English and most main Western languages but not for languages that use many different characters. Unicode has many more characters than GSM. Normally, you're best off using GSM unless you have a reason to use Unicode.

- **Reply Path** Select this check box if you want to ensure that any reply the recipient sends comes through the same message center that you sent your message through. Normally, you don't need to do this—getting the reply via any available message center works fine.

Choose Multimedia Message (MMS) Settings

In the Multimedia Message (MMS) Settings area of the Settings screen for the Messaging app, you can set the following settings:

- **Delivery Reports** Select this check box if you want to get a delivery report confirming that each MMS message you send has arrived. Usually, this isn't necessary—especially if you expect to receive replies to your messages.
- **Read Reports** Select this check box if you want to receive a read report when a recipient opens an MMS message you've sent. Given that MMS messages tend to travel much more slowly than plain text messages because of their bulk, getting read reports can be useful.
- **Auto-Retrieve** Select this check box if you want the Messaging app to automatically retrieve MMS messages. Clear this check box if you want to control when the Galaxy Tab picks up the messages.
- **Roaming Auto-Retrieve** Select this check box if you want the Messaging app to automatically retrieve MMS messages when you're roaming on other data networks. Because retrieving the messages while roaming may rack up extra charges, you may prefer to keep this check box cleared and retrieve the messages manually when it's convenient.
- **Creation Mode** To control the MMS creation mode the Messaging app uses for creating messages, tap this button, and then tap the appropriate option button in the Select Creation Mode dialog box (shown here). Your choices are

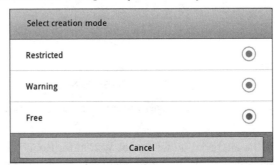

- **Restricted** Choose this option button to restrict messages' sizes and contents to the guidelines in the message class.
- **Warning** Choose this option button to be able to create messages with larger sizes and different content than the guidelines approve, but to have the Messaging app warn you that the messages may not transfer successfully.
- **Free** Choose this option button to be able to make messages as large as you want or to include the content types you want.

Choose Push Message Settings

In the Push Message Settings area of the Settings screen for the Messaging app, you can set these two settings:

- **Push Messages**   Select this check box to have messages "pushed" from the messaging server to your Galaxy Tab when the messages are received. Clear this check box if you prefer the messages to wait at the server until you check for messages.
- **Service Loading**   Tap this button to display the Service Loading dialog box (shown here). You can then control service loading by tapping the Always option button, the Prompt option button (which prompts you to load services), or the Never option button. Tapping the option button closes the dialog box.

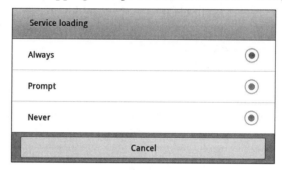

Choose Cell Broadcast (CB) Settings

Cell Broadcast (CB) is a feature that carriers use to broadcast messages to all the cell phones connected to base stations in a particular area. Beyond sharing an abbreviation, it has nothing to do with the Citizens' Band widely used by truckers in the 1980s. If your Galaxy Tab model doesn't have 3G capability, you won't see the Cell Broadcast settings.

Normally, you won't need to turn on the Cell Broadcast feature unless you're in an area where you expect warnings to be broadcast—for example, because you're expecting to experience an earthquake, hurricane, tropical storm, tsunami, or other form of elemental retaliation against humanity's relentless spread.

In the Cell Broadcast (CB) Settings area of the Settings screen for the Messaging app, you can set the following settings:

- **CB Activation**   Select this check box if you want to turn on the Cell Broadcast feature so that you can receive messages your carrier broadcasts to all the cell phones in the area you happen to be in.

- **Channel Configuration** If you select the CB Activation check box, you can tap this button to display the Channel Configuration screen, on which you can set up Cell Broadcast channels. Here, you can tap the Receiving Channel button, and then tap the All Channels option button (normally the best choice) or the My Channel option button (for when you have a hotline to authorities) in the Receiving Channel dialog box. If you choose the My Channel option button, tap the Add Channel button in the My Channels list, and then use the Add Channel dialog box to specify the channel name and number.
- **Language** If you select the CB Activation check box, you can tap this button to display the Language screen, and then select the check box for each language in which you want to receive the Cell Broadcast alerts.

Choose Notification Settings

In the Notification Settings area of the Settings screen for the Messaging app, you can set the following settings:

- **Notifications** Select this check box to make the Galaxy Tab display notifications of incoming messages in the notifications bar. This is usually helpful.
- **Select Ringtone** Tap this button to display the Ringtones screen, on which you can select exactly the right ringtone for instant messages.

Choose Text-to-Speech Settings

In the Text-to-Speech area of the Settings screen for the Messaging app, you can set these settings:

- **Read Out New Message Notification** Select this check box to have the Galaxy Tab automatically read out new message notifications.
- **Read Out Message Contents** If you select the Read Out New Message Notification check box, you can select this check box to have the Galaxy Tab read out the content of messages as well.

When you've finished choosing settings on the Settings screen, tap the Back button to return to the Messaging screen.

 How to... **Reset Your Messaging Settings to Their Defaults**

If you mess up your settings for the Messaging app, don't worry—you can quickly reset them to their defaults.

To reset the settings, open the Settings screen, tap the Menu button, and tap Restore Default Settings.

Send Instant Messages

To send a new instant message, follow these steps:

1. From the Messaging app's main screen, tap the New Message button (the button that shows a sheet of paper and a pen or an envelope and a pen, depending on your Galaxy Tab model). The Messaging app displays the New Message screen, the top part of which appears in the next illustration.

2. With the focus in the To area, enter the recipient's name in one of these ways:
   - **Start typing the name or number**   When the Messaging app displays a list of matching contacts, as shown here, tap the correct one. Use this method to quickly add contacts one at a time.

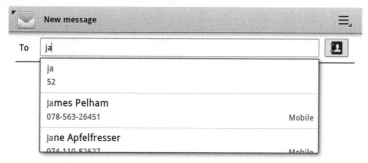

   - **Choose from your Contacts**   Tap the Contacts button (the button to the right of the To box) to open the Contacts app, and then select the check box for each contact you want to include. For example, tap the Contacts tab to display your full list of contacts, and then select check boxes there, as shown in the next illustration. Tap the Done button when you've finished selecting recipients. Use this method to quickly address a message to multiple people.

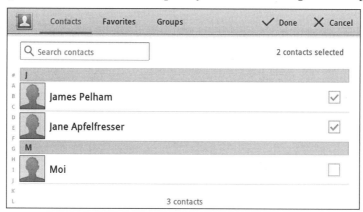

- **Type the whole number** To send a message to someone who's not a contact, type in the whole phone number.

3. Tap the Enter Message Here box at the bottom of the screen (as shown in the next illustration), and then enter the message. You can type it in using the keyboard, paste in text you've copied from elsewhere, or import it from a contact record, a calendar event, or a memo (see the nearby sidebar "Import Text into an Instant Message" for details).

4. If you want to give the message a subject, follow these steps:
   a. Tap the Menu button to display the menu panel.
   b. Tap the Add Subject button to display the subject box above the message box.
   c. Type in the subject for the message.

5. If you want to attach a file to the message, tap the Attach button (the paperclip icon) to display the Attach dialog box (shown here). Tap the button for the attachment type you want, and then use the resulting screen to attach the item. For example, tap the Capture Picture button to launch the Camera app, take the photo, and then tap the Save button.

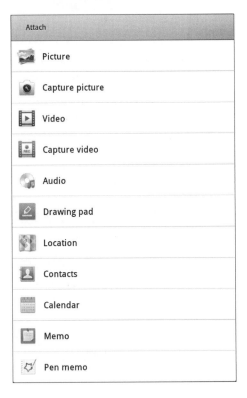

After you create a multimedia message, tap the Preview button to get a better idea of how the message will look to the recipient. If you don't like the effect, tap the attachment to select it, and then tap the Delete button on the keyboard to remove it.

6. When you finish the message, tap the Send button to send it.

If you tap the Back button while creating a message, the Messaging app stores the message as a draft. You can then open the message again from the main Messaging screen when you're ready to continue working on it.

How to...   # Import Text into an Instant Message

You can quickly import text into an instant message from your contacts, your calendar, or your memos. This is a great way of saving time and effort when one of these sources contains the information you want to put in the instant message.

To import text into an instant message, follow these steps:

1. Start the instant message as usual.
2. Tap the text field.
3. Tap the Menu button to display the menu panel.
4. Tap the Import Text button to display the Import Text dialog box (shown here).

Import text
Location
Contacts
Calendar
Memo

5. Tap the button for the source of the information:
   - **Location**   Tap this button to display a map, and then tap the location you want to add to the message.
   - **Contacts**   Tap this button to display your Contacts list. Tap the contact you want, and then select the check box for each piece of information you want to import—for example, the contact's name, e-mail address, and phone number. Then tap the Done button.
   - **Calendar**   Tap this button to display your calendar. Select the check box for each event whose details you want to import, and then tap the Add button.
   - **Memo**   Tap this button to display your memos. Select the check box for each memo you want to import, and then tap the Done button.

Receive Instant Messages

When you receive an instant message, the Galaxy Tab plays the incoming message sound (if you've set one, as described earlier in this chapter) and displays the first part of the message's text in the notifications area, as shown here.

Tap the notifications area to display the notification panel, and then tap the message's button in the panel to jump straight to the message in its thread in the Messaging app (see Figure 10-4). If you want to move even faster, tap the Reply button contained in the message's button to start a reply and display it so that you can continue.

FIGURE 10-4 Open an instant message in its thread in the Messaging app so that you can read the message's full text in context and reply to it if necessary.

To reply to the message, tap in the text box at the bottom (which shows the prompt Enter Message Here), type your message, and then tap the Send button. Your replies appear as a conversation, as shown here.

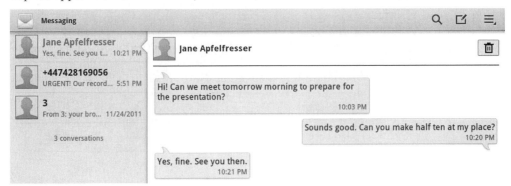

If you want to change the size of the font the Messaging app uses for the conversation bubbles, tap the Menu button to display the menu panel, and then tap the Font Size button to display the Font Size dialog box. Tap the Smallest option button, the Smaller option button, the Medium option button, the Larger option button, or the Largest option button, as needed.

How to... Protect an Instant Message Against Deletion

If you want to make sure you don't delete a particular instant message by accident, apply protection to it. Follow these steps:

1. Open the message in its thread.
2. Tap the message and hold down until the Message Options dialog box (shown here) appears.
3. Tap the Protection On button. The Messaging app closes the Message Options dialog box and displays a lock icon at the bottom of the message, as shown here.

Message options
Forward
Delete message
Copy message text
Copy to SIM
Protection on
Details

The unlock key for the file is LVFY75$@Fz (case sensitive).
🔒 5:46 AM

When you need to remove protection from the message, repeat these steps, but this time tap the Protection Off button.

Forward Instant Messages

To forward an instant message, follow these steps:

1. Open the message in its thread.
2. Tap the message you want to forward and hold down until the Message Options dialog box opens.
3. Tap the Forward button to display the New Message dialog box (shown here).

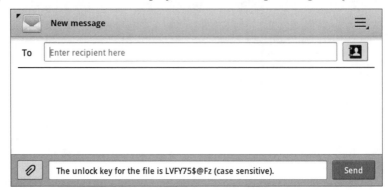

4. Enter the recipient or recipients for the forwarded message by typing in the To text box or by selecting from your Contacts list.
5. Tap the Send button to send the message.
6. Tap the option button for the message you want to forward.
7. Tap the Forward button. The Messaging app opens a new message that incorporates the forwarded message.
8. Address the message, and then send it as usual.

Delete Instant Messages

Did you know the average American teenager sends an average of seven instant messages per waking hour? And the number is rising relentlessly.

Even if you're slacking on the texting front, you'll probably need to delete your old threads so that the Messaging app isn't swamped with them. You can delete either an entire thread or just some of the messages from a thread.

Delete an Entire Thread

To delete a thread, follow these steps:

1. From the main Messaging screen, tap the Menu button to display the menu panel.
2. Tap the Delete Threads button. The Messaging app displays a check box to the right of each thread.

3. Select the check box for each thread you want to delete.
4. Tap the Delete button. The Messaging app displays the Delete dialog box shown here.
5. Select the Include Protected Message check box if you want to delete protected messages as well as regular messages.

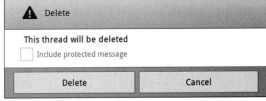

6. Tap the Delete button. The Messaging app deletes the thread or threads.

Delete Messages from a Thread

To delete just some of the messages from a thread, follow these steps:

1. Tap the thread in the left column to display its messages.
2. Tap the Delete button, the one with the trashcan icon in the upper-right corner of the screen. The Messaging app displays a check box to the right of each message in the thread (see Figure 10-5).
3. Select the check box for each message you want to delete.
4. Tap the Delete button in the upper-right corner of the screen.

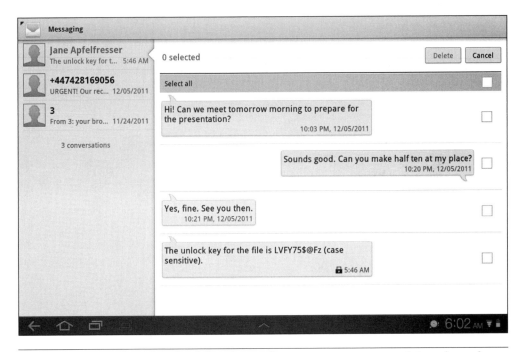

FIGURE 10-5   Select the check box for each message you want to delete from the thread, and then tap the Delete button.

11

Read e-Books, Newspapers, and Magazines on Your Galaxy Tab

HOW TO...

- Read e-books and PDF files using the eBook app
- Create e-books and PDF files from your own documents
- Read newspaper and magazine articles with the Pulse newsreader

In this chapter, we'll look at how to enjoy e-books, newspapers, and magazines on your Galaxy Tab.

Most Galaxy Tab models include the eBook app for reading e-books and PDF files and the Pulse newsreader for keeping up with news. If your Galaxy Tab doesn't have these apps, you can download either these apps or similar apps from Android Market.

 Your Galaxy Tab may also include the Amazon Kindle app, which you can use to get books from Amazon's online store. Amazon has a huge selection of free books as well as books you must pay for, so you may want to install the Kindle app if your Galaxy Tab doesn't already have it. Some Galaxy Tab models also come with an app called Readers Hub, which gives you access to a selection of newspapers, magazines, and books.

Read e-Books and PDF Files Using the eBook App

The best place to get started with reading e-books on your Galaxy Tab is to use the eBook app that comes with it. With this app, you can buy e-books online, find free books online, or load e-books you acquire from other sources. You can also read PDF files, which is a great way of catching up on white papers and similar reading.

FIGURE 11-1 The eBook app displays your books and PDF files on a virtual bookshelf.

Launch the eBook App

To launch the eBook app, tap and hold the Recent Applications button until the Apps screen appears, and then tap the eBook icon. The eBook app launches and displays your bookshelf with an icon for each book it contains. Figure 11-1 shows the bookshelf with a modest population of books and PDF files. This view is called Icon view.

When you first launch the eBook app, your bookshelf may contain only sample books, or it may be completely bare. If you need to add books or PDF files immediately, see the section "Import Books and PDF Files into the eBook App," later in this chapter, for instructions.

Find the Book or PDF You Want to Read

If your bookshelf contains only a few books or PDF files, as in Figure 11-1, you can see all of them at once, and you'll have no difficulty finding the book or PDF file you want to read.

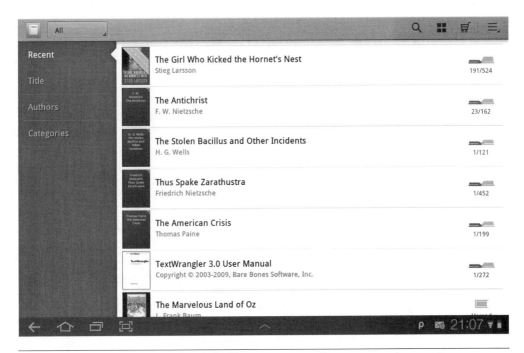

FIGURE 11-2   Switch your bookshelf to List view when you need to navigate quickly through your books and PDF files.

If your bookshelf is full of books and PDF files, use these moves to find the one you want:

- **Scroll**   If your bookshelf is too long to fit on the screen all at once, scroll down to see the rest of it.
- **Switch to List view**   To navigate a long list of books or PDF files more easily, tap the List view button, the third button from the right on the toolbar. The eBook app displays your books and PDF files in List view, as shown in Figure 11-2. You can filter the books and PDF files by tapping the Recent button, the Title button, the Authors button, or the Categories button in the left pane.
- **Display only books or only PDF files**   Tap the drop-down menu in the upper-left corner of the eBook app's screen, and then tap the Book item or the PDF item, as needed. To switch back to displaying all items, tap the drop-down menu again, and then tap the All item.

When you find the book or PDF file you want to read, tap it to open it.

How to... **Choose Between the ePub e-Book Format and PDF Format for Putting Your Own Documents on the Galaxy Tab**

If you enjoy reading using the eBook app, you'll probably want to put your own files on the Galaxy Tab to read. You can do this by creating either ePub files or PDF files.

Choosing between the two formats can be difficult. ePub files are harder to create, but they contain the text in a way in which the eBook app can resize and reflow it as needed. Being able to change the font size—and the font if you like—makes reading much easier.

PDF files are easier to create, but because the PDF format is essentially a picture of the laid-out document, a reader app such as the eBook app can't change the layout, the fonts, or the font size. When viewing a PDF, you can zoom in to make the text larger, but when you have zoomed in, you may need to scroll around the page to see different parts of it.

I'll show you how to create both ePub files and PDF files from your own documents later in this chapter.

Read a Book or PDF File in the eBook App

After you tap a book or PDF file on your bookshelf, the eBook app opens it at the beginning (if you haven't opened it before) or at the place you last stopped reading. You can then start reading—you don't need me to tell you how to do that—and turn the page by dragging your finger from the right side of the screen to the left (see Figure 11-3).

Note When you're reading an e-book, the eBook app animates the page turn, as shown in Figure 11-3. When you're reading a PDF file, there's no animation.

When you need to annotate the page, change how it appears, or take other actions, tap the page to bring up the reading controls shown in Figure 11-4. You can then take the following actions:

- **Highlighter** Tap this button to turn on the Highlighter, and then tap and drag to highlight text. Tap the button again when you're ready to turn off the Highlighter.

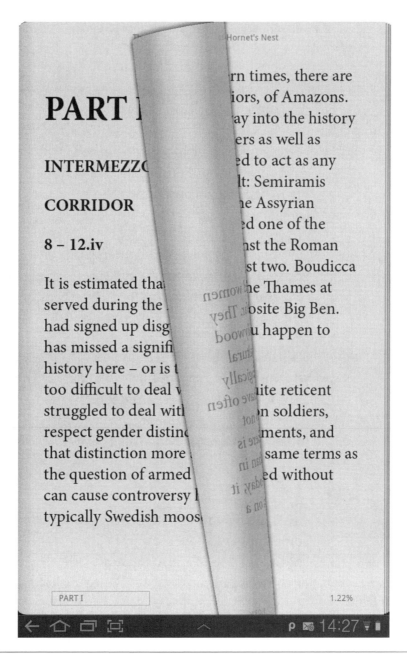

FIGURE 11-3   Drag your finger from the right side of the screen to the left to turn the page forward. Drag the other way to turn the page back.

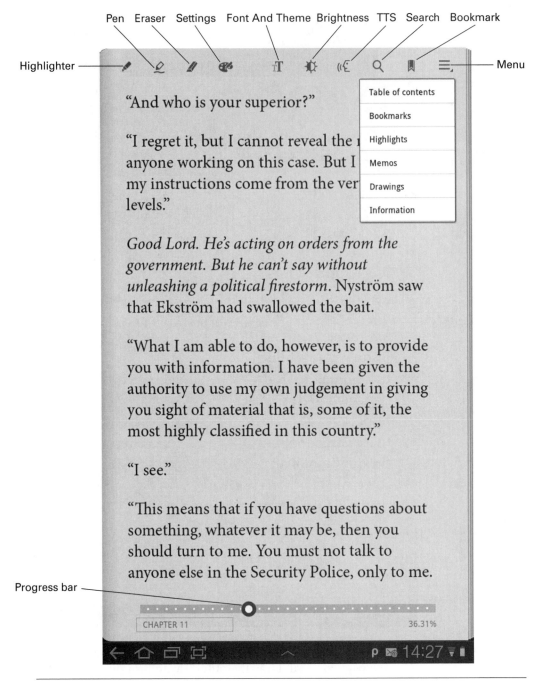

FIGURE 11-4 Tap the screen to display the controls at the top and the bottom.

- **Pen**   Tap this button to turn on the Pen, with which you can draw on the page. Tap this button again to turn the Pen off.
- **Eraser**   Tap this button to turn on the Eraser. With the Eraser on, tap the highlighting or pen annotation you want to remove. Tap the Eraser button again when you want to turn the Eraser off.
- **Settings**   Tap this button to display the Settings dialog box (shown here), in which you can choose the pen thickness, style, and color, and the highlight color. Tap the Settings button again when you're ready to close the Settings dialog box.

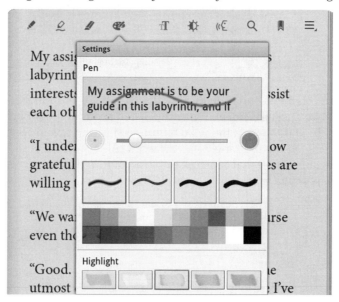

- **Font And Theme**   Tap this button to display the Font And Theme dialog box (shown here), and then choose the font size and the theme you want. Select the Page Turn Sound check box if you want the eBook app to play a sound when you turn a page. Tap the Font And Theme button again to close the Font And Theme dialog box.

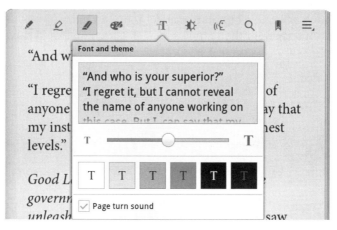

- **Brightness** Tap this button to display the Brightness dialog box (shown here), and then drag the slider until the brightness is the way you like it. Select the Automatic Brightness check box if you want the eBook app to adjust the brightness automatically to suit the light conditions. Tap the Brightness button again to close the Brightness dialog box.

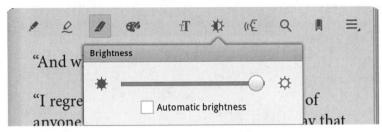

- **TTS** Tap this button to display the TTS dialog box (shown here; TTS stands for Text To Speech). Tap and drag the Speed slider and the Pitch slider to your desired levels, and then tap the Read button to start the text-to-speech reading. Getting the speed and the pitch right can be awkward, because you must stop playback (tap the Stop button that replaces the Read button) to change them. Tap the TTS button when you're ready to close the TTS dialog box.

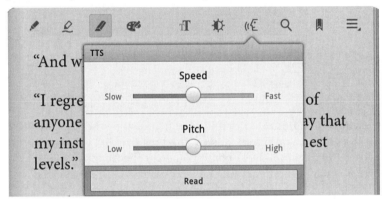

- **Search** Tap this button to display the Search dialog box (shown here), type your search term, and then tap Enter. The Search dialog displays matching results. Tap the result you want to see.

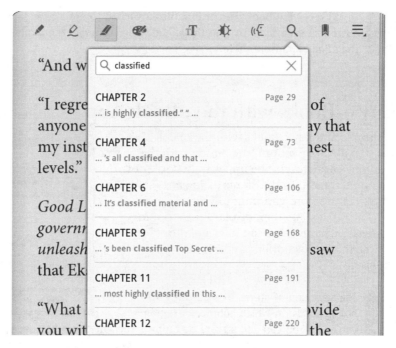

- **Bookmark**   Tap this button to place a bookmark at the current page. The bookmark indicator appears in the upper-right corner of the page. Tap the button again to remove an existing bookmark from this page.
- **Menu**   Tap this button to display the menu, shown in Figure 11-4, which provides commands for displaying the table of contents, your bookmarks, your highlights, your memos, your pen drawings, or the book's information (author, file format, size, and download date).
- **Progress bar**   Tap and drag the slider to change your place in the book swiftly.

To stop reading the book or PDF file, tap the Back button. The eBook app displays your bookshelf again, and you can tap another book or PDF file to open it.

Import Books and PDF Files into the eBook App

If you already have e-books or PDF files, you can quickly import them into the eBook app. Follow these steps:

1. In the eBook app, display the home screen.
2. Choose Menu | Import to display the My Files app.
3. Navigate to the folder that contains the file or files you want to add.
4. Select the check box for each file.
5. Tap the Done button. You'll see the e-books or PDF files appear on your bookshelf.

If you receive e-book files or PDF files attached to e-mail messages, tap the Save button to save them to your Download folder. You can then import the files into the eBook app from there.

Buy e-Books with the eBook App

To browse and buy e-books with the eBook app, tap the Shop button (the button with the shopping-cart icon) in the upper-right corner of the home screen. In the Stores dialog box (shown here), tap the store you want to visit.

The Galaxy Tab then displays the store in a browser window. You can navigate the store, browse the books it offers, and buy any you choose to.

 The selection of stores in the Stores dialog box depends on which country or region you're in. You can add a store by tapping the Add Store button, typing the name and URL in the New Store dialog box that opens, and then clicking the OK button. Conversely, you can remove a store from the Stores dialog box by tapping the Delete button, selecting the check box to the right of the store's name, and then tapping the Delete button.

Remove a Book or PDF File from the eBook App

To remove a book or PDF file from the eBook app, follow these steps:

1. Tap the Menu button to display the menu.
2. Tap the Edit item. The eBook app displays a – button at the upper-right corner of each book or PDF file, as shown here.

How to... Create Your Own e-Books in the ePub Format

If you like reading e-books on the Galaxy Tab, you may want to turn your own content into e-books so that you can easily read them. You can do so using commercial software you may already have or free software you can download from the Internet.

Here are four easy ways to create e-books in the ePub format on your computer:

- **LibreOffice with Writer2ePub plug-in**   LibreOffice (www.libreoffice.org) is the latest port of the free office suite originally called OpenOffice.org. By adding the Writer2ePub plug-in (http://extensions.services.openoffice.org/en/node/4615?), you can export documents from the Writer module of LibreOffice as ePub documents.
- **Adobe InDesign**   The Adobe InDesign layout desktop-publishing application includes a built-in feature for creating ePub documents. If you have InDesign, this will likely be your top choice for creating ePub documents; if not, InDesign is an expensive option, because it's aimed at the professional market.
- **Pages**   Apple's Pages application, which is part of the iWork productivity suite, includes a built-in feature for exporting a document in ePub format. If you have iWork, Pages should be your first choice for creating ePub documents; if not, Pages is relatively affordable, but it runs only on the Mac.
- **eCub**   eCub (www.juliansmart.com/ecub) is a free application for creating e-book files in formats that include ePub. eCub is cross-platform—it runs on Windows, Mac OS X, Linux, and other operating systems.

3. Tap the – button for the book or PDF file you want to delete. The eBook app displays the Delete dialog box shown here.

4. Tap the OK button.
5. When you finish deleting books or PDF files, tap the Done button on the toolbar.

How to... Create PDF Files from Windows Documents

Windows doesn't include a built-in feature for creating PDF files, so you need to add extra software if you want to create PDF files from your documents.

Here are the top three ways of creating PDF files on Windows:

- **Microsoft Office** Most versions of Microsoft Office include a command for creating PDF files from files such as Word documents. For example, in Microsoft Word 2010:
  1. Open the document.
  2. Choose File | Share to display the Share pane in Backstage view.
  3. Click the Create PDF/XPS Document item. The Create A PDF/XPS Document pane appears.
  4. Click the Create A PDF/XPS button. The Publish As PDF Or XPS dialog box appears.
  5. In the Save As Type drop-down list, choose PDF.
  6. Specify the filename and location.
  7. Click the Publish button.
- **Freeware tools** You can find various freeware tools on the Internet for creating PDF files on Windows. Try CutePDF Writer (www.cutepdf.com/products/cutepdf/writer.asp) or PDFCreator (www.pdfforge.org/pdfcreator).
- **Adobe Acrobat** Adobe Acrobat is professional-grade software for creating and editing PDF files. Unfortunately, Acrobat has a professional-grade price too—Acrobat X Standard costs $299 and Acrobat X Professional costs $449—so it's worth considering only if you create and edit many PDF files.

How to... Create PDF Files on Mac OS X

Mac OS X includes a built-in feature for creating PDF files, so you can easily create a PDF file from just about any document you can view onscreen. This is a great way to create PDF files for viewing in the eBook app.

To create a PDF file from a document, follow these steps:

1. Open the document in the application you usually use for it. For example, fire up Microsoft Word, and then open the Word document you want to create a PDF file from.
2. Choose File | Print—or press the standard ⌘-P keyboard shortcut—to display the Print dialog box.
3. Click the PDF button in the lower-left corner of the Print dialog box to display the PDF pop-up menu, shown here.

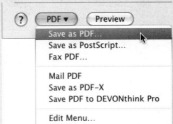

4. Click the Save As PDF item to display the Save dialog box (shown here).

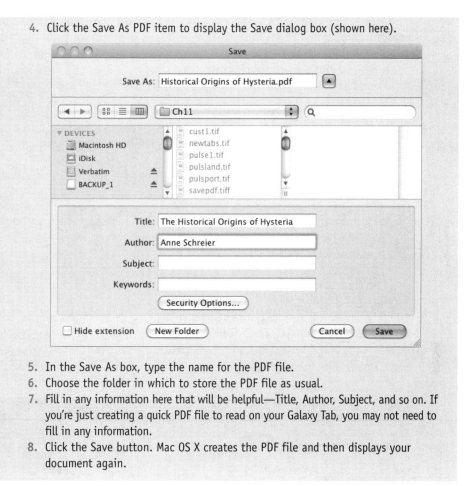

5. In the Save As box, type the name for the PDF file.
6. Choose the folder in which to store the PDF file as usual.
7. Fill in any information here that will be helpful—Title, Author, Subject, and so on. If you're just creating a quick PDF file to read on your Galaxy Tab, you may not need to fill in any information.
8. Click the Save button. Mac OS X creates the PDF file and then displays your document again.

Read Newspaper and Magazine Articles with the Pulse Newsreader

Pulse is a newsreader app that gives you quick access to a wide range of news sources. You can choose which news sources to view and you can arrange them on the Pulse home page and on other pages you create. When viewing a news source, you can open an article for reading.

Some of the news sources featured in Pulse provide full articles that you can read freely. Others provide only a taster of the article, together with a link that you can tap to visit the news source's web site to read the rest of the article. Some of these web sites require you to subscribe to read the full articles.

At this writing, the news sources to which Pulse gives you access are free. If you want to save stories to read later, send stories to bookmarking services, or sync your news so that you can view it on different devices, you need to sign up for a Pulse account—but this account too is free.

Launch Pulse

To get started with Pulse, launch it by following these steps:

1. Tap and hold the Recent Applications button to display the Apps screen.
2. Tap the Pulse button.

 If Pulse displays an introductory screen with a message such as "Your sources everywhere!", tap anywhere on the screen to dismiss the message and to get started with Pulse.

You then see the Pulse screen with its default selection of news. Figure 11-5 shows an example of this screen.

You can scroll sideways to view more articles in a news source; scroll down to display more newspapers, magazines, and headlines; and open an article by tapping it. But what you'll probably want to do first is customize the selection of news, so let's look first at how to do that.

FIGURE 11-5 At first, the Pulse screen presents a default selection of news.

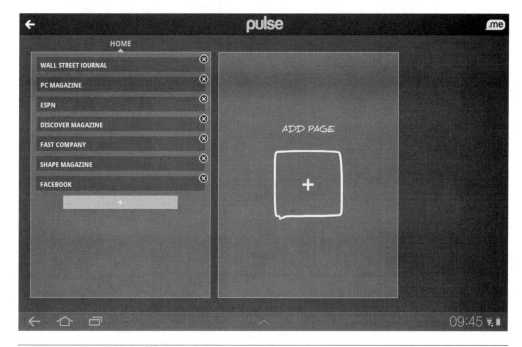

FIGURE 11-6   On the Customize screen, you can remove existing news sources, add other news sources, or add further pages to organize your reading material.

Customize the Selection of News

To customize the selection of news, tap the cog icon in the upper-left corner of the Pulse screen to display the Customize screen (see Figure 11-6).

From here, you can take the following actions:

- **Remove an existing source**   Tap the × button at the right end of the item's bar to remove it from the list.
- **Add a new source**   Tap the blue + button at the bottom of the Home page to display the Sources screen (see Figure 11-7). At the top, tap the category you want—Social, Featured, Art & Design, Business, Entertainment, Food, and so on—to display the list of related sources in the lower part of the screen. Scroll left or right if necessary to see other categories. Scroll down the list to find a source you want to add, and then tap the + button to add it. A check mark indicates that you're already using the source.

Tip   You can also tap the Search button (the magnifying glass icon) at the top of the Sources screen and then type a search term to find matching results. Again, tap the + button to add a source to your list.

FIGURE 11-7 At the top of the Sources screen, tap the category of reading material you want. In the list of sources that appears, tap the + button for any source you want to add to your page.

- **Rearrange your existing sources** Tap the button for a source, and then drag it up or down the list to where you want it. You can also drag the source to another page after you create one (as discussed later in this list).
- **Add a new page** Pulse gives you a Home page to start with, but if you have many news sources or want to organize your sources into different categories, you can add other pages. To add a page, tap the Add Page button on the right of the Customize screen. Pulse adds a new page to the right of the existing page and gives it a default name, such as PAGE2 (see Figure 11-8); you can rename it as discussed in the "Rename a page" bullet below.
- **Add content to a new page** The quick way to add content to a page is by tapping the button to add a pack of sources. For example, tap the Science button in the Choose A Pack area to add the Science pack. Tap the > button to display more packs you can add. If you prefer to add sources one by one, tap the + button under the Browse Our Catalog heading, and then add sources using the Sources screen, as described earlier in this section.
- **Rename a page** To rename a page, tap and hold its name until Pulse displays the Rename Page dialog box (shown here). Type the new name for the page, and then tap the Save button.
- **Delete a page** To delete a page you've added, delete all of its sources by tapping each × button in turn. When you delete the last source, Pulse removes the page.

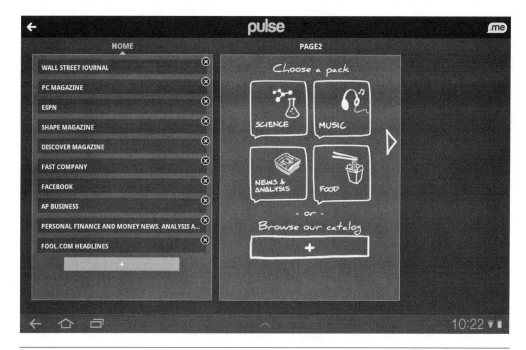

FIGURE 11-8   Pulse gives each new page a default name. You can populate the page either with an existing pack of sources, such as Science or Food, or tap the Browse Our Catalog button to add sources one at a time.

When you finish setting up your sources, tap the Back button in the upper-left corner of the Customize screen to return to the Pulse home screen. Any new pages you added appear as tabs in the upper-right corner of the screen, as shown here. Tap a tab to display its page so that you can access the articles on it.

You can quickly add another page by tapping the + button at the right end of the bar containing the page tabs.

Navigate Among Your News Sources and Read Articles

When you've chosen your sources, you're ready to start reading articles in them. Here's how to navigate quickly and easily among your sources in Pulse:

- **Switch from page to page**   Tap the tab for the page you want to view.
- **View sources that are further down the page**   Tap and scroll up to view the lower parts of the page.
- **Scroll through the articles in a source**   Scroll the articles left or right.

When you find an article you want to read, tap it to open it.

If you are holding the Galaxy Tab in landscape orientation when you open an article, Pulse displays the article only on the right side of the screen, as shown in Figure 11-9. This lets you quickly navigate to other articles by tapping their buttons on the left side of the screen (scroll as needed to see other buttons).

When you find an article you want to read in full, you'll normally do best to turn the Galaxy Tab to portrait orientation to view the article full screen (see Figure 11-10). Scroll left to display the next article, or scroll right to display the previous article.

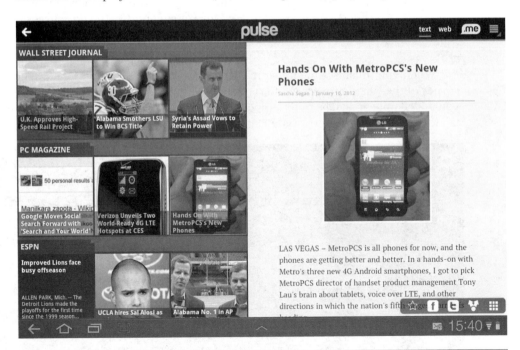

FIGURE 11-9   In landscape orientation, Pulse splits the screen between the sources (left) and the article you've opened (right).

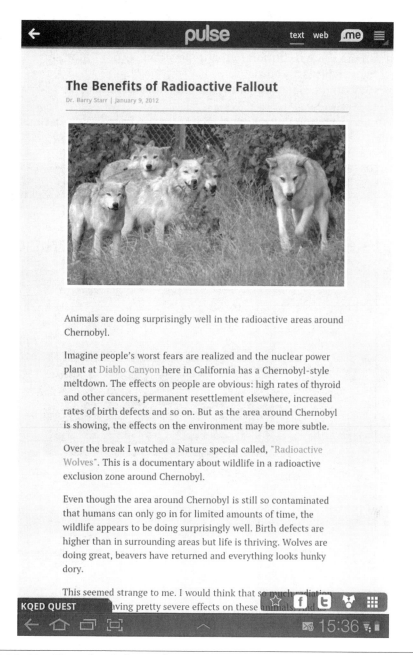

FIGURE 11-10 Turn the Galaxy Tab to portrait orientation when you want to concentrate on an article.

In either landscape orientation or portrait orientation, Pulse at first displays the article in Text view, which presents the text formatted for easy reading onscreen. You can tap the Web button in the upper-right corner of the screen to switch to Web view, which displays the article as a web page. Figure 11-11 shows part of a page in Text view on the right side of the Galaxy Tab screen; Figure 11-12 shows the same page in Web view.

To return to the Pulse home screen, tap the Back button in the upper-left corner of the screen.

FIGURE 11-11 Text view shows the article formatted for easy reading onscreen.

FIGURE 11-12   Web view displays the article formatted as a web page.

Sign Up for a Pulse Account

If you like Pulse and want to take your usage of it to the next level, you can sign up for a Pulse account. This is free but requires you to provide your e-mail address.

To set up a Pulse account, tap the .Me button in the upper-right corner of the Pulse window, and then follow through the signup process.

How to... Change the Way Pulse Looks

If you find Pulse's default look hard to read, you can change it. To do so, go back to the home screen (shown in Figure 11-5, earlier in the chapter) if you're at any other screen, tap the Menu button to display the menu panel, and then tap the Settings item.

In the Display section of the Settings screen (shown here), you can choose the following settings:

- **Article Font Size** Tap this button to display the Article Font Size dialog box, and then tap the Small option button, the Medium option button, the Large option button, or the Extra Large option button, as needed.

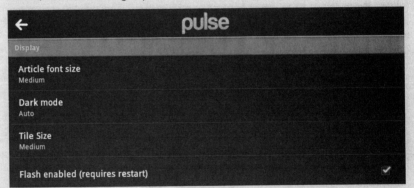

- **Dark Mode** Pulse's Dark mode can automatically darken the screen in low light conditions to make reading easier on the eyes. To control how Pulse uses Dark mode, tap the Dark Mode button, and then tap the Auto option button, the On option button, or the Off option button in the Dark Mode dialog box that opens.
- **Tile Size** To control the size of the tiles on which Pulse presents the articles, tap the Tile Size button, and then tap the Small option button or the Medium option button in the Tile Size dialog box that opens.
- **Flash Enabled** To control whether Pulse displays content that uses Adobe's Flash technology, select or clear the Flash Enabled check box. You need to restart Pulse to make this change take effect.

12

Make the Most of Apps

HOW TO...

- Use the apps that come with the Galaxy Tab
- Add third-party apps from Android Market
- Add apps from other sources
- Reinstall apps you've purchased but uninstalled or lost
- Create app shortcuts on the home screen
- Manage your apps
- Uninstall an app by using the Market app
- Clear RAM or stop services to make the Galaxy Tab run faster

Perhaps the most powerful feature of the Galaxy Tab is the wide range of apps that it can run. With its Android operating system, the Galaxy Tab can tap into the hundreds of thousands of apps available on Google's Android Market—many of them free, and others at very reasonable cost. You can also run non-Market apps if you're sure you want to.

This chapter shows you how to get the most out of apps on the Galaxy Tab. We'll start by recapping the essentials of running the apps that come with the Galaxy Tab. We'll then look at how to add third-party apps from Android Market, how to create shortcuts on the home screen so you can run apps quickly, and how to manage the apps on the Galaxy Tab.

Along the way, you'll also learn how to reinstall apps you've purchased from Android Market but then uninstalled (or lost), and how to shut down services when Android starts acting hinky.

Roll up your sleeves, and we'll dig in.

Use the Apps That Come with the Galaxy Tab

The Galaxy Tab usually comes with a solid basic selection of apps ranging from Alarm and Browser to World Clock and YouTube. To see the full range of apps installed on your Galaxy Tab model, tap the Home button to return to the home screen, and then tap the Apps icon in the upper-right corner of the screen.

Tip You can also display the Apps screen by tapping and holding the Recent Apps button.

Figure 12-1 shows the first Apps screen on my Galaxy Tab; yours probably has a different selection of apps, but many of the core apps are likely to be the same. You can drag the screen to the left to display the next Apps screen or to the right to display the previous Apps screen—the screens wrap around in exactly the helpful way that the home screen panels don't.

Launch an App

As you've seen earlier in the book, you launch an app from the Apps screen by tapping its icon. The Galaxy Tab displays that app in front of all the other apps you're running, and you can start using it.

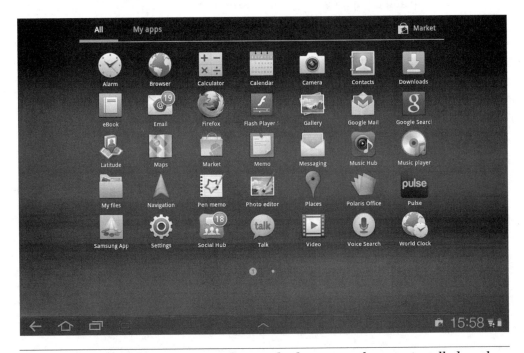

FIGURE 12-1 Use the Apps screen for standard access to the apps installed on the Galaxy Tab.

For apps you need to run frequently, you can create shortcuts on your home screen panels as discussed in Chapter 2. You can then run these apps from the home screen panels without needing to display the Apps screen.

Close an App

When you finish using an app, you can close it by tapping the Back button. You may need to tap the Back button several times to close the app, as each tap takes you back to the previous screen until you reach the app's initial screen.

 Most apps close when you tap the Back button from their initial screen. But if an app doesn't close, you can close it by using the Task Manager, as discussed later in this chapter.

If you think you'll need to use an app again soon, you don't need to close it. Instead, just tap the Home button to leave the app running in the background while you switch to another app.

 Most Galaxy Tab models come with enough memory to run between 6 and 12 normal-size apps at the same time. (If the apps are bigger than normal, you get to run fewer of them at once.) You'll soon notice if you're running too many apps for the Galaxy Tab to handle, as the Galaxy Tab will respond more slowly to your commands. When you notice this happening, it's time to close some apps.

Switch Among Apps

You can switch from one app to another in these ways:

- **Use the Recent Apps list**   To switch to one of the last apps you've used, tap the Recent Apps button in the lower-left corner of the screen. On the menu of apps that appears, tap the button for the app you want.
- **Go back to the home screen**   You can launch or switch to any app by using the home screen or the Apps screen. Tap the Home button to display the home screen, and then either tap the app's shortcut on one of its panels, or tap the Apps button to display the Apps screen, and then tap the app's icon.

 Some apps launch other apps. When you've launched one app from another, you can return to the previous app by tapping the Back button in the app you've launched. As before, you may need to tap the Back button several times.

See Which Apps You're Running

To see which apps you're running, open the Task Manager and look at the Active Applications screen.

To open the Task Manager, tap and hold the Home button. The Task Manager displays the Active Applications screen at the front, as shown here.

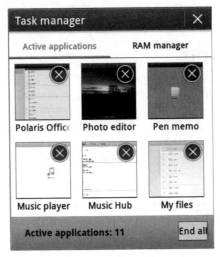

From here, you can switch to an app, end an app, or end all the apps:

- **Switch to an app** Tap the app's button in the Task Manager (but don't tap the × button).
- **End an app** Tap the × button for the app.

 Before ending an app, make sure that you've saved any unsaved data in it. If you think the app may contain unsaved data, switch to the app by tapping the Back button and then close it, instead of closing it using the × button on the Active Applications screen.

- **End all the apps** Tap the End All button at the bottom of the Active Applications screen.

Add Third-Party Apps from Android Market

When you need to add apps to the Galaxy Tab to get more out of it, your first stop should be Android Market. Android Market is Google's online store of approved apps for Android devices such as the Galaxy Tab. Android Market offers a wide range of apps that covers most needs; the prices are reasonable; and the built-in Market app makes it easy to access.

Open the Market App

To find apps on Android Market, first open the Market app like this:

1. Tap and hold the Recent Apps button to display the Apps screen.
2. Tap the Market icon.

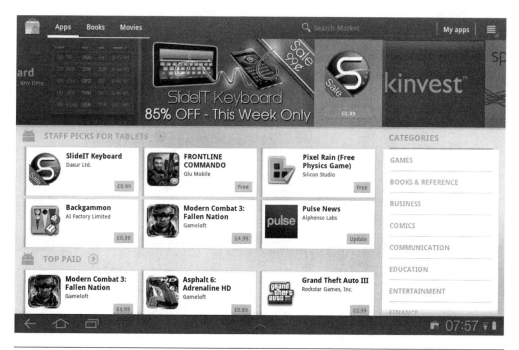

FIGURE 12-2   From the Apps tab on the Market app's home screen, you can browse apps, books, or movies, go to your My Apps list, or search for apps.

Figure 12-2 shows the Market app's home screen. If the Apps tab in the upper-left corner isn't already selected (with a thicker white bar under it), tap the Apps tab to make sure you're looking at apps rather than books or movies.

Find the Apps You Need

From the Market app's home screen, you can find apps in several ways:

- **Browse the Featured list and Staff Picks list**   The Featured list on the scrolling bar at the top of the Apps tab is worth a quick look, especially if you're interested in the latest and supposedly greatest apps. Below this, the Staff Picks list shows apps recommended by the Android Market staff.
- **Browse apps by category**   In the Categories list on the right of the Apps tab, tap the category of apps you want to see—for example, Games, Books & Reference, or Business. Figure 12-3 shows the Business category.
- **View the My Apps list**   Tap the My Apps icon in the upper-right corner to display the My Apps list (shown in Figure 12-4). You can then update apps you've installed or reinstall apps you've deleted.

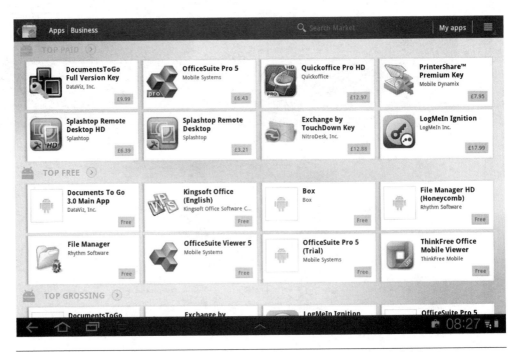

FIGURE 12-3 You can browse apps by a particular category, such as the Business category shown here.

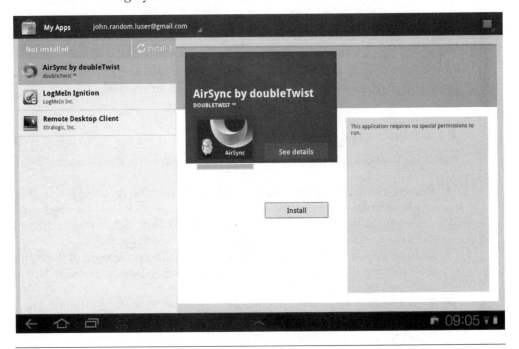

FIGURE 12-4 From the My Apps list, you can quickly update installed apps, or reinstall apps you've purchased or downloaded but deleted.

From the My Apps list, tap the button in the upper-left corner to go back to the Market screen.

- **Search for an app**   Tap in the Search Market box on the toolbar at the top of the Market app's home screen (or most other Market app screens), type your search term, and then tap the Enter button.

Download and Install an App

When you find an app you want to know more about, tap its button to display an information screen, as shown in Figure 12-5. You can tap the More button in the lower-right corner of the screen to display more details about the app.

The first time you try to download a free app or buy a paid app, the Market app walks you through the process of creating an account. The first time you buy an app, the Market app takes your payment details.

When you've found an app you want to buy or get, tap the Buy button or the Free button. The notifications area shows a notification as the download starts, and you can open the notifications panel to see the progress of the download.

FIGURE 12-5   On an app's information screen, you can tap the More button in the lower-right corner to display more information, or tap the Buy button or the Free button to get the app.

If you do open the notifications panel, when the app's button shows that the download has completed, you can tap the button to launch the app. Otherwise, tap and hold the Recent Apps button to display the Apps screen, and then tap the app's icon as usual to launch it.

 Add Apps from Other Sources

For most Galaxy Tab users, the best way to install apps is to download them from Android Market as described earlier in this chapter. This way, you get apps that have been checked for compatibility with the Android operating system and that are certified as not containing malicious code.

But sometimes, for special purposes, you may need to install apps that aren't available on Android Market. To do so, you must select the Unknown Sources check box on the Applications screen in Settings. Follow these steps:

1. From the home screen, tap the notifications area to display the notifications panel.
2. Tap the Settings button to display the Settings screen.
3. Tap the Applications button to display the Applications screen.
4. Select the Unknown Sources check box. The Galaxy Tab displays the Attention dialog box (shown here).
5. Tap the OK button.

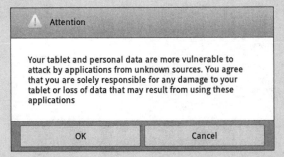

After selecting the Unknown Sources check box, you can install apps in either of these ways:

- **Use an installer** From Android Market, download an installer such as Fast Installer or z-App Installer. Download the package file for the app you want to install, and copy it to the root directory of the Galaxy Tab's file system. Run the installer, select the app when it shows you the contents of the root directory, and install the app.
- **Install the Android SDK** If you get heavily into installing non-Market apps, and you're using a Windows PC rather than a Mac, download the Android Software Development Kit (SDK) from the Android Developers web site (http:/developer .android.com/sdk/), together with the Google USB Driver (http://developer.android .com/sdk/win-usb.html). You can then install apps from your PC to the Galaxy Tab.

Update Your Apps

To get the best performance out of the Galaxy Tab and the apps you've installed, you'll want to install updates to the apps. To do so, follow these steps:

1. Open the Market app.
2. On the Market app's home screen, tap the My Apps button to display the My Apps screen.
3. Tap the Update button for an app to update that app.
4. If the Market app displays the Allow Access dialog box (see Figure 12-6), review the access the app needs, and then tap the OK button if you want to proceed.

 To set an app for automatic updating, tap the app's button on the My Apps screen to display the screen for the app, and then select the Allow Automatic Updating check box.

FIGURE 12-6   In the Allow Access dialog box, make sure you're okay with the access the app needs before you tap the OK button to update the app.

How to...

Reinstall Apps You've Purchased but Uninstalled or Lost

Sometimes you may purchase an app, find you don't like it, delete it—and then have second thoughts and decide you want it back. Or you may need to restore the Galaxy Tab to factory settings (as described in Chapter 14) to clear up problems; this process removes any apps you've installed, so you'll need to reinstall them.

To reinstall the apps, follow these steps:

1. Open the Market app.
2. Tap the My Apps button to go to the My Apps screen.
3. Reinstall either all the apps at once or individual apps one by one:
   - **Reinstall all the apps at once** Tap the Install button on the right of the Not Installed bar (shown here).
   - **Reinstall apps one by one** In the Not Installed list, tap the app you want to install, and then tap the Install button below its name.

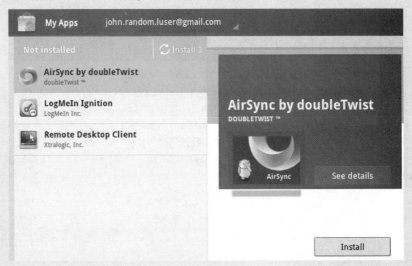

4. Tap the OK button when the Market app prompts you to accept permissions.

The download begins, and runs as normal.

Create App Shortcuts

To make your apps easy to run, you'll want to add shortcuts for your most used apps to the home screen panels. You can create a shortcut to an app in either of these ways:

- **Drag the shortcut to the home screen panel on which you want it**   Follow these steps:
  1. Tap and hold the Recent Apps button to display the Apps screen.
  2. Tap and hold the app you want to create a shortcut for. After a moment, the Galaxy Tab displays miniature versions of the home screen panels at the bottom of the Apps screen.
  3. Drag the app's icon to the home screen panel you want to create the shortcut on, as shown in the example in Figure 12-7.
- **Use the Add To Home Screen Options screen**   Follow these steps:
  1. Tap the Home button to display the home screen.
  2. Tap the Customize (+) button in the upper-right corner, or tap and hold on blank space anywhere in the main part of the screen, to display the Add To Home Screen Options screen.

Drag an app's icon to a home
screen panel to create a shortcut

FIGURE 12-7   You can quickly create an app shortcut by tapping and holding the app's icon on the Apps screen, then dragging it to the miniature of the relevant home screen panel.

3. Tap the App Shortcuts tab to display the apps.
4. Tap an app and drag it to the appropriate miniature home screen panel at the top of the screen.

Manage Your Apps

To keep your Galaxy Tab running smoothly, you'll sometimes need to manage the apps it runs. Sometimes you may need to force an app to stop running; other times, you may want to uninstall apps you no longer use. You can also check how much memory and battery power the apps are using, choose development settings, and select settings for Samsung apps.

To manage your apps, you work from the Applications screen in the Settings app—so what you need to do first is open the Applications screen.

Open the Applications Screen in Settings

To open the Applications screen in Settings, follow these steps:

1. From the home screen, tap the notifications area to display the notifications panel.
2. Tap the Settings button to display the Settings screen.
3. Tap the Applications button to display the Applications screen (shown in Figure 12-8).

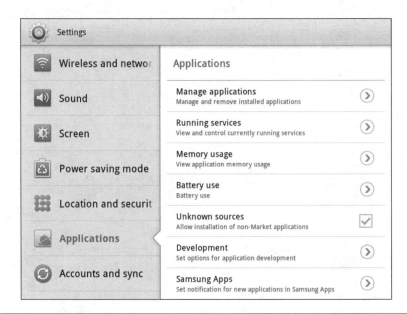

FIGURE 12-8   From the Applications screen in Settings, you can manage or remove installed apps, view memory and battery usage, and choose whether to install apps from sources other than Android Market.

FIGURE 12-9   The Manage Applications screen first shows the Downloaded tab, which lists the apps you've downloaded.

From here, you can choose settings and manage apps, as discussed in the following subsections.

Open the Manage Applications Screen

To start managing your apps, tap the Manage Applications button on the Applications screen in the Settings to display the Manage Applications screen. At first, the Galaxy Tab displays the Downloaded tab (see Figure 12-9), which lists only the apps you've downloaded and installed on your Galaxy Tab.

You can tap the All tab to see the full list of apps, as shown on the left in Figure 12-10. Or you can tap the Running tab to view the list of system services that are now running, as shown on the right in Figure 12-10.

On the Downloaded tab and the All tab, the apps at first appear sorted by name. To sort the apps by size in descending order, tap the Sort By Size button in the upper-right corner of the screen. To sort the apps by name again, tap the Sort By Name button, which replaces the Sort By Size button. On the Running tab, you can tap the Show Cached Processes button in the upper-right corner of the screen to display the system processes that are cached (held in memory) rather than running; tap the Show Services In Use button to switch back to viewing the services that are running.

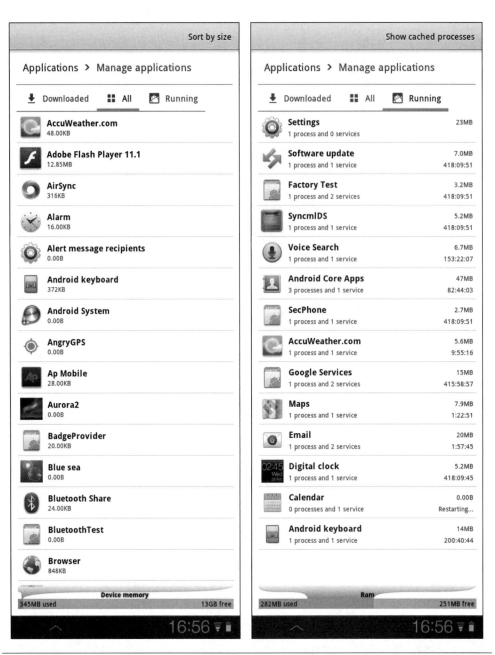

FIGURE 12-10 Tap the All tab (left) of the Manage Applications screen when you want to see the full list of apps installed on your Galaxy Tab. Tap the Running tab (right) when you want to see only the system services that are actually running.

Use the Application Info Screen to Stop or Uninstall an App

When you locate the app you're looking for on the Manage Applications screen, tap the app's button to display the Application Info screen for the app. Figure 12-11 shows the Application Info screen for the Firefox web browser app.

FIGURE 12-11   From the Application Info screen for an app, you can force the app to stop, clear its data, clear its cache, or clear its defaults. If the app is one you've installed, you can uninstall it.

From here, you can take the following actions:

- **Force the app to stop running** If you can't stop the app using the Task Manager, as described earlier in this chapter, tap the Force Stop button. In the Force Stop dialog box that opens (shown here), tap the OK button.

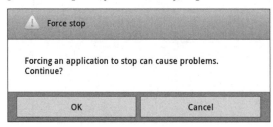

- **Uninstall the app** If the app is one you've installed, you can uninstall it by tapping the Uninstall button, and then tapping the OK button in the confirmation dialog box that appears (shown here).

- **Clear the app's data** To clear any data the app has stored (for example, your user name and password), tap the Clear Data button in the Storage area of the Application Info screen, and then tap the OK button in the Delete dialog box that appears (shown here).

- **Clear the app's cache** If the app caches data in the hope of delivering that data more quickly the next time you need it, you can clear the cache. Tap the Clear Cache button in the Cache area of the Application Info screen to clear this data. The Galaxy Tab doesn't ask you to confirm clearing the cache.
- **Clear the defaults** If the app is set to launch by default, you can tap the Clear Defaults button in the Launch By Default area of the Application Info screen to remove this default setting.

How to...   **Uninstall an App by Using the Market App**

You can also uninstall an app by using the Market app. Follow these steps:

1. Tap and hold the Recent Apps button to display the Apps screen.
2. Tap the Market button to launch the Market app.
3. Tap the My Apps button to display the My Apps screen.
4. Tap the button for the app you want to uninstall. The screen for the app appears.
5. Tap the Uninstall button. The Galaxy Tab uninstalls the app without asking for confirmation.

- **View the app's permissions**   The Permissions area at the bottom of the Application Info screen shows which permissions the app has—for example, Firefox can get your location information, access the Internet, modify or delete items on USB storage, use the hardware controls to take pictures and videos, and use system tools to change network connectivity and prevent the Galaxy Tab from going to sleep.

If the Show All button appears at the bottom of the Permissions section, you can tap it to display further details on the app's permissions.

Check How Much Memory the Apps Are Using

From the Applications screen in Settings, you can tap the Memory Usage button to display the Memory Usage screen (see Figure 12-12). As with the Manage Applications screen, the Memory Usage screen has three tabs:

- **Downloaded**   Tap this tab to see the memory usage for apps you've added to the Galaxy Tab.
- **All**   Tap this tab to see the memory usage for the full list of apps.
- **Running**   Tap this tab to see the memory usage for the services that are running.

Check Which Apps and Features Are Using the Most Battery Power

To see which apps and features are using the most battery power, tap the Battery Use button on the Applications screen in Settings. The Battery Use screen (see Figure 12-13) appears, showing a simple list sorted by the greediest app or feature. Usually, the Screen is the clear winner here, especially when you've been using the Galaxy Tab.

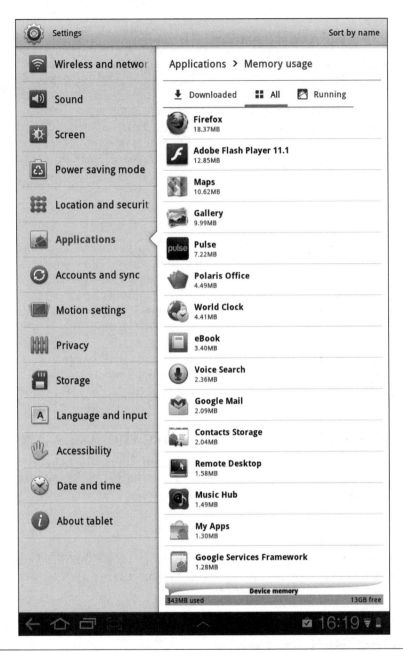

FIGURE 12-12 Display the Memory Usage screen to see how much memory each of the apps is using.

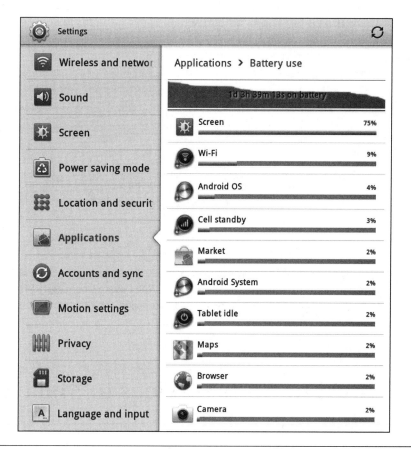

FIGURE 12-13   Open the Battery Use screen to see which apps and features have been consuming the most power.

    Tap the Refresh button (the button with two arrows circling clockwise) at the upper-right corner of the Battery Use screen to refresh the information.

From the Battery Use screen, you can tap an item's button to display the Usage Details screen for the feature or app, which includes options for controlling it. For example, the left screen in the next illustration shows the Usage Details screen for the Screen feature, where you can tap the Screen Settings button to open the Screen Settings screen. The right screen in the next illustration shows the Usage Details screen for the Wi-Fi feature; similarly, you can tap the Wi-Fi Settings button to display the options for controlling Wi-Fi.

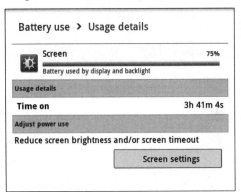

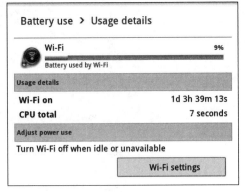

Tip For coverage of the Applications screen's Development button and its corresponding screen, see the section "Set Development Options" in Chapter 2. For coverage of the Samsung Apps button and screen, see the section "Choose Samsung Apps Settings" in Chapter 2.

Clear RAM or Stop Services to Make the Galaxy Tab Run Faster

If the Galaxy Tab seems to be running more slowly than usual, or if apps respond jerkily rather than smoothly, you may be running out of RAM. If this is the case, you can recover some of the RAM to make the Galaxy Tab run faster or more smoothly. You can also stop system services, although this is something you shouldn't normally need to do.

Clear RAM

To see how much of the Galaxy Tab's RAM the apps you're running are using, and to clear some RAM if you're running short, follow these steps:

1. Tap and hold the Home button until the Task Manager window appears onscreen.

 Before you use the Clear Memory feature, manually shut any apps you're no longer using. On the Active Applications tab of the Task Manager window, tap the × button for each app you want to close.

2. Tap the RAM Manager tab in the upper-right corner of the Task Manager window to display the RAM Manager tab (shown here). The RAM Status readout at the top shows how much of the Galaxy Tab's memory you're using and how much is left.

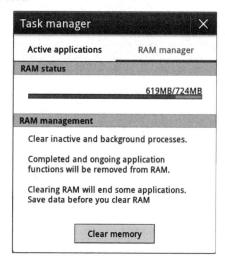

3. Click the Clear Memory button. The Galaxy Tab clears inactive processes and processes that are running in the background. You should see the RAM Status readout indicate that more RAM is available.
4. Tap the × button to close the Task Manager window.

Shut Down an Android Service

In computer terms, a *service* is a module of code that performs a particular task for an operating system. For example, the Galaxy Tab typically runs services such as the Samsung Keypad service, which controls the onscreen keypad you use to type in content.

Normally the Android operating system manages services automatically for you, starting some automatically when you fire up the Galaxy Tab and starting others when you take an action that demands them. For example, when you turn on Bluetooth, Android automatically starts the Bluetooth Share service—you don't need to turn on the Bluetooth Share service yourself in order to share files using Bluetooth.

Sometimes, when things go wrong, you may need to shut down one or more services yourself. To shut down a service, follow these steps:

1. From the home screen, tap the notifications area to display the notifications panel.
2. Tap the Settings button to display the Settings screen.
3. Tap the Applications button to display the Applications screen.

4. Tap the Running Services button to display the Running tab of the Manage Applications screen (shown on the right in Figure 12-10, earlier in this chapter).

5. Tap the button for the service you're thinking of stopping. The Galaxy Tab displays the Active Application screen for the service. The following illustration shows examples of the Active Application screen for a service you can stop (left) and for a service you can't stop (right).

6. If the service has a Stop button, tap the Stop button to stop the service. If the service doesn't have a Stop button, you can't stop the service because it's vital to the system.

13

Learn Three Tricks to Take the Galaxy Tab to the Max

HOW TO...

- Connect computers and other devices to the Internet through the Galaxy Tab
- Connect the Galaxy Tab to a work network via virtual private networking
- Install a digital certificate on the Galaxy Tab
- Control your PC or Mac from the Galaxy Tab anywhere

In this chapter, I'll show you how to perform three advanced maneuvers to take your use of the Galaxy Tab to the next level.

First, you'll learn how to connect other computers and devices to the Internet through the Galaxy Tab's cellular connection. This capability can be a real timesaver when you're on the road. You can either connect a single PC via tethering—lassoing the Galaxy Tab's Internet connection with the USB cable—or connect up to five computers or devices via Wi-Fi. As you'd imagine, this capability works only with Galaxy Tab models that have cellular connectivity.

Second, you'll learn how to connect the Galaxy Tab to your work network via virtual private networking. By doing this, you can connect to network resources even when you're halfway around the world. You may need to install a digital certificate for authentication; I'll walk you through the installation process.

Last, I'll show you how to take control of your PC or Mac from the Galaxy Tab—no matter where you happen to be. This remote control enables you to get work done on your computer when you're elsewhere, so it can save you time and effort.

Connect Computers and Other Devices to the Internet Through the Galaxy Tab

When the Galaxy Tab has an Internet connection but your computer doesn't, you can share the Galaxy Tab's connection to get your computer online. The easy way to do this is by using USB tethering, making the Galaxy Tab share its Internet connection via a USB connection to your computer.

Other times, you may need to use the Galaxy Tab to put several computers or other devices online. You can do this by turning the Galaxy Tab into a portable Wi-Fi hotspot (in other words, a mobile wireless access point) that can share its Internet connection with up to five other computers or devices.

Both these capabilities are great when you're on the road, either alone or with colleagues or family. But you can also use them at home if necessary—for example, when your landline fails.

Use Tethering to Connect a Windows PC to the Internet

When you need to connect a Windows PC to the Internet via the Galaxy Tab's Internet connection, use USB tethering. Tethering sounds like what you'd do to your pet goat to stop it wandering off, but in this context it means connecting your computer via a cable to the Galaxy Tab so that the computer can share the Galaxy Tab's Internet connection.

At this writing, USB tethering doesn't work with Macs. To connect a Mac to the Internet via the Galaxy Tab, use the mobile access point feature instead, as described in the next section.

 Tethering makes your computer use the Galaxy Tab's Internet connection, so it inevitably increases the use of your data plan. If you've got a generous plan, you may be able to use tethering as your normal way of connecting your computer to the Internet. If your plan is limited, use tethering for emergencies only—for example, when your broadband connection fails.

Set the Galaxy Tab to Share Its Internet Connection via USB Tethering

To set the Galaxy Tab to share its Internet connection via USB tethering, follow these steps:

1. Connect the Galaxy Tab to your PC with the USB cable.
2. Tap the Home button to display the home screen.

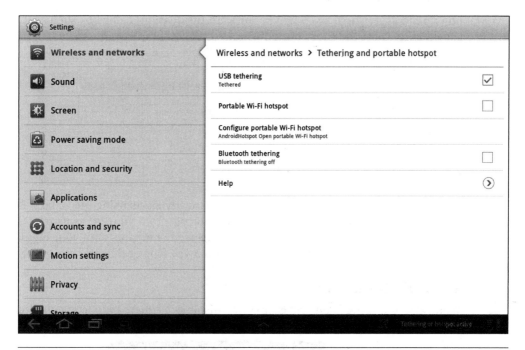

Settings

Wireless and networks

Sound

Screen

Power saving mode

Location and security

Applications

Accounts and sync

Motion settings

Privacy

Storage

Wireless and networks > Tethering and portable hotspot

USB tethering
Tethered   ☑

Portable Wi-Fi hotspot   ☐

Configure portable Wi-Fi hotspot
AndroidHotspot Open portable Wi-Fi hotspot

Bluetooth tethering
Bluetooth tethering off   ☐

Help   ⊙

Tethering or hotspot active

FIGURE 13-1   On the Tethering And Portable Hotspot screen, select the USB
Tethering check box to turn on USB tethering. The Galaxy Tab
displays the "Tethering Or Hotspot Active" message in the
notifications area for a moment, and displays the USB symbol in the
indicator icons area.

3. Tap the notifications area to display the notifications panel, and then tap the
   Settings button to display the Settings screen.
4. Tap the Wireless And Networks button in the left pane to display the Wireless
   And Networks screen.
5. Tap the Tethering And Portable Hotspot button to display the Tethering And
   Portable Hotspot screen (see Figure 13-1).
6. Select the USB Tethering check box to turn on tethering.

Install the Samsung Android USB Remote Network Driver on Windows

The first time you turn on tethering, Windows installs the driver for the Samsung
Android USB Remote NDIS Network Device. You'll see a pop-up message in the
notifications area saying that Windows is installing driver software. If you click the

pop-up message, you'll see a Driver Software Installation dialog box such as the one shown here. Click the Close button when Windows completes the installation.

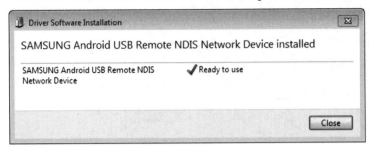

With the driver in place, Windows automatically starts using the Galaxy Tab's Internet connection, so you can access the Internet from your PC as usual. Depending on how the Galaxy Tab's Internet connection speed compares with your regular Internet connection, accessing the Internet may be slower than usual.

Turn Off Tethering

When USB tethering is on, the Galaxy Tab displays a square blue icon containing a USB symbol at the left end of the notifications area, as you see here.

You can use USB tethering and the portable Wi-Fi hotspot at the same time if you want. But as you'd imagine, the more devices that share the Galaxy Tab's Internet connection, the farther performance drops.

When you've finished using the Galaxy Tab as a mobile access point, turn it off. Follow these steps:

1. Tap the Home button to display the home screen.
2. Tap the USB icon to display its pop-up panel.
3. Tap the Tethering Or Hotspot Active icon on the pop-up panel to display the Tethering And Portable Hotspot screen in the Settings app.
4. Clear the USB Tethering check box.

Use the Galaxy Tab as a Portable Wi-Fi Hotspot

When you need to connect multiple computers or devices to the Internet via your Galaxy Tab's Internet connection, you can turn the Galaxy Tab into a portable Wi-Fi hotspot—a mobile wireless access point. The Galaxy Tab creates a wireless network that it shares its Internet connection on. You then connect the computers or devices—up to five of them—to the Galaxy Tab's wireless network just as you would to any other wireless network.

Using the Galaxy Tab as a mobile access point for several devices can go through your data plan faster than teenagers devouring pizza. Unless you have a generous plan, you'll probably want to use the Galaxy Tab as a mobile access point only for short periods or for emergencies.

Set Up the Galaxy Tab as a Portable Wi-Fi Hotspot

To set up the Galaxy Tab as a portable Wi-Fi hotspot, follow these steps:

1. Tap the Home button to display the home screen.
2. Tap the notifications area to display the notifications panel, and then tap the Settings button to display the Settings screen.
3. Tap the Wireless And Networks button in the left pane to display the Wireless And Networks screen.
4. Tap the Tethering And Portable Hotspot button to display the Tethering And Portable Hotspot screen.
5. Tap the Configure Portable Wi-Fi Hotspot button to display the Configure Portable Wi-Fi Hotspot dialog box (shown here with settings chosen).
6. In the Network SSID text box, type the name

you want to give the wireless network. SSID is the abbreviation for *service set identifier*—in other words, the name for the wireless network.

 The Galaxy Tab's Configure Portable Wi-Fi Hotspot dialog box offers two security options: Open and WPA2 PSK. Open uses no security, so anybody can connect to it. Unless you control all wireless devices within range of the Galaxy Tab, this lack of security is usually a bad idea. WPA2 PSK uses Wi-Fi Protected Access version 2 (WPA2) with a pre-shared key (PSK)—what most people call a password. You should use this setting for your Galaxy Tab's wireless network.

7. Tap the Security pop-up button, and then tap WPA2 PSK on the pop-up menu. The dialog box expands to display the Password text box.
8. Type the password in the Password text box. Samsung recommends using at least eight characters. This is normally a good idea, but using a shorter password (six characters or more) is okay for short-term use.
9. Tap the Save button to close the Configure Portable Wi-Fi Hotspot dialog box. The Galaxy Tab returns you to the Tethering And Portable Hotspot screen.
10. Select the Portable Wi-Fi Hotspot check box. If the Galaxy Tab is using Wi-Fi to connect to the Internet, it automatically switches to the cellular connection. The Galaxy Tab displays the Portable Wi-Fi Hotspot icon to the left of the notifications area, as shown here.

The Galaxy Tab is now acting as a portable Wi-Fi hotspot. While it does so, you can use the Galaxy Tab as normal—but the Internet connection speed will appear to be slower when other computers and devices are using the connection.

Keep an eye on the Portable Wi-Fi Hotspot icon in the indicator icons area. It's easy to forget that the portable Wi-Fi hotspot stays on even when the Galaxy Tab goes to sleep.

Connect a Computer or Device to the Galaxy Tab's Wireless Network

After you turn on the Galaxy Tab's Portable Wi-Fi Hotspot feature, you can connect a computer or device to the wireless network just as you would to any other wireless network. For example:

- **Windows 7** Click the wireless network icon in the system tray, and then click the name of the Galaxy Tab's network in the list of wireless networks. Click the Connect button, as shown on the left in the next illustration. In the Connect To A Network dialog box that Windows displays (shown on the right in the illustration), type the password in the Security Key text box, and then click the OK button.

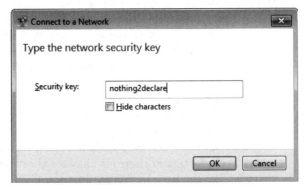

- **Mac OS X** On the menu bar, click the Wi-Fi icon (on Lion) or AirPort icon (on Snow Leopard or Leopard), and then click Turn Wi-Fi On (on Lion) or Turn AirPort On (on Snow Leopard or Leopard), unless Wi-Fi or AirPort is on already. Click the Wi-Fi icon or AirPort icon again, and then click the name of the Galaxy Tab's wireless network, as shown on the left in the next illustration. In the dialog box that opens (shown on the right in the next illustration), type the password, select the Remember This Network check box if you want to be able to use the network again, and then click the Join button.

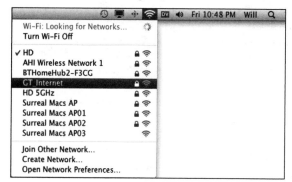 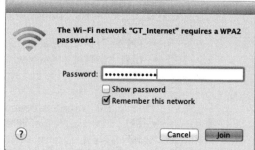

Turn Off the Mobile Access Point

When you've finished using the Galaxy Tab as a mobile access point, turn it off. Follow these steps:

1. Tap the Home button to display the home screen.
2. Tap the Portable Wi-Fi Hotspot icon on the system bar to display a pop-up panel.
3. Tap the Tethering Or Hotspot Active icon on the pop-up panel to display the Tethering And Portable Hotspot screen in the Settings app.
4. Clear the Portable Wi-Fi Hotspot check box.

Connect to a Work Network via Virtual Private Networking

If you need to connect to the network at your workplace from elsewhere, you can create a virtual private network connection on the Galaxy Tab. By using virtual private networking, you establish a secure tunnel through an insecure public network (usually the Internet), so that the Galaxy Tab is connected securely to your workplace's network.

Most virtual private networks use a password or a digital certificate to *authenticate* (verify the identity of) the user or computer who is trying to connect. A password authenticates the user; you simply type it in on the Galaxy Tab. A digital certificate authenticates the Galaxy Tab itself; you need to install the digital certificate, as discussed in the sidebar "Install a Digital Certificate on the Galaxy Tab," later in this chapter.

Did You Know?

Essential VPN Abbreviations and Acronyms

Apart from VPN itself (*virtual private network* or *virtual private networking*, depending on the context), you need to have at least a nodding acquaintance with the following abbreviations and acronyms:

- **PPTP**   PPTP is the abbreviation for Point-to-Point Tunneling Protocol.
- **L2TP**   L2TP is the abbreviation for Layer 2 Tunneling Protocol.
- **IPSec**   IPSec is the acronym for IP Security. (IP is the abbreviation for Internet Protocol.)
- **PSK**   PSK is the abbreviation for *pre-shared key*—essentially a password.
- **CRT**   In the context of VPNs, CRT stands for *certificate* rather than *cathode-ray tube*. This is a digital certificate that you must install on the Galaxy Tab before you can set up the VPN.

Get the Information You Need for the VPN

To set up a VPN connection, you'll need to know the following information:

- **Encryption type**   The Galaxy Tab can use PPTP, L2TP, L2TP/IPSec with PSK, or L2TP/IPSec with CRT. If your eyes just glazed over at that explosion of abbreviations, see the nearby sidebar titled "Essential VPN Abbreviations and Acronyms."
- **VPN server**   The server address can be either a hostname (for example, vpnserv. surrealpcs.com) or an IP address (for example, 212.1.12.101).
- **DNS search domains**   You may need to tell the VPN connection where to search for DNS information. Some VPN connections do not need you to specify DNS search domains.

Set Up a Virtual Private Network Connection

Once you've gathered the information detailed in the previous section, you're ready to set up a VPN connection. To do so, follow these steps:

1. Tap the Home button to display the home screen.
2. Tap the notifications area to display the notifications panel, and then tap the Settings button to display the Settings screen.
3. Tap the Wireless And Networks button to display the Wireless And Networks screen.

4. Tap the VPN Settings button to display the VPN Settings screen, the top of which is shown here. At first, the list of VPNs will probably be empty, as in this example.

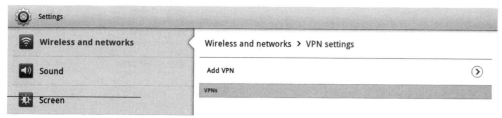

5. Tap the Add VPN button to display the Add VPN screen (shown here).

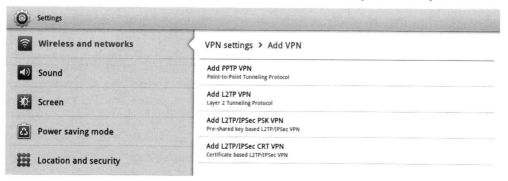

6. Tap the button for the type of security the VPN uses:
   • **Add PPTP VPN**   Tap this button to create a VPN connection using PPTP.
   • **Add L2TP VPN**   Tap this button to create a VPN connection using L2TP.
   • **Add L2TP/IPSec PSK VPN**   Tap this button to create a VPN using either L2TP or IPSec with a pre-shared key (a password).
   • **Add L2TP/IPSec CRT VPN**   Tap this button to create a VPN using either L2TP or IPSec with a digital certificate.
7. When you tap the button, the Galaxy Tab displays the Add PPTP VPN screen (shown in the upper-left corner of Figure 13-2), the Add L2TP VPN screen (shown in the upper-right corner), the Add L2TP/IPSec PSK VPN screen (shown in the lower-left corner), or the Add L2TP/IPSec CRT VPN screen (shown in the lower-right corner).
8. For any type of VPN, tap the VPN Name button, type a descriptive name in the VPN dialog box that opens, and then tap the OK button.
9. For any type of VPN, tap the Set VPN Server button, type the VPN server's hostname or IP address in the Set VPN Server dialog box, and then tap the OK button.
10. Set up the security method for the VPN:
    • **PPTP VPN**   Select the Enable Encryption check box.
    • **L2TP VPN**   Select the Enable L2TP Secret check box. Then tap the Set L2TP Security button, type the password in the Set L2TP Security dialog box, and tap the OK button.

```
VPN settings  >  Add PPTP VPN

VPN name
VPN name not set

Set VPN server
VPN server not set

Enable Encryption                              ☑
PPTP encryption enabled

DNS search domains
DNS search domains not set
```

```
VPN settings  >  Add L2TP VPN

VPN name
VPN name not set

Set VPN server
VPN server not set

Enable L2TP secret                             ☐
L2TP secret disabled

Set L2TP security
L2TP secret not set

DNS search domains
DNS search domains not set
```

```
VPN settings  >  Add L2TP/IPSec PSK VPN

VPN name
VPN name not set

Set VPN server
VPN server not set

Set IPsec pre-shared key
IPsec pre-shared key not set

Enable L2TP secret                             ☐
L2TP secret disabled

Set L2TP security
L2TP secret not set

DNS search domains
DNS search domains not set
```

```
VPN settings  >  Add L2TP/IPSec CRT VPN

VPN name
VPN name not set

Set VPN server
VPN server not set

Enable L2TP secret                             ☐
L2TP secret disabled

Set L2TP security
L2TP secret not set

Set user certificate
User certificate not set

Set CA certificate
Certificate authority (CA) certificate not set

DNS search domains
DNS search domains not set
```

FIGURE 13-2   Set up the details of the VPN connection on the Add PPTP VPN screen (top left), the Add L2TP VPN screen (top right), the Add L2TP/IPSec PSK VPN screen (lower left), or the Add L2TP/IPSec CRT VPN screen (lower right). Each type of connection needs different items of information.

- **L2TP/IPSec VPN using a pre-shared key**   Tap the Set IPSec Pre-Shared Key button, type the key in the Set IPSec Pre-Shared Key dialog box, and then tap the OK button. Next, select the Enable L2TP Secret check box. Then tap the Set L2TP Security button, type the password in the Set L2TP Security dialog box, and tap the OK button.

- **L2TP/IPSec VPN using a certificate**   Select the Enable L2TP Secret check box. Then tap the Set L2TP Security button, type the password in the Set L2TP Security dialog box, and tap the OK button. Next, tap the Set User Certificate button to display the Set User Certificate dialog box (shown below on the left), then tap the option button for the user certificate you want to install. (There may be only a single certificate available, as in this example.) Tap the Set CA Certificate button to display the Set CA Certificate dialog box (shown below on the right), then tap the option button for the certificate.

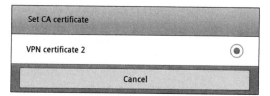

11. For any type of VPN, if you need to set DNS search domains for the VPN connection, tap the DNS Search Domains button, type the addresses of the search domains in the DNS Search Domains dialog box that opens, and then tap the OK button. For example, if you enter **surrealpcs.com** as a search domain, you'll be able to connect to corp.surrealpcs.com by simply entering **corp** rather than the full address.

12. When you've finished choosing all the settings for the VPN, tap the Menu button in the upper-right corner of the screen to display the menu (shown here), and then tap the Save button to save the VPN configuration.

13. If the Set Password dialog box (shown here) appears, type the password to use for credential storage in the New Password box and the Confirm New Password box. The password must be eight characters or more. Then tap the OK button.

When you finish setting up the VPN, it appears in the VPNs list on the VPN Settings screen in Wireless And Networks Settings.

Install a Digital Certificate on the Galaxy Tab

If you need to use a digital certificate to connect to a VPN, you must first install that digital certificate on the Galaxy Tab. You may need two digital certificates—a user certificate and a certificate authority (CA) certificate.

The easiest way to install the digital certificate or digital certificates on the Galaxy Tab is to e-mail the digital certificate to yourself, open the e-mail message, and then open the attached file containing the digital certificate. When the Galaxy Tab prompts you to type a name for the certificate, do so.

To use your digital certificates, you will also need to allow the Galaxy Tab's apps to access them. To make sure the apps can access your digital certificates, follow these steps:

1. Tap the Home button to display the home screen.
2. Tap the notifications area to display the notifications panel, and then tap the Settings button to display the Settings screen.
3. Tap the Location And Security button in the left column to display the Location And Security screen.
4. In the Credential Storage area, select the Use Secure Credentials check box.

From the Location And Security screen, you can also install digital certificates you've copied to a drive that you've connected to the Galaxy Tab via USB. To do so, tap the Install From USB Storage button in the Credential Storage area, and then follow the instructions for entering the password protecting the certificates and choosing the names under which to store them.

 To delete a VPN connection, go to the VPN Settings screen, and then tap and hold down its button in the VPNs list. In the dialog box that opens, tap the Delete Network button.

Connect via Your Virtual Private Network Connection

To connect to the remote network using your VPN, follow these steps:

1. Tap the Home button to display the home screen.
2. Tap the notifications area to display the notifications panel, and then tap the Settings button to display the Settings screen.
3. Tap the Wireless And Networks button to display the Wireless And Networks screen.
4. Tap the VPN Settings button to display the VPN Settings screen.

5. Tap the button for the VPN you want to connect to. The Galaxy Tab displays the Connect To dialog box (shown here).

```
Connect to L2TP VPN

      User name:       aconnor

      Password:        ·········

                  ☑ Remember user name

            Connect                    Cancel
```

6. Type your user name in the User Name text box.
7. Type your password in the Password text box.
8. Select the Remember User Name check box if you want the Galaxy Tab to remember your user name. This is usually helpful.
9. Tap the Connect button. The Galaxy Tab closes the Connect To dialog box and shows *Connecting* on the VPN's button on the VPN Settings screen as it connects.

When the Galaxy Tab establishes the connection, the notifications area briefly displays a message telling you it has connected.

After the message disappears, the notifications area continues to display the VPN symbol to remind you that you're connected.

You can now work on the network as if you were directly connected to it from within the network, but data will transfer only at the speed of your Internet connection or more slowly.

Disconnect from the VPN

When you have finished using the VPN, disconnect from it like this:

1. Tap the Home button to display the home screen.
2. In the notifications area of the System bar, tap the VPN's button to jump to the VPN Settings screen.
3. Tap the button for the VPN that's connected. You can also tap and hold down on the VPN's button in the notifications area to display the dialog box for the VPN, and then tap the Disconnect From Network button.

Control Your PC or Mac from the Galaxy Tab Anywhere

Connecting to your work network via VPN is useful, but you may need to take your presence a step further, and take control of your PC or Mac remotely from the Galaxy Tab.

Taking control enables you to work on your PC or Mac pretty much as if you were sitting at it. The main differences are practical: You can see only as much of the screen as fits on the Galaxy Tab's screen; you're stuck with an onscreen keyboard unless you connect a keyboard; and you point with a touch screen rather than a mouse unless you connect a mouse. But if you're patient, it works fine. And if it means you can take care of a project update or troubleshoot a sick server without having to drive to the office, you can probably find the patience.

At this writing, you can get various Android applications for controlling your PC or Mac remotely. In this section, I'll introduce you to the three main contenders for your money.

Did You Know?

Why RDP Beats VNC Hands Down for Controlling Windows PCs

If you need to take remote control of a Windows PC, you have two main mechanisms for doing so: Microsoft's Remote Desktop Protocol (RDP), and Virtual Network Computing (VNC), a standard protocol that works on most operating systems, including Windows, Mac OS X, and Linux.

Normally, you'll want to use RDP if you can. RDP has two main advantages:

- **Screen size** In an RDP session, the remote computer specifies the size of the screen it wants to use. So even if you connect to a PC that has a high-resolution monitor attached, your Windows session runs only at the Galaxy Tab's native resolution. In the same situation, VNC gives you a window the size of the Galaxy Tab's screen on the larger desktop, so you need to scroll around.
- **Discretion** When you connect via RDP, you log in on the PC, which makes the PC's screen display the login screen. As you work, anybody observing the PC can't see what you're doing. By contrast, with VNC, you share the remote computer's screen, observing and optionally controlling it. But even when you're controlling it, everything appears on the screen connected to the remote computer. If you're controlling your work computer, this may be a concern. (You can turn on your web cam to see who's watching...)

The only bugbear about RDP is that not all versions of Windows include the Remote Desktop feature that enables you to connect via RDP. All version of Windows Server include Remote Desktop, but only the "business" versions of regular Windows have it. These are Windows XP Professional; Windows Vista Business, Enterprise, and Ultimate; and Windows 7 Professional, Enterprise, and Ultimate.

Connect with Wyse PocketCloud RDP/VNC

The remote-control application you'll probably want to start with is Wyse PocketCloud, which you can download for free from Android Market. Wyse PocketCloud is the starter version of Wyse PocketCloud Pro, which costs around $15 and offers full features. PocketCloud can connect to both Windows PCs and Macs. For Windows PCs, you can use either RDP or VNC; for Macs, VNC is the only option.

Wyse has crippled PocketCloud by limiting it to a single saved connection and saddling it with ads. So if you find PocketCloud works for you, you'll probably want to upgrade to the Pro version. Figure 13-3 shows PocketCloud accessing a Mac.

 PocketCloud has an Auto Discovery Setup feature that requires downloading and installing the PocketCloud companion software on the PC or Mac. Once you've done this, Auto Discovery Setup can grab the information automatically across the network by using your Gmail account.

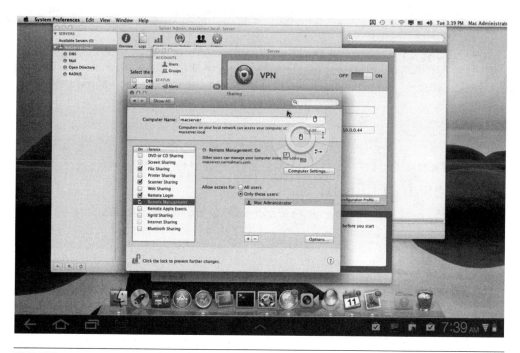

FIGURE 13-3 Wyse PocketCloud is an easy-to-use client for both RDP and VNC.

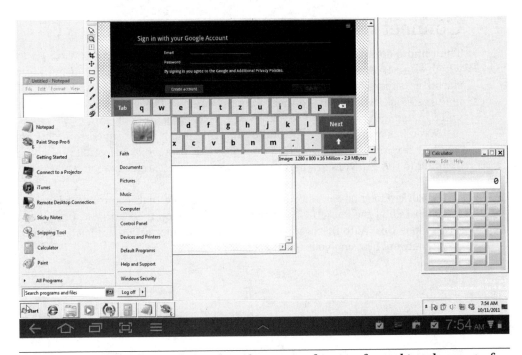

FIGURE 13-4   Remote Desktop Client has strong features for making the most of RDP connections to Windows PCs. Here, Remote Desktop Client has resized the desktop to fit the Galaxy Tab's screen, making navigation much easier.

Connect to Windows PCs with Remote Desktop Client

If you need to connect only to Windows PCs, try Remote Desktop Client from Xtralogic, Inc. (around $25). Remote Desktop Client (shown in Figure 13-4 controlling a PC running Windows 7) offers strong features for optimizing and managing RDP connections. For example, you can resize the Windows desktop to fit the Galaxy Tab's screen, choose whether to transmit graphical information such as desktop backgrounds and themes, and play sounds from the remote PC on the Galaxy Tab.

Connect Across the Internet with LogMeIn Ignition

When you need to connect to your PC or Mac across the Internet without having to configure a firewall to pass traffic on particular ports or track your computer's IP address, you can use a tool such as LogMeIn Ignition from LogMeIn, Inc. (around $30).

LogMeIn Ignition uses three components:

- **LogMeIn service**   This online site (www.logmein.com) passes information between the computer you're using (for example, the Galaxy Tab) and the remote computer. You need to create an account at this site to use LogMeIn Ignition.
- **LogMeIn Ignition**   This application runs on the Galaxy Tab (and on many other devices).
- **LogMeIn program**   This program runs on your PC or Mac and keeps in touch with the LogMeIn service.

Once you have set up your account, installed and configured LogMeIn Ignition on the Galaxy Tab, and installed and configured the LogMeIn program on the PC or Mac, LogMeIn works smoothly and effectively. Figure 13-5 shows LogMeIn Ignition accessing a Mac across the Internet.

LogMeIn Ignition also has a lot of neat tricks, such as enabling you to easily change the resolution on the remote computer to better suit the device you're using. For example, when using LogMeIn Ignition on the Galaxy Tab, you'll probably want to lower the resolution so that you can see things at a reasonable size without having to scroll the screen all the time.

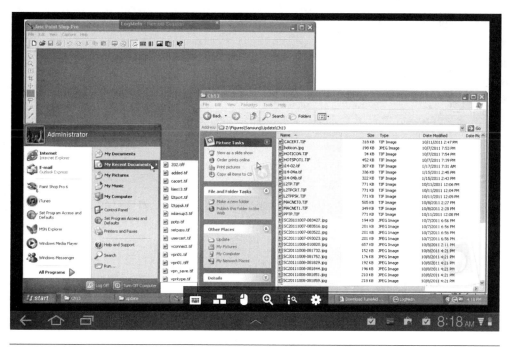

FIGURE 13-5   LogMeIn Ignition gives you remote access to a Mac (shown here) or PC across the Internet without your needing to reconfigure your firewall or router.

14

Troubleshoot and Update the Galaxy Tab

HOW TO...

- Deal with an app that has crashed
- Force close an app
- Recover from operating system crashes
- Restart when the Galaxy Tab stops responding to the touch screen
- Back up your data and settings
- Restore the Galaxy Tab from a backup on your PC
- Reinstall the Kies driver on your PC
- Restore the Galaxy Tab to factory settings
- Restore the Galaxy Tab to factory settings if Android won't load
- Update the Galaxy Tab's firmware to the latest version
- Avoid causing problems with the firmware upgrade

In this chapter, I'll show you how to troubleshoot problems you're likely to run into with the Galaxy Tab. We'll start by looking at how to deal with app crashes, then move on to operating system crashes and touch-screen sulkiness before covering backup and restoration—including how to restore the Galaxy Tab to its factory settings when things go seriously awry.

You'll also learn how to keep the Galaxy Tab in good shape by installing firmware updates.

How to... **Force Close an App**

When the Galaxy Tab notices that an app has crashed in the background, it brings the app under control, and then displays the Sorry! dialog box. Click the Force Close button to force the app to close—there's no alternative—and then launch the app again if you still need to run it.

Deal with an App That Has Crashed

When an app crashes, it may simply disappear from view; it may spread digital detritus all over the screen; or it may simply keep displaying whichever screen you were on, and resolutely refuse to acknowledge button taps.

If the app is still visible, follow these steps to close it:

1. Tap and hold the Home button until the Task Manager dialog box appears on the screen with the Active Applications tab at the front (see Figure 14-1). This screen shows a list of all the apps that are running.
2. Tap the × button for the app you want to close.
3. When you finish closing apps, tap the × button in the upper-right corner of the Task Manager dialog box to close it.

FIGURE 14-1 On the Active Applications tab in the Task Manager dialog box, tap the × button for the app you want to close.

From the Active Applications tab in the Task Manager, you can also end all the running apps by tapping the End All button. Normally, you don't need to do this, but it may sometimes become necessary.

Recover from Operating System Crashes

Normally the Galaxy Tab's operating system, which is called Android, runs smoothly and stably for days or weeks on end. But if Android crashes, you'll need to shut the Galaxy Tab down to recover.

Before shutting down the Galaxy Tab, make sure that Android has crashed rather than just taken a timeout—you may find that the Galaxy Tab has stopped responding for a moment while Android knocks some misbehaving chunk of code on the head and heaves it overboard, so give the Galaxy Tab a few seconds to start responding to your caresses again. If you're not getting a response from the main part of the touch screen, try tapping the Home button. If that works, you should be back in business—or you should at least be able to open the Task Manager and end any apps that seem to be causing problems.

If you get no response to the Home button, press and hold down the power button until the Tablet Options dialog box (shown here) appears. Tap the Power Off button to display the Power Off dialog box, then tap the OK button to power the Galaxy Tab down.

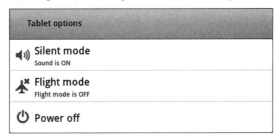

If the Tablet Options dialog box doesn't appear, keep holding down the power button for a few more seconds until the Galaxy Tab shuts down.

Whichever way you shut the Galaxy Tab down, give it a few seconds to contemplate the meaning of nothingness while you savor your potency. Then press and hold down the power button for a couple of seconds until the Galaxy Tab logo appears on the screen and the device starts booting.

Restart When the Galaxy Tab Stops Responding to the Touch Screen

If the Galaxy Tab responds only slowly or jerkily to the touch screen, the problem may be that your fingers are too cold or dirty to give the screen the electrical sensations it spends its whole life longing for. Assess your fingers for ice or grime, strip off any offending substance, and try again.

Because the Galaxy Tab's screen is designed to respond to fingers, you can't use the screen with full-fingered gloves on, though fingerless gloves or gloves with the thumb and trigger finger free work pretty well. But if you need to use the Galaxy Tab in conditions severe enough to freeze your fingertips, you may be able to use a jerky-style smoked sausage instead. This tip comes from South Korea, where the ambient temperature can be even frostier than the diplomatic relations with its northern neighbor.

If the Galaxy Tab stops responding to the touch screen altogether, you'll usually need to restart it. Use the technique described earlier in this chapter. A restart normally clears minor bugs that have cropped up.

If you've managed to break the touch screen, take the Galaxy Tab to a service center.

As I mentioned in Chapter 1, arming the Galaxy Tab's screen with a screen protector is usually a good idea. But you have to get the right kind of screen protector. If your screen protector is thick enough to prevent the Galaxy Tab from reading your taps accurately, junk the screen protector and get a more sensitive one. You can get standard screen protectors from eBay for a dollar or two, but you may prefer to go with heavier-duty ones such as those made by Zagg (www.zagg.com).

Back Up Your Data and Settings

Like most tablet computers, the Galaxy Tab is designed to be your constant companion through daily life (but perhaps not share your shower or your bed) and to take its ration of life's daily knocks.

In case you damage or lose the Galaxy Tab, you'll want to back up your settings and your data so that you can restore them to the Galaxy Tab when you repair or replace it.

To keep your settings safe, you can set the Galaxy Tab to back them up to Google's servers and to automatically restore them as needed. To keep your data safe, you can back it up to your PC using Kies.

Android Market automatically keeps a list of the apps you've installed on the Galaxy Tab. You can reinstall the apps you've purchased without paying for them again.

Back Up Your Settings and Data to Google's Servers

To keep your Galaxy Tab's settings protected, back them up to Google's servers like this:

1. From the home screen, tap the notifications area to display the notifications panel.
2. Tap the Settings button to display the Settings screen.
3. Tap the Privacy button to display the Privacy screen (shown here).

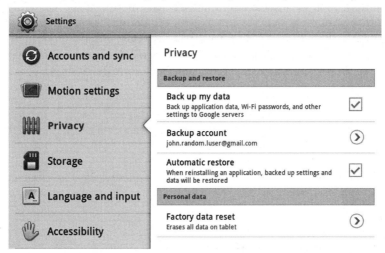

4. In the Backup And Restore area, select the Back Up My Data check box.
5. Look at the Backup Account button. If the readout shows a different account than the one you want to use, tap the Backup Account button to display the Set Backup Account dialog box (shown here), and then tap the account to use. If the account doesn't appear in the Set Backup Account dialog box, tap the Add Account button and follow the steps to add it.

6. While you're on the Privacy screen, select the Automatic Restore check box as well. This setting makes the Galaxy Tab automatically restore your backed-up settings and data when you restore an app.

Back Up the Galaxy Tab to Your PC

To keep your data safe, back it up to your PC using Kies so that you can restore it when you need to.

 At this writing, Kies for the Mac doesn't provide backup and restore features.

It's a good idea to back up regularly as a matter of course—daily, weekly, or however frequently you can manage consistently. But you should also back up immediately before you perform any heavy-duty troubleshooting moves, such as restoring the Galaxy Tab to factory settings (as discussed in the next section).

To back up the Galaxy Tab to your PC, follow these steps:

1. Connect the Galaxy Tab to your PC.
2. Launch Kies if it doesn't automatically launch itself.
3. Wait for the Galaxy Tab's item to appear in the Connected Devices list at the top of the left pane in the Kies window.
4. If Kies doesn't automatically select the Galaxy Tab's item in the Connected Devices list, click the Galaxy Tab's item to display the control screens.
5. Click the Back Up/Restore tab to display the Back Up/Restore screen (see Figure 14-2).

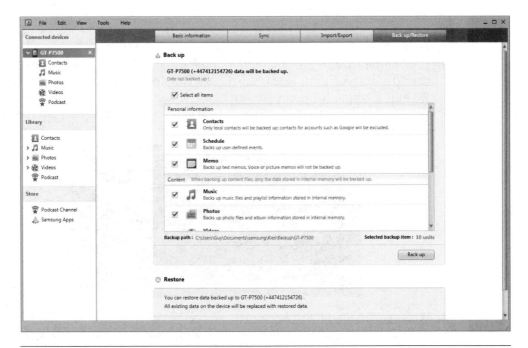

FIGURE 14-2 On the Back Up/Restore screen in Kies, select the check box for each item you want to back up. Select the Select All Items check box if you want to back up everything.

6. In the Back Up box, select the check box for each item you want to back up. Kies divides the data into three categories:
   - **Personal Information**   Select the Contacts check box, the Schedule check box, and the Memo check box, as needed.
   - **Content**   Select the Music check box, the Photos check box, the Videos check box, and the Miscellaneous Content Files check box, as needed.

 If you keep many songs, photos, and videos on your Galaxy Tab, backing them up will take a long time and plenty of disk space. If you have put these files on your Galaxy Tab by copying them from your computer, and the original files are still on your computer, you may prefer not to back up the files from the Galaxy Tab, because you can easily put them back on the Galaxy Tab from the computer if necessary.

   - **Account Information And Settings**   Select the Preferences And Ringtones check box, the Network Settings And Bookmarks check box, and the Email Account Information check box, as needed.
7. Click the Back Up button to start the backup running. Kies displays the Data Backup dialog box with a progress readout (see Figure 14-3) as it creates the backup.
8. When the Data Backup dialog box shows the message Backup Completed, click the Complete button to close the dialog box.
9. You can now unplug the Galaxy Tab from your PC and start using it.

FIGURE 14-3   The Data Backup dialog box shows you the progress of the backup.

Restore the Galaxy Tab from a Backup on Your PC

To restore the Galaxy Tab from a backup on your PC, follow these steps:

1. Connect the Galaxy Tab to your PC.
2. Launch Kies if it doesn't automatically launch itself.
3. Wait for the Galaxy Tab's item to appear in the Connected Devices list at the top of the left pane in the Kies window.
4. If Kies doesn't automatically select the Galaxy Tab's item in the Connected Devices list, click the Galaxy Tab's item to display the control screens.
5. Click the Back Up/Restore tab to display the Back Up/Restore screen (shown in Figure 14-2, earlier in this chapter).
6. In the Restore box, click the Restore button. Kies displays the Restore Data dialog box (see Figure 14-4).
7. In the Select The Backup File To Restore list box, click the backup file you want to use. The files are identified by their date and time—for example, 20111221T194018.sbu is from 7:40:18 P.M. on December 21, 2011—and by the Galaxy Tab's model number (which can be useful if you sync multiple Samsung

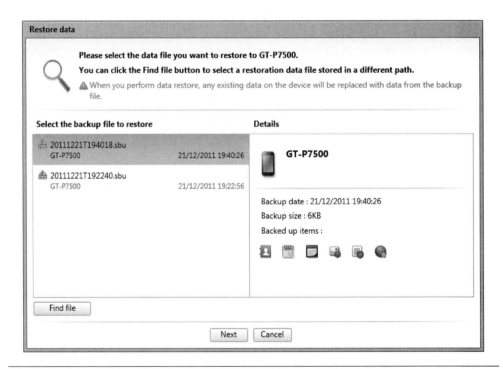

FIGURE 14-4 In the Restore Data dialog box, choose the backup from which you want to restore the Galaxy Tab.

devices with Kies). When you click the backup, its details appear in the Details box on the right, where they're easier to read.

8. Look at the Details box and make sure the backup's details look right.

If you've put your backups somewhere other than where Kies is looking for them, click the Find File button in the Restore Data dialog box, use the Open dialog box to select the backup file, and then click the Open button.

9. Click the Next button to start the restore process. The Restore Data dialog box displays the Please Select Items And Types Of Memory To Restore screen (see Figure 14-5).

10. Select the check box for each type of data you want to restore. If you want to select all the check boxes immediately, select the Select All check box. (You can also clear the Select All check box to clear all the other check boxes.)

11. Click the Next button to start the restore operation running. The Restore Data dialog box shows you its progress (see Figure 14-6).

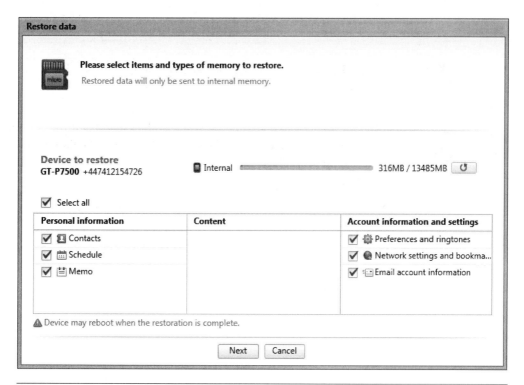

FIGURE 14-5 On the Please Select Items And Types Of Memory To Restore screen of the Restore Data dialog box, select the check box for each item you want to restore.

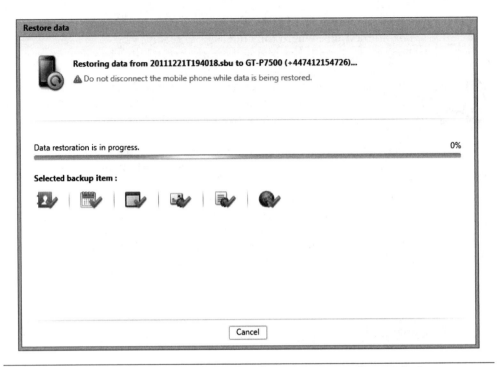

FIGURE 14-6 The Restore Data dialog box keeps you up to date with the progress of the restore operation.

 Be prepared for the restore operation to take a while, especially if the backup contains lots of music, photos, and videos. Don't disconnect the Galaxy Tab until the backup is complete—doing so can mess up your data.

12. When the Restore Data dialog box shows that the restore operation is complete, click the Complete button. The Restore Data dialog box closes.

At this point, your Galaxy Tab may restart to refresh its memories of what's loaded on it. If you see a mysterious dialog box such as the BnR dialog box shown here saying that the connection to your Galaxy Tab has been lost, just click the OK button and wait for the Galaxy Tab to find its feet again.

How to... **Reinstall the Kies Driver on Your PC**

Sometimes the Kies driver on your PC gets confused. When this happens, you won't be able to connect the Galaxy Tab successfully via USB. You'll often see a message telling you that Kies doesn't support the current connection method (which is clearly a lie) and that you need to "reconnect the device in Samsung Kies (PC Studio) mode."

The first thing to do is to try unplugging the Galaxy Tab's USB cable and plugging it into a different USB port on your PC. This works sometimes and is the quickest fix.

If Kies just gives you the same error message, disconnect the USB cable, then click the Troubleshoot Connection Error button or choose Tools | Troubleshoot Connection Error. Then follow through the wizard that opens. This wizard removes and then reinstalls the Kies driver, which typically takes several minutes.

When the wizard finishes, connect the USB cable again. You'll see Windows detect the Galaxy Tab as a new device and install the driver for it. After this, Kies should establish the connection to the Galaxy Tab as normal, and you'll be back in business.

Restore the Galaxy Tab to Factory Settings

When things go so wrong with the Galaxy Tab that restarting it doesn't help, you may need to restore the device to factory settings. Make sure you've backed up the Galaxy Tab before restoring the device, because this is a serious move. Restoring to factory settings deletes the following data from the Galaxy Tab:

- Your Google account
- Your system and app data and settings
- All the apps you've downloaded

Restoring the Galaxy Tab to factory settings doesn't delete the Galaxy Tab's system software and its bundled apps. This is because the Galaxy Tab installs a fresh copy of the system software and bundled apps from its ROM storage.

To restore the Galaxy Tab to factory settings, follow these steps:

1. From the home screen, tap the notifications area to display the notifications panel.
2. Tap the Settings button to display the Settings screen.
3. Tap the Privacy button to display the Privacy screen.

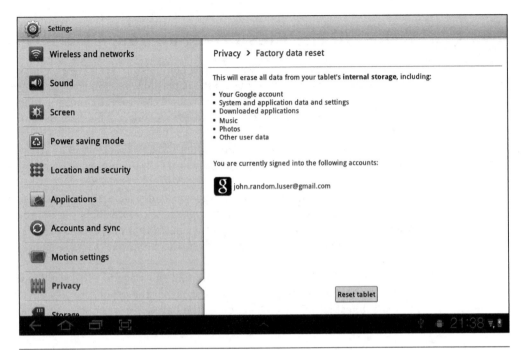

FIGURE 14-7 On the first Factory Data Reset screen, tap the Reset Tablet button.

4. In the Personal Data area, tap the Factory Data Reset button to display the first Factory Data Reset screen (see Figure 14-7), which shows a sober list of what you're about to erase.
5. Tap the Reset Tablet button. The Galaxy Tab displays the Confirm Reset screen (shown here), which displays a more excitable warning.

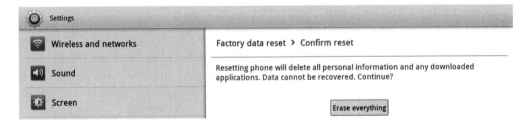

6. Tap the Erase Everything button if you're sure you want to proceed. (If not, tap the Back button a few times to step out of the Factory Data Reset zone.)

After resetting the Galaxy Tab to factory settings, you'll need to go through the initial setup routine as described in Chapter 1.

Restore the Galaxy Tab to Factory Settings if Android Won't Load

If the Android operating system won't load at all, you can't reach the Privacy screen and restore the Galaxy Tab to factory settings from there. Instead, you need to use this hardware move:

1. If the Galaxy Tab is on, turn it off. The easiest way is to press and hold down the power button for around eight seconds, but you can also use the Tablet Options dialog box like this:
   a. Press and hold down the power button until the Tablet Options dialog box appears.
   b. Tap the Power Off button to display the Power Off dialog box.
   c. Tap the OK button to shut down the Galaxy Tab.
2. Press and hold the Volume Down button (the side of the volume rocker button that's nearer to the power button).
3. Press and hold down the power button for a few seconds until the Galaxy Tab starts booting.
4. When you see the Galaxy Tab logo or carrier logo appear on the screen, release the power button but keep holding down the Volume Down button.
5. When the Android System Recovery/Downloading screen appears, release the Volume Down button.
6. At this point, you'll see the Downloading icon blinking, indicating that it's active. Press the Volume Down button once to make the Android System Recovery icon active, so that the Android System Recovery icon (the icon showing a box being unpacked) starts blinking.
7. Press the Volume Up button once to select the Android System Recovery icon. The Galaxy Tab displays the Android System Recovery screen, which starts with a menu of text options like this:

```
Android system recovery <3e>


Volume up/down to move highlight;
power button to select.


reboot system now
apply update from /sdcard
wipe data/factory reset
wipe cache partition
```

8. Press the Volume Down button three times to highlight the Wipe Data/Factory Reset item on the menu.

(Continued)

9. Press the power button to select the Wipe Data/Factory Reset item. The Galaxy Tab displays a confirmation screen that looks like this:

```
Android system recovery <3e>

Confirm wipe of all user data?
  THIS CAN NOT BE UNDONE.


No
No
No
No
No
No
Yes -- delete all user data
No
No
No
```

10. Press the Volume Down button several times to highlight the Yes -- Delete All User Data item.
11. Press the power button to select the Yes -- Delete All User Data item.
12. The Galaxy Tab wipes out the data and displays the Android System Recovery screen again.
13. Make sure the Reboot System Now item is highlighted. (If not, press the Volume Up button or the Volume Down button to move the highlight to it.)
14. Press the power button to select the command. The Galaxy Tab then restarts.

Update the Galaxy Tab's Firmware

To keep the Galaxy Tab running as fast, smoothly, and stably as possible, it's a good idea to install any firmware updates Samsung releases for the device. We'll look at the process first on the Galaxy Tab, then on Windows, and finally on the Mac.

Update the Galaxy Tab Without Using a PC or Mac

To update the Galaxy Tab's firmware without using a PC or Mac, follow these steps:

1. Tap the Home button to display the home screen.

 If you have a 3G-capable Galaxy Tab, make sure it's connected to a wireless network before running Software Update. Downloading updates over 3G can eat through your data plan quickly, so use Wi-Fi for updates.

2. Tap the notifications area to display the notifications panel.

How to...   ## Avoid Causing Problems with the Firmware Upgrade

Upgrading the Galaxy Tab's firmware isn't brain surgery, but it does involve replacing files deep in the Galaxy Tab's file system. Some of these files are critical to the Galaxy Tab being able to run, so it's vital not to interrupt the upgrade—if you do, you may "brick" the Galaxy Tab, preventing it from ever working again.

This potential for disaster is why Kies keeps reminding you not to disconnect the Galaxy Tab from your PC or Mac while the upgrade is running. It's also why you should back up all the Galaxy Tab's data (or all the data that you care about) before performing the upgrade.

To make sure the upgrade runs okay, you should also:

- **Recharge the battery fully before upgrading**   Even though the Galaxy Tab remains connected to your PC or Mac throughout the upgrade, you should make sure it has plenty of battery power for the parts of the upgrade when it stops drawing power from the computer.
- **Remove other devices from the USB chain**   Ideally, your Galaxy Tab would be the only device connected to your computer via USB while the upgrade is running, simply to avoid possible confusion. In practice, you may have a USB keyboard or mouse that you can't unplug. But do unplug any nonessential devices—such as your printer, scanner, digital camera, and USB thumb drive—until the upgrade is complete.
- **Not use the Galaxy Tab during the upgrade**   Don't press any of the Galaxy Tab's buttons while the upgrade is running.

3. Tap the Settings button to display the Settings screen.
4. Tap the About Tablet button at the bottom of the left pane to display the About Tablet screen.
5. Tap the Software Update button to display the Software Update screen (shown here).

If you haven't yet set up a Samsung account on the Galaxy Tab, you'll need to accept the Samsung Account agreement and then sign in with an existing account or sign up for a new account. You can then use Software Update.

6. Tap the Update button to display the Software Update dialog box (shown here).

7. Click the OK button. The Galaxy Tab checks for updates.
8. If any updates are available, follow the prompts for installing them. If no updates are available, the Galaxy Tab displays a dialog box saying so; click the OK button, and go back to your work or play.

Update the Galaxy Tab's Firmware on Windows

When an update is available, and you've connected the Galaxy Tab to your PC, Kies displays the Samsung Kies: A New Firmware Version Is Available dialog box (see Figure 14-8) to notify you, so all you have to do is click the Update button.

 Updating the Galaxy Tab's firmware can take up to two hours, especially if your Internet connection isn't rugged, windswept, and handsome or if Samsung's servers are suffering a surfeit of Internet connections that do match that description. So you may need to put off the update until a convenient time.

FIGURE 14-8 Click the Update button in the Samsung Kies: A New Firmware Version Is Available dialog box to start the process of updating the firmware.

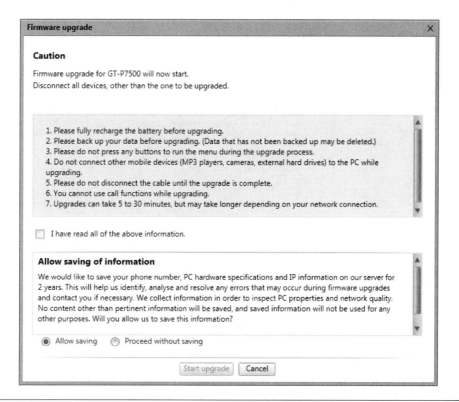

Firmware upgrade   ✕

Caution

Firmware upgrade for GT-P7500 will now start.
Disconnect all devices, other than the one to be upgraded.

1. Please fully recharge the battery before upgrading.
2. Please back up your data before upgrading. (Data that has not been backed up may be deleted.)
3. Please do not press any buttons to run the menu during the upgrade process.
4. Do not connect other mobile devices (MP3 players, cameras, external hard drives) to the PC while upgrading.
5. Please do not disconnect the cable until the upgrade is complete.
6. You cannot use call functions while upgrading.
7. Upgrades can take 5 to 30 minutes, but may take longer depending on your network connection.

☐ I have read all of the above information.

Allow saving of information

We would like to save your phone number, PC hardware specifications and IP information on our server for 2 years. This will help us identify, analyse and resolve any errors that may occur during firmware upgrades and contact you if necessary. We collect information in order to inspect PC properties and network quality. No content other than pertinent information will be saved, and saved information will not be used for any other purposes. Will you allow us to save this information?

◉ Allow saving   ◯ Proceed without saving

[Start upgrade]   [Cancel]

FIGURE 14-9   In the Firmware Upgrade dialog box, read the warnings, select the I Have Read All Of The Above Information check box, and choose whether to allow Samsung to save your phone number, IP address, and PC hardware specifications. Then click the Start Upgrade button.

When you do click the Update button, Kies displays the Firmware Upgrade dialog box (see Figure 14-9).

Read the warnings, and then select the I Have Read All Of The Above Information check box. In the Allow Saving Of Information box at the bottom of the Firmware Upgrade dialog box, read the details of the information Samsung would like to save about your PC, and then select the Allow Saving option button or the Proceed Without Saving option button, as needed.

Click the Start Upgrade button when you're ready to run the upgrade.

Next, the updater displays the Data Backup: Back Up Data dialog box (see Figure 14-10), which lets you choose which data to back up.

If your Galaxy Tab contains no data that you care about, you can click the Skip Backup button here. But normally it's best to select the check box for each item you want to back up (or select the Select All check box to select all the other check boxes in one move), and then click the Continue button. You can also click the Cancel button if you want to cancel the upgrade—for example, because you want to transfer data from the Galaxy Tab to another computer.

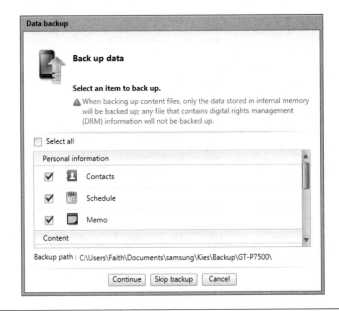

FIGURE 14-10 In the Data Backup: Back Up Data dialog box, choose which items to back up before the upgrade. Normally, you'll want to back up everything.

Once the backup is going, it takes a few minutes—enough for a couple of Facebook updates if you're quick. When the backup is complete, Kies displays the Backup Completed dialog box (see Figure 14-11), and you need to click the Proceed With The Upgrade button to proceed with the firmware upgrade.

Next, Kies displays the Prepare For Firmware Upgrade dialog box (see Figure 14-12), reminding you not to disconnect the cable that connects the Galaxy Tab to your PC. Smile benignly and wait while Kies downloads the firmware upgrade components from Samsung's servers.

After Kies finishes downloading the installer, it runs the firmware update. Unless you've turned off Windows' protective User Account Control feature, User Account Control then pops up a warning dialog box (as shown here) to make sure you want to run the Samsung Kies UAC Command Agent. Click the Yes button to proceed.

FIGURE 14-11   Click the Proceed With The Upgrade button in the Data Backup: Backup Completed dialog box to move along.

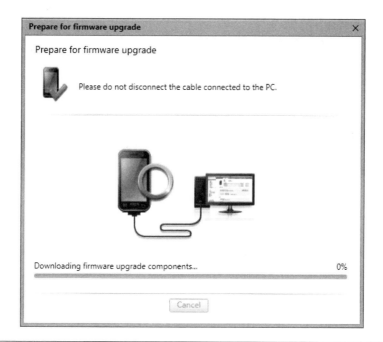

FIGURE 14-12   Kies warns you not to disconnect the Galaxy Tab while it downloads the firmware upgrade.

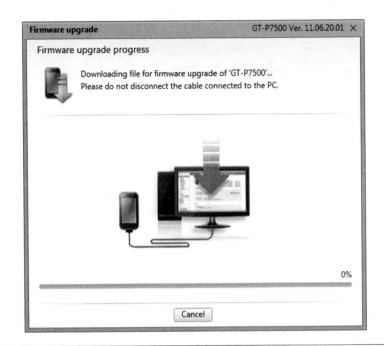

FIGURE 14-13 Kies displays its progress as it updates the Galaxy Tab's firmware.

Kies then prepares the upgrade and installs it, displaying the Firmware Upgrade: Firmware Upgrade Progress readout as it does so (see Figure 14-13). This too takes a while—and don't even think about disconnecting the Galaxy Tab from the PC until the update is finished, Kies has restored your data, and you see the Galaxy Tab's screen again. Interrupting the update can "brick" the Galaxy Tab, turning it into an expensive paperweight with no way back to functionality.

Update the Galaxy Tab's Firmware on the Mac

When an update is available, and you've connected the Galaxy Tab to your Mac, Kies displays the Samsung Kies: A New Firmware Version Is Available dialog box (see Figure 14-14) to let you know.

To go ahead with the update, click the Update button. Kies then displays the first Firmware Upgrade dialog box (see Figure 14-15), which makes sure you know how you should prepare for the update. See the sidebar titled "Avoid Causing Problems with the Firmware Upgrade," earlier in this chapter, for some do's and don'ts.

 At this writing, the Mac OS X version of the Firmware Update software hogs the focus on the Mac: Immediately after you click another app to activate it, the Firmware Update app grabs the focus back. This means that you can't get anything done on your Mac while the update is running.

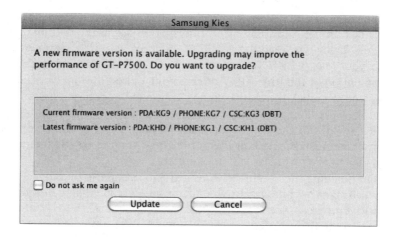

FIGURE 14-14   Click the Update button in the Samsung Kies: A New Firmware Version Is Available dialog box to start the process of updating the firmware.

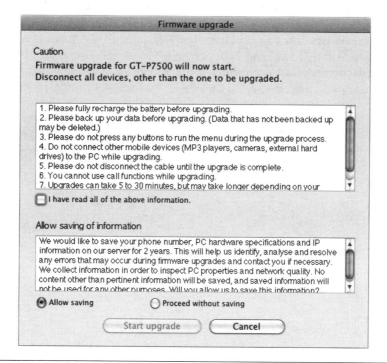

FIGURE 14-15   In this Firmware Upgrade dialog box, read the warnings, select the I Have Read All Of The Above Information check box, and choose whether to allow Samsung to save your phone number, IP address, and "PC hardware specifications"—in other words, your Mac's details. Then click the Start Upgrade button.

Read the warnings, and then select the I Have Read All Of The Above Information check box. In the Allow Saving Of Information box at the bottom of the Firmware Upgrade dialog box, read the details of the information Samsung would like to save about your Mac (which Kies refers to as a "PC"), and then select the Allow Saving option button or the Proceed Without Saving option button, as needed.

When you click the Start Upgrade button to begin the upgrade, Kies displays the next Firmware Upgrade dialog box (see Figure 14-16), which shows a progress readout as Kies downloads the file for the firmware upgrade. Depending on the speed of your Internet connection and how busy Samsung's servers are, this may take a while. It's a good idea to allow at least half an hour.

On finishing the download, Kies starts to install the update across the USB cable. This also takes a while. Again, the Firmware Upgrade dialog box keeps you informed about the progress (see Figure 14-17).

When the firmware upgrade is complete, the Firmware Upgrade dialog box tells you so, as shown in Figure 14-18. This dialog box also tells you to take two actions:

- **Restart the Galaxy Tab** You'll normally find the Galaxy Tab restarts itself automatically after the firmware upgrade finishes. This restart may take longer than usual, because during the restart and boot process, Android needs to shuffle some of the new files into place. So let the Galaxy Tab restart completely, even if restarting takes several minutes. Don't restart the Galaxy Tab manually unless you're sure it has hung—for example, it has been unresponsive for 15 minutes.
- **Disconnect and reconnect the USB cable** After the Galaxy Tab has finished restarting, disconnect the USB cable, wait a few seconds, and then reconnect it.

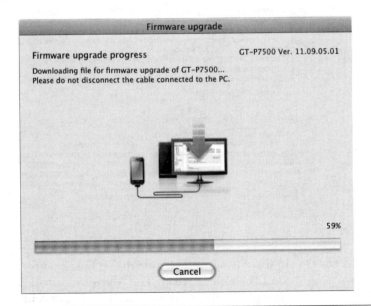

FIGURE 14-16 This Firmware Upgrade dialog box shows you Kies's progress downloading the file for the firmware update.

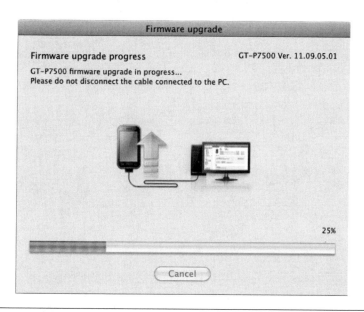

FIGURE 14-17   This Firmware Upgrade dialog box shows you how the process of installing the firmware on the Galaxy Tab is going.

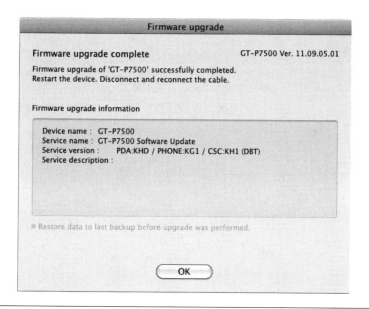

FIGURE 14-18   When the firmware upgrade finishes, you may need to restart the Galaxy Tab and then disconnect and reconnect its USB cable.

Index

Numbers

3G networks
    Cell Broadcast (CB) settings in Messaging app, 277–278
    connecting to Google servers, 7
    Galaxy Tab models and, 4
    switching from Wi-Fi to mobile data, 85
24-hour format, time settings, 73

A

AAC (Advanced Audio Coding), 25
access points
    turning off mobile access point, 337
    using Galaxy Tab as portable Wi-Fi hotspot, 334–336
accessibility settings, 71–72
accessories
    external keyboards, 87–88
    outputting videos and photos to TV, 88
    screen protectors and cases, 86–87
    stand for hands-free use, 88
accounts
    adding to Social Hub, 252–254
    backing up, 65
    setting up Google account, 6–8
    setting up Market app account, 315
    setting up YouTube account, 156–157
    signing up for Pulse account, 307
    sync settings, 62
accounts, email
    account settings, 227–228
    adding, 217–219
    deleting, 232
    general settings, 229–230
    notification settings, 231

setting up Exchange account, 226–227
    setting up IMAP account, 224–226
    setting up manually, 219–220
    setting up POP3 account, 220–224
    switching between, 227
accounts, Gmail
    setting up, 242–243
    settings, 245–249
Acrobat, Adobe, 298
action photos, 169, 181–182
Active Applications screen
    closing running apps, 351
    dealing with crashed app, 350
    viewing running apps, 311–312
ActiveSync, 253. *see also* Microsoft Exchange
Address Book (Mac), syncing to Galaxy Tab, 103
administrators, 56
Adobe Acrobat, 298
Adobe Flash Player, 192, 308
Adobe InDesign, 297
Advanced Audio Coding (AAC), 25
advanced settings, Browser app, 208–210
alarm tones, using song as, 144
albums
    browsing for music, 133, 135
    title, 138
alerts, security, 55–56
Amazon MP3, buying music online, 130
Amazon.com, as music store, 132
Android Market
    apps available from, 309
    downloading installer from, 316
    downloading Wyse PocketCloud from, 345
    reinstalling purchased apps, 318, 352
    Staff Picks, 313
    third-party apps from, 312

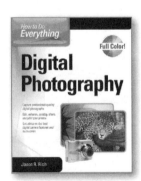